**Copyright © 2021 by Amber Southee -All rights reserved.**

No part of this publication may be reproduced, distributed, or transmitted in any form or by any means, including photocopying, recording, or other electronic or mechanical methods, without the prior written permission of the publisher, except in the case of brief quotations embodied in reviews and certain other non-commercial uses permitted by copyright law.

This Book is provided with the sole purpose of providing relevant information on a specific topic for which every reasonable effort has been made to ensure that it is both accurate and reasonable. Nevertheless, by purchasing this Book you consent to the fact that the author, as well as the publisher, are in no way experts on the topics contained herein, regardless of any claims as such that may be made within. It is recommended that you always consult a professional prior to undertaking any of the advice or techniques discussed within.This is a legally binding declaration that is considered both valid and fair by both the Committee of Publishers Association and the American Bar Association and should be considered as legally binding within the United States.

# CONTENTS

**INTRODUCTION** .................................................. 9
   The Benefits of Owning Your Own Cuisinart Ice Cream Maker .............................. 9
   How To Use Your Ice Cream Maker! ............. 10
**CANDY BAR FUSION ICE CREAM** ............... 12
   1. Zero Soft Serve Ice Cream ........................... 12
   2. Take 5 Soft Serve Ice Cream ....................... 12
   3. Oh, Henry! Soft Serve Ice Cream ................ 12
   4. Mounds Soft Serve Ice Cream ..................... 12
   5. 3 Musketeers Soft Serve Ice Cream ............ 13
   6. Whatchamacallit Soft Serve Ice Cream ....... 13
   7. Nestlé Crunch Soft Serve Ice Cream ........... 13
   8. Sky Bar Soft Serve Ice Cream ..................... 13
   9. Charleston Chew Soft Serve Ice Cream ...... 13
   10. Almond Joy Soft Serve Ice Cream ............ 14
   11. Kit Kat Soft Serve Ice Cream .................... 14
   12. Baby Ruth Soft Serve Ice Cream .............. 14
   13. Caramello Dreamin Soft Serve Ice Cream 14
   14. Heath Bar Soft Serve Ice Cream ............... 15
   15. Snickers Soft Serve Ice Cream ................. 15
   16. 100 Grand Soft Serve Ice Cream .............. 15
   17. Mr. Goodbar Soft Serve Ice Cream ........... 15
   18. Milky Way Soft Serve Ice Cream .............. 16
   19. 5th Avenue Soft Serve Ice Cream ............. 16
   20. Hershey Bar Soft Serve Ice Cream ........... 16
   21. Twix Soft Serve Ice Cream ....................... 16
   22. Pay Day Soft Serve Ice Cream .................. 17
   23. Mars Bar Soft Serve Ice Cream ................ 17
   24. Skor Bar Soft Serve Ice Cream ................. 17
   25. Krackel Soft Serve Ice Cream ................... 17
   26. Butterfinger Soft Serve Ice Cream ........... 18
**FRUITILICIOUS ICE CREAM** ........................ 19
   27. Kickin' Key Lime Sorbet ........................... 19
   28. Orange Chocolate Almond Vegan Ice Cream ........................................................ 19
   29. Chocolate Peppermint Banana Vegan Milkshake .................................................. 19
   30. Going Guava Milkshake ............................ 20
   31. Double Bliss Berry Delight Frozen Yogurt 20
   32. Chocolate Raspberry Pistachio Vegan Gelato ........................................................ 20
   33. Nutella & Bananas Soft Serve Ice Cream 20
   34. Cinnamon Soy Vanilla Vegan Soft Serve Ice Cream .................................................. 21
   35. Big Blueberry Chocolate Gelato ................ 21
   36. Juicy Strawberry Honey Frozen Yogurt 21
   37. Pineapple Strawberries N Cream Tofu Vegan Ice Cream ........................................ 22
   38. Kickin' Kiwi Lime Ice Cream .................... 22
   39. Blackberry Lemon Coconut Vegan Frozen Yogurt .......................................................... 22
   40. Caramel Cookie Crunch Soft Serve Ice Cream ........................................................ 23
   41. Grapelicious Ice Cream ............................. 23
   42. "bursting" Blueberry Maple Syrup Soft Serve Ice Cream ........................................ 23
   43. Chunky Cherry Sorbet ............................... 23
   44. Blueberry Chocolate Vegan Soft Serve Ice Cream ........................................................ 24
   45. Vanilla Apple Cinnamon Ice Cream ......... 24
   46. Carob Chip Mint Soy Vanilla Vegan Ice Cream ........................................................ 24
   47. Peanut Butter White Chocolate Soft Serve Ice Cream .................................................. 25
   48. Sassy Strawberry Lime Sorbet .................. 25
   49. Rosemary Soft Serve Ice Cream ................ 25
   50. Bursting Banana Nut Gelato ..................... 26
   51. Lemon Lime Milkshake ............................. 26
   52. Peaches And Cream Soft Serve Ice Cream 26
   53. Mango Madness Coconut Raspberry Sorbet ........................................................ 26
   54. Lemon Chocolate Blueberry Vegan Gelato 27
   55. Double Cherry Chocolate Milkshake ........ 27
   56. Caribbean Pineapple Sorbet ...................... 27
   57. Astounding Apricot Almond Ice Cream ... 27
   58. Tropical Mango Soft Serve Ice Cream ..... 28
   59. Apricot Honey Gelato ................................ 28
   60. Basil Chocolate Vegan Soft Serve Ice Cream ........................................................ 28
   61. Raspberry Pumpkin Spice Vegan Soy Frozen Yogurt ............................................. 29
   62. Chocolate Cherry Cocoa Banana Vegan Milkshake .................................................. 29
   63. Pulsating Pomegranate Mint Frozen Yogurt .......................................................... 29
**THE CLASSICS ICE CREAM** ........................ 31
   64. Mint Cookies 'n Cream "silkshake" .......... 31
   65. Daiquiri Lime Soda Frozen Yogurt ........... 31
   66. The Guinness Chocolate Milkshake ......... 31
   67. Chocolate Chip Cookie Dough Frozen Yogurt .......................................................... 31
   68. "tasty" Tequila Sunrise Gelato .................. 32
   69. Lemon Tequila "sunset" Gelato ................ 32

70. Strawberry Cinnamon Margarita Soft Serve Ice Cream ...................................32
71. Very Strawberry Gelato ......................33
72. Grown Folks "old Fashioned" Ice Cream33
73. Miraculous Double Mint Chip Ice Cream33
74. Orange Tequila "sunrise" Gelato .............33
75. "adults Old Fashioned" Ice Cream ...........34
76. Sunrise Strawberry Daiquiri Milkshake34
77. Chunky Chocolate Chip Soft Serve Ice Cream ...................................................34
78. California Cookies-n-cream Soft Serve Ice Cream ...............................................35
79. Runnin' Rum And Coke Gelato ..................35
80. Lickin' Lime Daiquiri Frozen Yogurt ......35
81. Cucumber Rosemary Honey Rum Sorbet36
82. Margarita Madness Soft Serve Ice Cream36
83. Kahlua & Pistachio Ice Cream....................36
84. Divine Coffee Frozen Yogurt......................36
85. Pralines And "oh So Creamy" Milkshake37
86. Mango Strawberry Mint Daiquiri Milkshake ................................................37
87. Creamy Kahlua Almond Delight Ice Cream ...................................................37
88. The Original "manhattan" Ice Cream .....38
89. Double Gin And Juice Vanilla Soft Serve Ice Cream ...............................................38
90. Tropical Coconut Rum And Coke Gelato38
91. "the Big Stout" Almond Chocolate Milkshake ................................................38
92. Double Gin And Tonic Soft Serve Ice Cream ...................................................39
93. Power Punch Pistachio Ice Cream............39
94. Tropical Piña Colada Frozen Yogurt.......39
95. Classic Vanilla Soft-serve Ice Cream .......40
96. Caribbean Colada Frozen Yogurt.............40
97. Radical Rocky Road Ice Cream..................40
98. Tropical Watermelon Lemon/lime Sorbet40
99. Chocolate Screwdriver Soft Serve Ice Cream ...................................................41
100. Double Dark Chocolate Gelato................41
101. Vanilla Screwdriver Soft Serve Ice Cream ...................................................41
102. "new York" Manhattan Ice Cream..........41
103. Cuddling Cucumber Basil Rum Sorbet42
**SIMPLE ICE CREAM................................ 43**
104. Basic Custard Ice Cream With Sea Salt43
105. All-american Double Vanilla Soft-serve Ice Cream ...............................................43
106. Orange Cola Soft Serve Ice Cream..........43
107. Crazy Cotton Candy Milkshake ............. 43
108. Chocolate Chip Turmeric Peppermint Chip Ice Cream ...................................... 44
109. Rocky Road Frozen Custard Ice Cream44
110. Dr. Pepper Ice Cream.............................. 44
111. Strawberry Matcha Custard Ice Cream45
112. Pineapple Ice Cream ............................... 45
113. Three Musketeer Gelato......................... 45
114. Kiwi Lime Strawberry Ice Cream ......... 46
115. Double Bubble Gum Soft Serve Ice Cream ...................................................... 46
116. Chocolate Pistachio Ice Cream .............. 46
117. Blackberry Ice Cream ............................. 47
118. Coffee Toffee Ice Cream.......................... 47
119. Apricot Ice Cream ................................... 47
120. Chocolate Ice Cream ............................... 47
121. Custard Cantaloupe Ice Cream ............. 48
122. Butter Toffee Popcorn Soft Serve Ice Cream ...................................................... 48
123. Barbados Custard Ice Cream.................. 48
124. Thermomix Licorice Ice Cream............. 49
125. Pumpkin Custard Ice Cream................... 49
126. "cool" Cake Batter Soft Serve Ice Cream50
127. Banana Custard Ice Cream...................... 50
128. Gummy Worm Cotton Candy Ice Cream50
129. Mocha Ice Cream ..................................... 51
130. Classic Root Beer Lemon Gelato ........... 51
131. Peanut Butter Cup Milkshake ................ 51
132. Circus Cotton Candy Milkshake ............ 52
133. Mango Ice Cream...................................... 52
134. Tangerine Soda Ice Cream ...................... 52
135. Turmeric Ice Cream ................................ 52
136. Vegan Ice Cream....................................... 53
137. Island Coconut Banana Sorbet .............. 53
138. Blueberry Honey Cake Batter Soft Serve Ice Cream ...................................................... 53
139. Butter Pecan Ice Cream .......................... 54
140. Chilled Cherry Soda Frozen Yogurt..... 54
141. My Delicious M&m Ice Cream................ 54
142. California Mango Lime Soft Serve Ice Cream ...................................................... 55
143. Vanilla Frozen Custard ........................... 55
144. Purple Taro Ice Cream............................. 55
145. Butterfinger Cinnamon Crunch Gelato56
146. Banana Pudding Ice Cream .................... 56
147. Blueberry Mint Soft Serve Ice Cream . 56
148. Cookies And Cream Ice Cream .............. 56
149. Nutella Ice Cream..................................... 57
150. Crunchy Cinnamon Butterfinger Gelato57

151. Mocha Madness Ice Cream .......................... 58
152. Cinnamon Ice Cream ................................. 58
153. "give Me More" S'mores Frozen Yogurt 58
154. Double Espresso Ice Cream ...................... 58
155. Rhubarb Swirl Ice Cream ........................... 59
156. "georgia Peach" Maple Syrup Soft Serve Ice Cream ............................................................ 59
157. Cinnamon Blackberry Pineapple Ice Cream ............................................................ 60
158. Cookies 'n Cream Rice Crispy Treat Frozen Yogurt ...................................................... 60
159. Cinnamon Chocolate Chip Soft Serve Ice Cream ............................................................ 60
160. Peach Ice Cream ........................................ 61
161. Red Velvet Raspberry Milkshake ............... 61
162. Red Velvet Milkshake ................................. 61
163. Caramel Corn Soft Serve Ice Cream .......... 61
164. Dark Chocolate Cheery Custard Ice Cream ............................................................ 62
165. Custard Chocolate Ice Cream .................... 62
166. Key Lime Ice Cream ................................... 63
167. Green Apple Musketeer Gelato ................. 63
168. Radical Root Beer Gelato .......................... 63
169. Dr. Pepper Cherry Lime Ice Cream ........... 63
170. Kiddo's Coca Cola Soft Serve Ice Cream 64
171. Bubble Gum Cola Soft Serve Ice Cream 64
172. Chocolate Cookie Rice Crispy Treat Frozen Yogurt ...................................................... 64
173. Honey Ice Cream ....................................... 65
174. Graham Cracker Peanut Butter Cup Milkshake ....................................................... 65
175. Cherry Blueberry Lime Soda Frozen Yogurt ................................................................ 65
176. Tropical Coconut Banana Animal Cracker Sorbet .................................................. 66
177. Sour Patch Chocolate Ice Cream .............. 66
178. Chicago Style Cookies-n-cream Soft Serve Ice Cream ................................................ 66
179. Eggless Pistachio Ice Cream ..................... 67
180. Malted Milk Chocolate Ice Cream ............. 67
181. Orange Creamsicle Ice Cream ................... 67
182. Peppermint Hibiscus Tea Ice Cream ....... 68
183. Custard Cream Gelato ............................... 68
184. Pralines And Cream Custard Ice Cream 68
185. Honey Matcha Tea Extreme Ice Cream ..... 69
186. "crispy" Caramel Graham Cracker Ice Cream ............................................................ 69
187. Fresh Strawberry Ice Cream ...................... 69
188. Screamin' Sour Patch Kids Ice Cream .. 70
189. Orange Almond Apricot Ice Cream ...... 70
190. S'mores Camp Fire Frozen Yogurt ....... 70
**VANILLA ICE CREAM ................................. 72**
191. Six Threes Ice Cream Recipe ................. 72
192. Caramel-apple Ice Cream ...................... 72
193. Coconut Ice Cream ................................. 72
194. Root Beer Float Ice Cream Recipe ........ 72
195. Vanilla Ice Cream Vi Recipe .................. 72
196. Ice Cream In A Can Recipe ................... 73
197. Peppermint Bark No-churn Ice Cream 73
198. Vanilla Ice Cream I Recipe .................... 73
199. Fruited Ice Cream Recipe ...................... 73
200. Tropical Avocado Ice Cream .................. 73
201. Healthy Chunky Monkey Ice Cream Recipe ....................................................... 74
202. Ice Cream Recipe ................................... 74
203. Easy Cherry-chocolate Chunk Ice Cream Recipe ....................................................... 74
204. Italian Crema Ice Cream (gelato Alla Crema) ...................................................... 74
205. Creamy Lemon Grass Ice Cream Recipe 75
206. Fast And Easy Creamy Ice Cream Recipe 75
207. Vanilla Ice Cream ................................... 75
208. Rosewater-and-saffron Ice Cream (bastani Irani)? ...................................................... 76
209. Lavender Honey Ice Cream Recipe ....... 76
210. Chocolate Snow Ice Cream Recipe ....... 76
211. Simple Mint Chocolate Chip Strawberry Ice Cream Recipe ........................................... 77
212. Salted Watermelon Ice Cream ............... 77
213. Peanut Butter Cup Ice Cream Recipe .. 77
214. Cherry Cheesecake Ice Cream ............... 78
215. Five Minute Ice Cream ........................... 78
216. Mocha Coconut Ice Cream Recipe ........ 78
217. Creamy Banana Ice Cream Recipe ....... 78
218. Lemon Ice Ii Recipe ............................... 78
219. Tart Lemon Ice Cream Recipe ............... 79
220. Coffee Ice Cream .................................... 79
221. Strawberry Ice Cream Recipe ................ 79
222. Maplenut Ice Cream Recipe ................... 80
223. Mocha Espresso Ice Cream Recipe ...... 80
224. Cheesecake Ice Cream Recipe .............. 80
225. Peach-blueberry Ice Cream ................... 80
226. Guinness Ice Cream With Chocolate-covered Pretzels .................................................. 81
227. Strawberry Snow Ice Cream Recipe .... 81
228. Peach Ice Cream Recipe ........................ 81
229. Vanilla Ice Cream With Brown Butter Crumble ................................................... 82

230. Cherry Ice Cream Recipe ........................... 82
231. Snow Ice Cream I Recipe........................... 82
232. Homemade Soft Serve Ice Cream .......... 82
233. Vanilla Ice Cream Iii Recipe ..................... 83
234. Lina And Jens' Delicious Vegan Chocolate Ice Cream Recipe ..................... 83
235. Easy Banana Ice Cream Recipe ............. 83
236. Ice Cream Bonbon Pops .......................... 83
237. Homemade Vanilla Ice Cream (plus 5 Delish Mix-ins) ............................................... 84
238. Easy And Delicious Strawberry Frozen Yogurt Recipe................................................... 84
239. Death By Chocolate Ice Cream .............. 84
240. Vegan Blueberry Coconut Ice Cream Recipe................................................................. 85
241. Easy Mint Chocolate Chip Ice Cream Recipe................................................................. 85
242. Super Lemon Ice Cream Recipe ............. 86
243. Chocolate-hazelnut Soy Ice Cream Recipe................................................................. 86
244. Homemade Mint Chocolate Chip Ice Cream Recipe .................................................. 86
245. Creamy Pomegranate Ice Cream Recipe 87
246. Dark Chocolate And Cinnamon Frozen Custard Recipe ................................................ 87
247. Matcha Green Tea Ice Cream Recipe ... 87
248. Easy Eggnog Ice Cream Recipe.............. 87
249. Cookie Butter No-churn Ice Cream ...... 88
250. Dark Brownie Fudge Ice Cream Recipe 88
251. Tropical Ice Cream Sandwiches Recipe 88
252. Mint-chip Coconut Milk Ice Cream Recipe................................................................. 88
253. No-churn Keto Ice Cream Recipe .......... 89
254. Snow Cream Recipe .................................. 89
255. Easy Snow Ice Cream Recipe ................. 89
256. Vanilla Ice Cream Viii Recipe ................... 89
257. French-style Ice Cream............................. 89
258. Peach-maple Ice Cream ........................... 90
259. Guinness Ice Cream Recipe..................... 90
260. Honey Vanilla Ice Cream Recipe............ 91
261. Vanilla Ice Cream Ix Recipe ..................... 91
262. Snow Ice Cream ......................................... 91
263. Vegan Snickers Ice Cream Recipe ......... 91
264. Salted Pecan-maple Ice Cream Recipe 92
265. Divine Cherry Chocolate Ice Cream Recipe................................................................. 92
266. Tropical Ice Cream Recipe ...................... 92
267. Peach-buttermilk Ice Cream.................... 93
268. Espresso Chip Ice Cream Recipe ........... 93
269. Strawberry Freeze Recipe....................... 93
270. Cinnamon Ice Cream Ii Recipe............... 94
271. Dairy-free Coconut Candy Bar Ice Cream Recipe .................................................. 94
272. Condensed-milk Ice Cream With Black Sesame Polvoron?......................................... 94
273. Pumpkin Pie Ice Cream Recipe ............. 95
274. Easy Banana Ice Cream With Milk Chocolate Chunks............................................ 95
275. The Captain's Mango Ice Cream Recipe 95
276. Mudslide No-churn Ice Cream............... 95
277. Coffee And Donuts Ice Cream Recipe . 96
278. Vanilla-almond Ice Cream With Cherries And Pistachios ................................ 96
279. Vanilla Ice Cream X Recipe..................... 97
280. Hazelnut Gelato Recipe........................... 97
281. Instant Strawberry Ice Cream Recipe  97
282. How To Make Vanilla Ice Cream ........... 97
283. Vanilla Bean Ice Cream ............................ 98
284. Roasted Peaches With Mascarpone Ice Cream ............................................................... 98
285. Vanilla Cherry Ice Cream Recipe .......... 99
286. Graham Cracker Ice Cream Recipe ...... 99
287. Vegan Pumpkin Ice Cream Recipe ....... 99
288. Orange-pineapple Ice Recipe ................ 99
289. Fresh Fruit Ice Cream In A Baggie Recipe ................................................................. 99
290. Chocolate Hazelnut Tartufo Recipe... 100
291. Truly Key Lime Pie Ice Cream Recipe 100
292. Key Lime Ice Cream Recipe .................. 101
293. Maple Walnut Ice Cream Recipe......... 101
294. Ricotta Ice Cream With Honey And Almonds ........................................................... 102
295. Chai Tea Ice Cream Recipe ................... 102
296. Peanut Butter-banana V'ice Cream ... 102
297. Pumpkin Ice Cream Recipe ................... 103
298. Granny's Ice Cream Recipe ................... 103
299. Cinnamon Ice Cream Recipe................. 103
300. Strawberry Rosewater Ice Cream Recipe............................................................... 103
301. Fig Ice Cream Recipe ............................. 104
302. Coffee And Doughnuts Ice Cream Recipe 104
303. Keto No-churn Strawberry Ice Cream Recipe............................................................... 104
304. Frozen Vanilla Custard ........................... 105
305. Ice Cream In A Bag................................. 105
306. Vanilla Ice Cream Vii Recipe................. 105
307. Ice Cream Base Recipe .......................... 106
308. Unicorn Ice Cream ................................... 106

309. Keto Strawberry Ice Cream Recipe ... 106
310. Easy Pistachio Ice Cream Recipe ........ 106
311. Roman's Dairy-free Chocolate-coconut Ice Cream ................................................. 107
312. Keto Ice Cream ............................... 107
313. Strawberry Shortcake No-churn Ice Cream ................................................. 107
314. Homemade Pumpkin Frozen Yogurt Recipe ................................................. 108
315. Homemade Peanut Butter Ice Cream Recipe ................................................. 108
316. Vanilla Ice Cream Ii Recipe ................ 108
317. Vanilla Ice Cream V Recipe ................ 108
318. Chocolate Syrup Ice Cream Recipe .... 108
319. Sparkling Ice Cream ........................... 109
320. Ice Cream Salad Recipe ..................... 109
321. Nesquik Frostee No-churn Ice Cream 109
322. Chunky Banana Nut Chip Ice Cream Recipe ................................................. 109
323. Easy Ice Cream In A Bag Recipe ......... 110
324. Chocolate Frosty Recipe .................... 110
325. Pecan Caramel Ice Cream Recipe ....... 110
326. Smooth Raspberry Ice Cream Recipe 110
327. Chef John's Strawberry Ice Cream Recipe ................................................. 111
328. Ice Cream Cones ............................... 111
329. Easy Chocolate Ice Cream Recipe ....... 111
330. Pumpkin Ice Cream ........................... 112
331. Richer Than Rich German Chocolate Ice Cream Recipe ........................................ 112
332. Cherry Cheesecake Frozen Yogurt Recipe ................................................. 113
333. Peanut Butter Ice Cream Recipe ......... 113
334. Quick Ice Cream Recipe ..................... 113
335. Irish Cream Ice Cream Recipe ............ 113
336. Peanut Butter Banana Ice Cream Recipe 113
337. Reese's N'ice Cream .......................... 114
338. No-cook Eggnog Ice Cream Recipe .... 114
339. Lavender Ice Cream Recipe ................ 114
340. Coconut-avocado Ice Cream Recipe .. 114
341. Gelato Recipe .................................... 115
342. Frozen Strawberry Yogurt Recipe ..... 115
343. Olive Oil Ice Cream ............................ 115
344. Spiced Ginger-peach Ice Cream Recipe 116
345. Strawberry, Lemon And Vanilla Ice Cream Parfait ....................................... 116
346. Pineapple Whip Recipe ...................... 116
347. Mint Mojito Coffee Ice Cream Recipe 116
348. Vegan Banana Ice Cream Recipe ........ 117
349. Cinnamon Black Walnut Ice Cream Recipe ................................................. 117
350. Snow Ice Cream Recipe ..................... 117
351. Mermaid Ice Cream ........................... 117
352. No-churn Cake Batter Ice Cream Recipe 117
**OTHER FAVORITE RECIPES ................ 119**
353. Strawberry Ice Cream Milk Shake ..... 119
354. Basil Soft Serve Ice Cream ................. 119
355. Strawberry English Muffin With Honey Ice Cream Sandwich .............................. 119
356. Vegan Chocolate Made Mint Milkshake 119
357. Berries Sorbet ................................... 120
358. Big Banana Nutella Soft Serve Ice Cream 120
359. Vegan Ridiculous Raspberry Coconut Frozen Yogurt ....................................... 120
360. White Chocolate Chip Cookie Dough Frozen Yogurt ....................................... 121
361. Pistachio Berry Frozen Yogurt ............ 121
362. Mouth Watering Maple Bacon Milkshake ............................................. 121
363. Amazing Key Lime Sorbet ................... 121
364. Cherry Fig Mint Milkshake .................. 122
365. Cinnamon Clove Coffee Frozen Yogurt 122
366. Vegan "oh So" Soy Vanilla Soft Serve Ice Cream ................................................. 122
367. Mulberry Ginger Sorbet ..................... 123
368. Ice Cream Pizza ................................. 123
369. Maple Frozen Yogurt .......................... 123
370. Deep Dark Chocolate Sorbet .............. 123
371. "crispy" Kit Kat Ice Cream .................. 124
372. Chocolate Frozen Yogurt .................... 124
373. Chocolate Peanut Butter Soft Serve Ice Cream ................................................. 124
374. Easy Coconut Sorbet .......................... 124
375. Double Fudge Chocolate Gelato ......... 125
376. Buttermilk Frozen Yogurt ................... 125
377. Mango Tango Sorbet .......................... 125
378. Watermelon Sorbet ........................... 125
379. Kiwi Sorbet ........................................ 126
380. Cinnamon Coconut Lemon Blackberry Gelato ................................................. 126
381. Blueberry Frozen Yogurt .................... 126
382. Vegan Radical Raspberry Chocolate Soft Serve Ice Cream .................................. 127
383. Oreo Ice Cream Bar Dessert ............... 127
384. Vanilla Ice Cream Sponge Cake .......... 127
385. Rhubarb Ice Cream Cake .................... 128
386. White Chocolate Citrus Rose Frozen Yogurt ................................................. 128

387. Walnut Mint Pomegranate Frozen Yogurt ................................................. 129
388. Ice Cream Sliders ........................ 129
389. Watermelon Strawberry Frozen Yogurt 129
390. Fun Fig Mint Milkshake .................... 129
391. Frozen Cantaloupe Yogurt ................ 130
392. Chocolate Matcha Gelato .................. 130
393. Grape Sorbet ................................ 130
394. Snicker Doodle Ice Cream Sandwiches 130
395. Agave Lemon Chocolate Sorbet .......... 131
396. Berry Ice Cream Cake ..................... 131
397. Dark Chocolate Coconut Frozen Yogurt 131
398. Succulent Waffle Cookie Ice Cream Sandwich ........................................ 132
399. Apple Chocolate Gelato .................... 132
400. Lemon Strawberry Sorbet ................ 132
401. Cinnamon Maple Bacon Milkshake ... 133
402. Orange Dream Soda Ice Cream .......... 133
403. Chocolaty Chocolate Pretzel Gelato .. 133
404. Blackberry Sugar-free Keto Frozen Yogurt ................................................. 134
405. Strawberry Basil Frozen Yogurt ......... 134
406. Vanilla Peanut Butter Layer .............. 134
407. Mint Greek Frozen Yogurt ................ 134
408. Aromatic Rose Gelato ..................... 135
409. Vegan Chunky Chocolate Banana Milkshake ........................................ 135
410. Lingering Lemon Mint Sorbet ............ 135
411. Aromatic Earl Grey Tea Ice Cream .... 136
412. Raspberry Lavender Sorbet ............. 136
413. Blueberry Pumpkin Spice Waffle Ice Cream Sandwich ............................... 136
414. Cherry Mango Sorbet ..................... 136
415. Lemon Frozen Yogurt ..................... 137
416. Caribbean Pineapple Mint Sorbet ...... 137
417. Neapolitan Frozen Yogurt ................ 137
418. Healthy Greek Frozen Yogurt ........... 137
419. Plum Sorbet ................................ 138
420. Orange Sorbet .............................. 138
421. Berry Pumpkin Spice Frozen Yogurt 138
422. Vegan Chocolate Soft Serve Ice Cream 138
423. Creamy White Chocolate Rose Frozen Yogurt ................................................. 139
424. Vegan Pistachio "punch" Chocolate Chunk Gelato .................................... 139
425. Lemon Scented Rose Gelato ............ 139
426. Frozen Nanaimo Pie ....................... 140
427. Vegan Chunky Chocolate Almond Ice Cream ............................................... 140
428. Strawberry Vanilla Frozen Yogurt ..... 140
429. Sugar Cookie Sandwich With Ice Cream 141
430. Pumpkin Frozen Yogurt ................... 141
431. Caramel & Pistachio Milkshake .......... 141
432. Vegan Big Blackberry Soy Frozen Yogurt ................................................. 142
433. Luscious Lavender Sour Cherry Sorbet 142
434. Brown Sugar Honey Mango Frozen Yogurt ................................................. 142
435. Mint Cookies 'n Sea Salt "silkshake" .. 142
436. Strawberry Lime Sorbet ................... 143
437. Cherry Pineapple Chocolate Milkshake 143
438. Dulce De Leche Frozen Yogurt ......... 143
439. Passion Fruit Sorbet ....................... 143
440. Vegan Sweet Chocolate Strawberry Chunk Gelato .................................... 144
441. Pumpkin Cinnamon Raisin Gingerbread Frozen Yogurt .................................... 144
442. Mango Pineapple Sorbet .................. 144
443. "stuffed" Snickers Soft Serve Ice Cream 145
444. Mulberry Frozen Yogurt ................... 145
445. Mango Madness Chili Lime Sorbet .... 145
446. Meyer Lemon Sorbet ...................... 145
447. Caramel Frozen Squares ................. 146
448. Banana Pineapple Coconut Gelato ..... 146
449. Lime-mango Sorbet ........................ 146
450. Candy Cane Ice Cream Sandwiches ... 147
451. Black Cherry Kiwi Cotton Candy Gelato 147
452. Mango Texas Toast Ice Cream Sandwich ........................................ 147
453. Clementine Sorbet ......................... 147
454. Peach Mango Frozen Yogurt ............ 148
455. Lemon Blueberry Frozen Yogurt ........ 148
456. Finger Lickin' Honey Lavender Milkshake ........................................ 148
457. Vegan Sensuous Strawberries N Cream Ice Cream ....................................... 148
458. Blueberry Honey English Muffin Ice Cream Sandwich ............................... 149
459. Wonderful Watermelon Sorbet .......... 149
460. Lemon Mint Melon Sorbet ............... 149
461. Avocado Sorbet ............................. 149
462. Honey Peach Gelato ....................... 150
463. Lemon Lime Soda Milkshake ............ 150
464. Matcha Ice Cream .......................... 150
465. Strawberry, Nectarine, Orange, Banana Sorbet ............................................. 151
466. Black Raspberry Clementine Sorbet . 151
467. Coconut Guava Raspberry Sorbet ..... 151

468. Peanut Butter Plum Sorbet ................... 151
469. Vegan Soy Vanilla And Carob Chip Ice Cream ........................................................ 152
470. Honey Cinnamon Blackberry English Muffin Ice Cream Sandwich ........................... 152
471. Peach Sorbet ........................................ 152
472. Honey Mint Heaven Milkshake ........... 152
473. Chili Lime Mango Sorbet ..................... 153
474. Sweet Pumpkin Gingerbread Frozen Yogurt ...................................................... 153
475. S'mores Ice Cream Dream Cookie Delight ..................................................... 153
476. Frozen Pistachio Ice Cream Dessert . 153
477. Peach Frozen Yogurt ........................... 154
478. Tart Frozen Yogurt .............................. 154
479. Chunky Cherry Apple Sorbet .............. 154
480. Kiwi Strawberry Gelato ....................... 154
481. Pineapple Sorbet ................................ 155
482. Cherry Chocolate Pretzel Gelato ......... 155
483. Summer Sorbet ................................... 155
484. Lime Sorbet ......................................... 156
485. Matcha Frozen Yogurt ......................... 156
486. Berry Frozen Yogurt ............................ 156
487. Mint Guava Milkshake ......................... 156
488. Feta Frozen Yogurt .............................. 156
489. Chocolate Bacon Frozen Yogurt .......... 157
490. Applesauce Waffle Cookie Ice Cream Sandwich ................................................... 157
491. Chocolate Olive Oil Frozen Yogurt ..... 157
492. Apple Cinnamon Almond Butter Top Roman Ice Cream Sandwich ........................ 158
493. Oreo Ice Cream Cake ........................... 158
494. Chocolate Almond Butter Top Roman Ice Cream Sandwich ................................. 158
495. Frozen Banana Split ............................ 158
496. Turtle Brownie Ice Cream ................... 159

# INTRODUCTION
## The Benefits of Owning Your Own Cuisinart Ice Cream Maker

What makes the Cuisinart Ice Cream Maker special is that it is designed to make ice cream making an easy task. In fact, it is very convenient and economical to make your own frozen desserts at home. Not only do you know what kinds of ingredients go into your ice cream, but you also have saved money as you can make frozen desserts with ingredients that you currently have at home. While these are the benefits of any ice cream maker, the Cuisinart Ice Cream maker offers so much more. Below are the benefits of owning your own Cuisinart Ice Cream Maker.

- **Adding ingredients is a breeze:** This kitchen appliance comes with an ingredient spout that allows you to add ingredients in a breeze. You can add nuts, chips, and other ingredients without interrupting the freezing cycle. This means that the internal temperature of the ice cream chamber is kept constant thus the consistency of the ice cream is better compared to conventional ice cream makers.

- **Transparent Lid:** The lid of the Cuisinart Ice Cream Maker is transparent so you can check the entire freezing process as well as the progress of your dessert. For security purposes, the lid easily locks to the base, so it does not come off easily during the churning process.

- **Comes with a powerful mixing arm:** Mixing troubles are all in the past thanks to the powerful mixing arm of the Cuisinart Ice Cream Maker. The mixing arm aerates the ingredients in the bowl so that you can create light and smooth ice cream.

- **Double insulated walls:** The insulated walls of the Cuisinart Ice Cream maker contain a cooling liquid that speeds up the freezing process. The double-insulated walls keep the internal temperature even, so everything freezes up properly.

- **Space saver:** The Cuisinart Ice Cream Maker comes with space-saving designs. It has rubber feet that allow the machine to be stable while on use. The rubber feet also keep the machine from slipping thus it can be placed on any kind of surface. Moreover, it also comes with a cord storage that keeps the counter neat.

# How To Use Your Ice Cream Maker!

**Easy As 1-2-3**

All these ideas are now flowing, you're ready to open up your creative genius, and all you want to do is get started. There are people waiting! First, let's make sure you know how to use the Cuisinart Ice-21 1.5 Quart or Cuisinart Pure Indulgence 2 Quart Frozen Yogurt-Sorbet & Ice Cream Maker.

**The Steps**

**1)** Make sure your ice cream maker is clean and ready to use (even wash it before first use). Remember, wipe the base with a damp cloth, and then the freezer bowl, lid, and mixing arm with warm water and dish soap.

**2) Freeze your bowl!** We touched on this earlier, but make sure to freeze the freezer bowl in your freezer for at least 6 hours prior to making ice cream, but no more than 22 hours. After you wash and dry your bowl before freezing it, make sure to wrap it in plastic wrap so it doesn't get freezer burn. Store it in the coldest part of your freezer: the back.

**3)** Prepare the ingredients in the recipes in a separate container beforehand. Make sure you can pour easily from your mixing container.

**4)** The bowl is designed to make no more than either 1.5 Quarts for the Cuisinart ICE-21 or 2 quarts for the Pure Indulgence, and make sure not to fill the freezer bowl all the way to the top, leaving at least ½" of room. The ingredients will increase the volume so be careful!

**5)** Attach the churning device/mixing arm. Don't be alarmed if the arm is not snug. It is designed to loosely rest in the bowl.

**6)** Secure the lid firmly.

**7)** Turn on the ice cream maker. The freezer bowl will then begin to rotate.

**8)** Pour your ingredients immediately, but slowly, through the top opening in the lid.

**9)** Let the creaming begin! Wait for 25-35 minutes depending on the recipe and then turn off the ice cream maker and transfer the concoction to another container, placing in the freezer for an additional 2 hours or more. Then enjoy!

**Recipe Tips**

As you can make many frozen recipes with the Cuisinart Ice Cream maker, it is crucial that you know important recipe tips so that you can make delicious recipes at the comfort of your own home:

- Unlike commercial frozen treats, frozen treats made from home do not contain any preservatives and additives such as gums that impart commercial flavor and consistency of the dessert. To achieve firmer consistency, always transfer the frozen treats into airtight containers and store in the freezer to achieve desired consistency.
- For recipes that use precooked ingredients, make sure that such ingredients are chilled overnight before using or chilled over the ice bath. Putting in hot or warm ingredients may increase or raise the temperature inside the freezer bowl affecting the entire freezing process.
- Substitute low-fat creams such as half and half as well as non-dairy milk for heavy cream and whole milk. The higher the fat content, the creamier, and richer the desserts will be. If you use lower-fat substitute because you are health conscious, use the same volume of the substitute as you would with the original recipe.
- For recipes that use alcohol, add alcohol during the last two minutes of the freezing process. Adding the alcohol earlier may impede the freezing process.
- When making the sorbet, make sure that you use ripe fruits. The freezing process often reduces the sweetness of the fruit so that it tastes less sweet than what you will expect. If the fruit tastes tart, add sugar to the recipe.
- Never fill the freezer bowl higher than ¼-inch from the top of the freezer bowl. You have to take note that the volume of the ingredient doubles during the freezing process.
- When making more than one recipe at a time, make sure that the freezer bowl is completely frozen before each use. You can purchase additional freezer bowls for ease and convenience.
- Ingredients such as nuts, and chips should be added 5 minutes before the recipe is complete. Once the dessert thickens, add the ingredients gradually through the ingredient spout. Make sure that they should be chopped into smaller pieces and not larger than a chocolate chip.

# CANDY BAR FUSION ICE CREAM

### 1. Zero Soft Serve Ice Cream

Servings: 6
Cooking Time: 35 Minutes
**Ingredients:**
- 2 cups heavy cream
- 1 cup milk
- 3/4 cup sugar
- 1 Tbs. vanilla extract
- 1 cup sliced Bananas
- 2 Zero Candy Bars.

**Directions:**
1. Refer to note at the beginning of the chapter about freezing bowl.
2. Place the milk & cream in a bowl. Mix together until well combined. Use a whisk to mix in the sugar. Continue to whisking 4 minutes until sugar dissolves. Then mix in the vanilla extract.
3. Place all the ingredients in a food processor or blender, and puree.
4. Pour ingredients into ice cream maker. Let it churn for 25 minutes.

### 2. Take 5 Soft Serve Ice Cream

Servings: 6
Cooking Time: 35 Minutes
**Ingredients:**
- 2 cups heavy cream
- 1 cup milk
- 3/4 cup sugar
- 1 Tbs. vanilla extract
- 1 cup sliced Bananas
- 2 Take 5 Candy Bars.

**Directions:**
1. Refer to note at the beginning of the chapter about freezing bowl.
2. Place the milk & cream in a bowl. Mix together until well combined. Use a whisk to mix in the sugar. Continue to whisking 4 minutes until sugar dissolves. Then mix in the vanilla extract.
3. Place all the ingredients in a food processor or blender, and puree.
4. Pour ingredients into ice cream maker. Let it churn for 25 minutes.
5. Serve immediately.

### 3. Oh, Henry! Soft Serve Ice Cream

Servings: 6
Cooking Time: 35 Minutes
**Ingredients:**
- 2 cups heavy cream
- 1 cup milk
- 3/4 cup sugar
- 1 Tbs. vanilla extract
- 1 cup sliced Bananas
- 2 Oh, Henry! Candy Bars.

**Directions:**
1. Refer to note at the beginning of the chapter about freezing bowl.
2. Place the milk & cream in a bowl. Mix together until well combined. Use a whisk to mix in the sugar. Continue to whisking 4 minutes until sugar dissolves. Then mix in the vanilla extract.
3. Place all the ingredients in a food processor or blender, and puree.
4. Pour ingredients into ice cream maker. Let it churn for 25 minutes.

### 4. Mounds Soft Serve Ice Cream

Servings: 6
Cooking Time: 35 Minutes
**Ingredients:**
- 2 cups heavy cream
- 1 cup milk
- 3/4 cup sugar
- 1 Tbs. vanilla extract
- 1 cup sliced Bananas
- 2 Mounds Candy Bars.

**Directions:**
1. Refer to note at the beginning of the chapter about freezing bowl.
2. Place the milk & cream in a bowl. Mix together until well combined. Use a whisk to mix in the sugar. Continue to whisking 4 minutes until sugar dissolves. Then mix in the vanilla extract.
3. Place all the ingredients in a food processor or blender, and puree.
4. Pour ingredients into ice cream maker. Let it churn for 25 minutes.

### 5. 3 Musketeers Soft Serve Ice Cream

Servings: 6
Cooking Time: 35 Minutes
**Ingredients:**
- 2 cups heavy cream
- 1 cup milk
- 3/4 cup sugar
- 1 Tbs. vanilla extract
- 1 cup sliced Bananas
- 2 3 Musketeers Candy Bars.

**Directions:**
1. Refer to note at the beginning of the chapter about freezing bowl.
2. Place the milk & cream in a bowl. Mix together until well combined. Use a whisk to mix in the sugar. Continue to whisking 4 minutes until sugar dissolves. Then mix in the vanilla extract.
3. Place all the ingredients in a food processor or blender, and puree.
4. Pour ingredients into ice cream maker. Let it churn for 25 minutes.

### 6. Whatchamacallit Soft Serve Ice Cream

Servings: 6
Cooking Time: 35 Minutes
**Ingredients:**
- 2 cups heavy cream
- 1 cup milk
- 3/4 cup sugar
- 1 Tbs. vanilla extract
- 1 cup sliced Bananas
- 2 Whatchamacallit Candy Bars.

**Directions:**
1. Refer to note at the beginning of the chapter about freezing bowl.
2. Place the milk & cream in a bowl. Mix together until well combined. Use a whisk to mix in the sugar. Continue to whisking 4 minutes until sugar dissolves. Then mix in the vanilla extract.
3. Place all the ingredients in a food processor or blender, and puree.
4. Pour ingredients into ice cream maker. Let it churn for 25 minutes.

### 7. Nestlé Crunch Soft Serve Ice Cream

Servings: 6
Cooking Time: 35 Minutes
**Ingredients:**
- 2 cups heavy cream
- 1 cup milk
- 3/4 cup sugar
- 1 Tbs. vanilla extract
- 1 cup sliced Bananas
- 2 Nestlé Crunch Candy Bars.

**Directions:**
1. Refer to note at the beginning of the chapter about freezing bowl.
2. Place the milk & cream in a bowl. Mix together until well combined. Use a whisk to mix in the sugar. Continue to whisking 4 minutes until sugar dissolves. Then mix in the vanilla extract.
3. Place all the ingredients in a food processor or blender, and puree.
4. Pour ingredients into ice cream maker. Let it churn for 25 minutes.
5. Serve immediately.

### 8. Sky Bar Soft Serve Ice Cream

Servings: 6
Cooking Time: 35 Minutes
**Ingredients:**
- 2 cups heavy cream
- 1 cup milk
- 3/4 cup sugar
- 1 Tbs. vanilla extract
- 1 cup sliced Bananas
- 2 Sky Bar Candy Bars.

**Directions:**
1. Refer to note at the beginning of the chapter about freezing bowl.
2. Place the milk & cream in a bowl. Mix together until well combined. Use a whisk to mix in the sugar. Continue to whisking 4 minutes until sugar dissolves. Then mix in the vanilla extract.
3. Place all the ingredients in a food processor or blender, and puree.
4. Pour ingredients into ice cream maker. Let it churn for 25 minutes.
5. Serve immediately.

### 9. Charleston Chew Soft Serve Ice Cream

Servings: 6
Cooking Time: 35 Minutes
**Ingredients:**

- 2 cups heavy cream
- 1 cup milk
- 3/4 cup sugar
- 1 Tbs. vanilla extract
- 1 cup sliced Bananas
- 2 Charleston Chew Candy Bars.

**Directions:**
1. Refer to note at the beginning of the chapter about freezing bowl.
2. Place the milk & cream in a bowl. Mix together until well combined. Use a whisk to mix in the sugar. Continue to whisking 4 minutes until sugar dissolves. Then mix in the vanilla extract.
3. Place all the ingredients in a food processor or blender, and puree.
4. Pour ingredients into ice cream maker. Let it churn for 25 minutes.

### 10. Almond Joy Soft Serve Ice Cream

Servings: 6
Cooking Time: 35 Minutes
**Ingredients:**
- 2 cups heavy cream
- 1 cup milk
- 3/4 cup sugar
- 1 Tbs. vanilla extract
- 1 cup sliced Bananas
- 2 Almond Joy Candy Bars.

**Directions:**
1. Refer to note at the beginning of the chapter about freezing bowl.
2. Place the milk & cream in a bowl. Mix together until well combined. Use a whisk to mix in the sugar. Continue to whisking 4 minutes until sugar dissolves. Then mix in the vanilla extract.
3. Place all the ingredients in a food processor or blender, and puree.
4. Pour ingredients into ice cream maker. Let it churn for 25 minutes.
5. Serve immediately.

### 11. Kit Kat Soft Serve Ice Cream

Servings: 6
Cooking Time: 35 Minutes
**Ingredients:**
- 2 cups heavy cream
- 1 cup milk
- 3/4 cup sugar
- 1 Tbs. vanilla extract
- 1 cup sliced Bananas
- 2 Kit Kat Candy Bars.

**Directions:**
1. Refer to note at the beginning of the chapter about freezing bowl.
2. Place the milk & cream in a bowl. Mix together until well combined. Use a whisk to mix in the sugar. Continue to whisking 4 minutes until sugar dissolves. Then mix in the vanilla extract.
3. Place all the ingredients in a food processor or blender, and puree.
4. Pour ingredients into ice cream maker. Let it churn for 25 minutes.

### 12. Baby Ruth Soft Serve Ice Cream

Servings: 6
Cooking Time: 35 Minutes
**Ingredients:**
- 2 cups heavy cream
- 1 cup milk
- 3/4 cup sugar
- 1 Tbs. vanilla extract
- 1 cup sliced Bananas
- 2 Baby Ruth Candy Bars.

**Directions:**
1. Refer to note at the beginning of the chapter about freezing bowl.
2. Place the milk & cream in a bowl. Mix together until well combined. Use a whisk to mix in the sugar. Continue to whisking 4 minutes until sugar dissolves. Then mix in the vanilla extract.
3. Place all the ingredients in a food processor or blender, and puree.
4. Pour ingredients into ice cream maker. Let it churn for 25 minutes.
5. Serve immediately.

### 13. Caramello Dreamin Soft Serve Ice Cream

Servings: 6
Cooking Time: 35 Minutes
**Ingredients:**
- 2 cups heavy cream
- 1 cup milk
- 3/4 cup sugar

- 1 Tbs. vanilla extract
- 1 cup sliced Bananas
- 2 Caramello Candy Bars.

**Directions:**
1. Refer to note at the beginning of the chapter about freezing bowl.
2. Place the milk & cream in a bowl. Mix together until well combined. Use a whisk to mix in the sugar. Continue to whisking 4 minutes until sugar dissolves. Then mix in the vanilla extract.
3. Place all the ingredients in a food processor or blender, and puree.
4. Pour ingredients into ice cream maker. Let it churn for 25 minutes.
5. Serve immediately.

### 14. Heath Bar Soft Serve Ice Cream

Servings: 6
Cooking Time: 35 Minutes
**Ingredients:**
- 2 cups heavy cream
- 1 cup milk
- 3/4 cup sugar
- 1 Tbs. vanilla extract
- 1 cup sliced Bananas
- 2 Heath Bar Candy Bars.

**Directions:**
1. Refer to note at the beginning of the chapter about freezing bowl.
2. Place the milk & cream in a bowl. Mix together until well combined. Use a whisk to mix in the sugar. Continue to whisking 4 minutes until sugar dissolves. Then mix in the vanilla extract.
3. Place all the ingredients in a food processor or blender, and puree.
4. Pour ingredients into ice cream maker. Let it churn for 25 minutes.
5. Serve immediately.

### 15. Snickers Soft Serve Ice Cream

Servings: 6
Cooking Time: 35 Minutes
**Ingredients:**
- 2 cups heavy cream
- 1 cup milk
- 3/4 cup sugar
- 1 Tbs. vanilla extract
- 1 cup sliced Bananas
- 2 Snickers Candy Bars.

**Directions:**
1. Refer to note at the beginning of the chapter about freezing bowl.
2. Place the milk & cream in a bowl. Mix together until well combined. Use a whisk to mix in the sugar. Continue to whisking 4 minutes until sugar dissolves. Then mix in the vanilla extract.
3. Place all the ingredients in a food processor or blender, and puree.
4. Pour ingredients into ice cream maker. Let it churn for 25 minutes.

### 16. 100 Grand Soft Serve Ice Cream

Servings: 6
Cooking Time: 35 Minutes
**Ingredients:**
- 2 cups heavy cream
- 1 cup milk
- 3/4 cup sugar
- 1 Tbs. vanilla extract
- 1 cup sliced Bananas
- 2 100 Grand Candy Bars.

**Directions:**
1. Refer to note at the beginning of the chapter about freezing bowl.
2. Place the milk & cream in a bowl. Mix together until well combined. Use a whisk to mix in the sugar. Continue to whisking 4 minutes until sugar dissolves. Then mix in the vanilla extract.
3. Place all the ingredients in a food processor or blender, and puree.
4. Pour ingredients into ice cream maker. Let it churn for 25 minutes.

### 17. Mr. Goodbar Soft Serve Ice Cream

Servings: 6
Cooking Time: 35 Minutes
**Ingredients:**
- 2 cups heavy cream
- 1 cup milk
- 3/4 cup sugar
- 1 Tbs. vanilla extract
- 1 cup sliced Bananas
- 2 Mr. Goodbar Candy Bars.

**Directions:**

1. Refer to note at the beginning of the chapter about freezing bowl.
2. Place the milk & cream in a bowl. Mix together until well combined. Use a whisk to mix in the sugar. Continue to whisking 4 minutes until sugar dissolves. Then mix in the vanilla extract.
3. Place all the ingredients in a food processor or blender, and puree.
4. Pour ingredients into ice cream maker. Let it churn for 25 minutes.
5. Serve immediately.

### 18. Milky Way Soft Serve Ice Cream

Servings: 6
Cooking Time: 35 Minutes
**Ingredients:**
- 2 cups heavy cream
- 1 cup milk
- 3/4 cup sugar
- 1 Tbs. vanilla extract
- 1 cup sliced Bananas
- 2 Milky Way Candy Bars.

**Directions:**
1. Refer to note at the beginning of the chapter about freezing bowl.
2. Place the milk & cream in a bowl. Mix together until well combined. Use a whisk to mix in the sugar. Continue to whisking 4 minutes until sugar dissolves. Then mix in the vanilla extract.
3. Place all the ingredients in a food processor or blender, and puree.
4. Pour ingredients into ice cream maker. Let it churn for 25 minutes.

### 19. 5th Avenue Soft Serve Ice Cream

Servings: 6
Cooking Time: 35 Minutes
**Ingredients:**
- 2 cups heavy cream
- 1 cup milk
- 3/4 cup sugar
- 1 Tbs. vanilla extract
- 1 cup sliced Bananas
- 2 5th Avenue Candy Bars.

**Directions:**
1. Refer to note at the beginning of the chapter about freezing bowl.
2. Place the milk & cream in a bowl. Mix together until well combined. Use a whisk to mix in the sugar. Continue to whisking 4 minutes until sugar dissolves. Then mix in the vanilla extract.
3. Place all the ingredients in a food processor or blender, and puree.
4. Pour ingredients into ice cream maker. Let it churn for 25 minutes.
5. Serve immediately.

### 20. Hershey Bar Soft Serve Ice Cream

Servings: 6
Cooking Time: 35 Minutes
**Ingredients:**
- 2 cups heavy cream
- 1 cup milk
- 3/4 cup sugar
- 1 Tbs. vanilla extract
- 1 cup sliced Bananas
- 2 Hershey Bar Candy Bars.

**Directions:**
1. Refer to note at the beginning of the chapter about freezing bowl.
2. Place the milk & cream in a bowl. Mix together until well combined. Use a whisk to mix in the sugar. Continue to whisking 4 minutes until sugar dissolves. Then mix in the vanilla extract.
3. Place all the ingredients in a food processor or blender, and puree.
4. Pour ingredients into ice cream maker. Let it churn for 25 minutes.
5. Serve immediately.

### 21. Twix Soft Serve Ice Cream

Servings: 6
Cooking Time: 35 Minutes
**Ingredients:**
- 2 cups heavy cream
- 1 cup milk
- 3/4 cup sugar
- 1 Tbs. vanilla extract
- 1 cup sliced Bananas
- 4 Twix Candy Bars.

**Directions:**
1. Refer to note at the beginning of the chapter about freezing bowl.

2. Place the milk & cream in a bowl. Mix together until well combined. Use a whisk to mix in the sugar. Continue to whisking 4 minutes until sugar dissolves. Then mix in the vanilla extract.
3. Place all the ingredients in a food processor or blender, and puree.
4. Pour ingredients into ice cream maker. Let it churn for 25 minutes.

### 22. Pay Day Soft Serve Ice Cream

Servings: 6
Cooking Time: 35 Minutes
**Ingredients:**
- 2 cups heavy cream
- 1 cup milk
- 3/4 cup sugar
- 1 Tbs. vanilla extract
- 1 cup sliced Bananas
- 2 Pay Day Candy Bars.

**Directions:**
1. Refer to note at the beginning of the chapter about freezing bowl.
2. Place the milk & cream in a bowl. Mix together until well combined. Use a whisk to mix in the sugar. Continue to whisking 4 minutes until sugar dissolves. Then mix in the vanilla extract.
3. Place all the ingredients in a food processor or blender, and puree.
4. Pour ingredients into ice cream maker. Let it churn for 25 minutes.

### 23. Mars Bar Soft Serve Ice Cream

Servings: 6
Cooking Time: 35 Minutes
**Ingredients:**
- 2 cups heavy cream
- 1 cup milk
- 3/4 cup sugar
- 1 Tbs. vanilla extract
- 1 cup sliced Bananas
- 2 Mars Bar Candy Bars.

**Directions:**
1. Refer to note at the beginning of the chapter about freezing bowl.
2. Place the milk & cream in a bowl. Mix together until well combined. Use a whisk to mix in the sugar. Continue to whisking 4 minutes until sugar dissolves. Then mix in the vanilla extract.
3. Place all the ingredients in a food processor or blender, and puree.
4. Pour ingredients into ice cream maker. Let it churn for 25 minutes.

### 24. Skor Bar Soft Serve Ice Cream

Servings: 6
Cooking Time: 35 Minutes
**Ingredients:**
- 2 cups heavy cream
- 1 cup milk
- 3/4 cup sugar
- 1 Tbs. vanilla extract
- 1 cup sliced Bananas
- 2 Skor Bar Candy Bars.

**Directions:**
1. Refer to note at the beginning of the chapter about freezing bowl.
2. Place the milk & cream in a bowl. Mix together until well combined. Use a whisk to mix in the sugar. Continue to whisking 4 minutes until sugar dissolves. Then mix in the vanilla extract.
3. Place all the ingredients in a food processor or blender, and puree.
4. Pour ingredients into ice cream maker. Let it churn for 25 minutes.
5. Serve immediately.

### 25. Krackel Soft Serve Ice Cream

Servings: 6
Cooking Time: 35 Minutes
**Ingredients:**
- 2 cups heavy cream
- 1 cup milk
- 3/4 cup sugar
- 1 Tbs. vanilla extract
- 1 cup sliced Bananas
- 2 Krackel Candy Bars.

**Directions:**
1. Refer to note at the beginning of the chapter about freezing bowl.
2. Place the milk & cream in a bowl. Mix together until well combined. Use a whisk to mix in the sugar. Continue to whisking 4 minutes until sugar

dissolves. Then mix in the vanilla extract.
3. Place all the ingredients in a food processor or blender, and puree.
4. Pour ingredients into ice cream maker. Let it churn for 25 minutes.

### 26. Butterfinger Soft Serve Ice Cream

Servings: 6
Cooking Time: 35 Minutes
**Ingredients:**
- 2 cups heavy cream
- 1 cup milk
- 3/4 cup sugar
- 1 Tbs. vanilla extract
- 1 cup sliced Bananas
- 2 Butterfinger Candy Bars.

**Directions:**
1. Refer to note at the beginning of the chapter about freezing bowl.
2. Place the milk & cream in a bowl. Mix together until well combined. Use a whisk to mix in the sugar. Continue to whisking 4 minutes until sugar dissolves. Then mix in the vanilla extract.
3. Place all the ingredients in a food processor or blender, and puree.
4. Pour ingredients into ice cream maker. Let it churn for 25 minutes.
5. Serve immediately.

# FRUITILICIOUS ICE CREAM

## 27. Kickin' Key Lime Sorbet

Servings: 4
Cooking Time: 3 Hours
**Ingredients:**
- 3 cups cold water
- 2 ¼ cup fresh key lime juice
- 2 3/4 cup sugar
- 1 tablespoon lime zest

**Directions:**
1. Refer to note at the beginning of the chapter about freezing bowl.
2. Mix together the water and sugar in a large sauce pan on medium heat. Allow the mixture to come to a boil. Then lower to low heat, and let the mixture simmer until the sugar dissolve. Allow the mixture to cool completely.
3. Mix the lime juice and zest with the cooled mixture.
4. Pour the ingredients into your ice cream maker, and let it churn for 25-30 minutes.
5. Place in an airtight container for up to 2 hours, until desired consistency is reached.

## 28. Orange Chocolate Almond Vegan Ice Cream

Servings: 9
Cooking Time: 10 Minutes
**Ingredients:**
- 3/4 cup water
- 1 1/4 cups full fat coconut milk or coconut cream (as thick as possible)
- 2/3 cup organic cane sugar
- 2/3 cup unsweetened cocoa powder
- 1/4 tsp sea salt
- 6 ounces vegan dark chocolate, finely chopped
- 1/2 tsp pure vanilla extract
- ½ cup chopped almonds
- ½ tsp orange extract

**Directions:**
1. NOTE: Freeze your ice cream bowl for at least 24hrs prior to starting!
2. Put the first 5 ingredients in a large saucepan, and heat it on medium-high heat. Mix the ingredients together using a whisk. Allow the mixture to come to a low boil. Continue to whisk often, and remain cooking on a low boil for 1 minute.
3. Take the pan off the heat, and mix in the chocolate and vanilla extract using the whisk. Continue to mix until the chocolate is melted.
4. Place the mixture in a blender, blend on high (30 seconds) and allow the mixture to cool.
5. Pour the ingredients into your ice cream maker, and let it churn for 25 minutes. About 5 minutes before the ice cream is done churning.
6. Put the ice cream in an airtight container and place in the freezer for around 2 hours. Allow the ice cream to thaw for 15 minutes before serving.

## 29. Chocolate Peppermint Banana Vegan Milkshake

Servings: 9
Cooking Time: 10 Minutes
**Ingredients:**
- 3/4 cup water
- 1 1/4 cups full fat coconut milk or coconut cream (as thick as possible)
- 2/3 cup organic cane sugar
- 2/3 cup unsweetened cocoa powder
- 1/4 tsp sea salt
- 6 ounces vegan dark chocolate, finely chopped
- 11/2 tsp peppermint extract
- ½ cup sliced frozen bananas

**Directions:**
1. NOTE: Freeze your ice cream bowl for at least 24hrs prior to starting!
2. Put the first 5 ingredients in a large saucepan, and heat it on medium-high heat. Mix the ingredients together using a whisk. Allow the mixture to come to a low boil. Continue to whisk often, and remain cooking on a low boil for 1 minute.
3. Take the pan off the heat, and mix in the chocolate and mint extract using the whisk. Continue to mix until the chocolate is melted.

4. Place mixture in a blender with the bananas, and blend on high speed for about 30 seconds.
5. Allow the mixture to cool
6. Pour the ingredients into your ice cream maker, and let it churn for 10-15 minutes, until desired consistency is reached.
7. Serve immediately.

### 30. Going Guava Milkshake

Servings: 6
Cooking Time: 25 Minutes
**Ingredients:**
- 2 cups heavy cream
- 1 cup milk
- 3/4 cup sugar
- 1 teaspoon vanilla extract
- 1 1/2 cups guava juice

**Directions:**
1. Refer to note at the beginning of the chapter about freezing bowl.
2. Place the milk and cream in a bowl, and mix them together until well combined. Use a whisk to mix in the sugar. Continue to whisk for about 4 minutes until the sugar dissolves. Then mix in the vanilla extract, and juice.
3. Pour the ingredients into your ice cream maker, and let it churn for 10-15 minutes, until desired consistency is reached.
4. Serve immediately.

### 31. Double Bliss Berry Delight Frozen Yogurt

Servings: 1 Quart
Cooking Time: 2 Hours 35 Minutes
**Ingredients:**
- 1 quart container full-fat plain yogurt
- ¼ teaspoon salt
- 1 cup sugar
- 1 tablespoon vanilla extract
- 1 cup raspberries
- 1 cup blueberries

**Directions:**
1. Refer to note at the beginning of the chapter about freezing bowl.
2. Puree the raspberries and blueberries in a food processor or blender
3. Place the yogurt in a bowl. Use a whisk to mix in the sugar and salt. Continue to whisk for about 4 minutes until the sugar dissolves. Then mix in the vanilla extract, and berry puree.
4. Pour the ingredients into your ice cream maker, and let it churn for 25 minutes.
5. Put the frozen yogurt in an airtight container and place in the freezer for at least 2 hours, until desired consistency is reached.

### 32. Chocolate Raspberry Pistachio Vegan Gelato

Servings: 4
Cooking Time: 2 Hours 35 Minutes
**Ingredients:**
- 2 cups shelled, roasted, salted pistachios
- 1 can coconut milk
- I/2 cup arrowroot
- ¾ cup sugar
- 1 teaspoon lime juice
- 4 ounces chopped vegan chocolate
- 1/4 cup raspberries

**Directions:**
1. NOTE: Freeze your ice cream bowl for at least 24hrs prior to starting!
2. Pulse the pistachios in a food processor for about 3 minutes
3. Place all ingredients EXCEPT the chocolate in a blender. Blend on high speed until smooth.
4. Pour the mixture into your ice cream maker, and let it churn for 25 minutes. About 5 minutes before the ice cream is done churning add the chocolate to your ice cream maker.
5. Put the gelato in an airtight container and place in the freezer for up to 2 hours, until desired consistency is reached.

### 33. Nutella & Bananas Soft Serve Ice Cream

Servings: 6
Cooking Time: 35 Minutes

**Ingredients:**
- 1 cup sliced Bananas
- 6 tbs. Nutella
- 2 cups heavy cream
- 1 cup milk
- 3/4 cup sugar
- 1 Tbs. vanilla extract

**Directions:**
1. NOTE: Freeze your ice cream bowl for at least 24hrs prior to starting!
2. Place the milk and cream in a bowl, and mix them together until well combined. Use a whisk to mix in the sugar. Continue to whisk for about 4 minutes until the sugar dissolves. Then mix in the vanilla extract.
3. Place all the ingredients in a food processor or blender, and puree.
4. Pour the ingredients into your ice cream maker, and let it churn for 25 minutes.
5. Serve immediately.

### 34. Cinnamon Soy Vanilla Vegan Soft Serve Ice Cream

Servings: Makes 1 Quart
Cooking Time: 35 Minutes
**Ingredients:**
- 1 pound silken tofu
- ½ cup plus 2 tablespoons organic or granulated sugar
- ½ teaspoon kosher salt
- 1 vanilla bean, split lengthwise
- ¾ cup refined coconut oil, melted, cooled slightly
- 2 teaspoons cinnamon

**Directions:**
1. NOTE: Freeze your ice cream bowl for at least 24hrs prior to starting!
2. Put the first 3 ingredients in a blender. Then add in the vanilla bean seeds. Puree the mixture until its smooth, around 15 seconds. Turn the blender to medium speed, and slowly drizzle in the coconut oil and cinnamon. Blend the mixture until its thick, but don't over blend it.
3. Pour the ingredients into your ice cream maker, and let it churn for 25 minutes.
4. Serve immediately.

### 35. Big Blueberry Chocolate Gelato

Servings: 4-6
Cooking Time: 2 Hours 35 Minutes
**Ingredients:**
- 1/2 cup heavy cream
- 2 cups milk
- 3/4 cup sugar
- 1 teaspoon vanilla extract
- 1 cup blueberries
- ½ cup finely chopped semi-sweet

**Directions:**
1. Refer to note at the beginning of the chapter about freezing bowl.
2. Puree the bananas in a food processor or blender.
3. Place the milk and cream in a bowl, and mix them together until well combined. Use a whisk to mix in the sugar. Continue to whisk for about 4 minutes until the sugar dissolves. Then mix in the vanilla extract and banana puree.
4. Pour the ingredients into your ice cream maker, and let it churn for 25 minutes. About 5 minutes before the ice cream is done churning add the chocolate to your ice cream maker.
5. Put the gelato in an airtight container and place in the freezer for up to 2 hours, until desired consistency is reached.

### 36. Juicy Strawberry Honey Frozen Yogurt

Servings: 1 Quart
Cooking Time: 2 Hours 35 Minutes
**Ingredients:**
- 1 quart container full-fat plain yogurt
- ¼ teaspoon salt
- 1 cup sugar
- 1 teaspoon vanilla extract
- 8 ounces strawberries
- 1/4 cup honey

**Directions:**
1. Refer to note at the beginning of the chapter about freezing bowl.
2. Puree the strawberries in a food processor or blender.
3. Place the yogurt in a bowl. Use a whisk to mix in the sugar and salt. Continue to whisk for about 4

minutes until the sugar dissolves. Then mix in the vanilla extract, honey and strawberry puree.
4. Pour the ingredients into your ice cream maker, and let it churn for 25 minutes.
5. Put the frozen yogurt in an airtight container and place in the freezer for at least 2 hours, until desired consistency is reached.

### 37. Pineapple Strawberries N Cream Tofu Vegan Ice Cream

Servings: Makes 1 Quart
Cooking Time: 35 Minutes
**Ingredients:**
- 1 pound silken tofu
- ½ cup plus 2 tablespoons organic or granulated sugar
- ½ teaspoon kosher salt
- 1 vanilla bean, split lengthwise
- ¾ cup refined coconut oil, melted, cooled slightly
- ½ cup sliced strawberries
- ½ cup pineapple

**Directions:**
1. NOTE: Freeze your ice cream bowl for at least 24hrs prior to starting!
2. Put the first 3 ingredients in a blender. Then add in the vanilla bean seeds, pineapples and strawberries. Puree the mixture until its smooth, around 15 seconds. Turn the blender to medium speed, and slowly drizzle in the coconut oil. Blend the mixture until its thick, but don't over blend it.
3. Pour the ingredients into your ice cream maker, and let it churn for 25 minutes.
4. Put the ice cream in an airtight container and place in the freezer for around 2 hours. Allow the ice cream to thaw for 15 minutes before serving.

### 38. Kickin' Kiwi Lime Ice Cream

Servings: 6
Cooking Time: 2 Hours 50 Minutes
**Ingredients:**
- 2 cups heavy cream
- 1 cup milk
- 3/4 cup sugar
- 1/2 teaspoon vanilla extract
- ½ teaspoon salt
- 1 kiwi, peeled
- Juice of one and a half limes

**Directions:**
1. Refer to note at the beginning of the chapter about freezing bowl.
2. Puree the kiwi in a food processor or blender.
3. Place the milk and cream in a bowl, and mix them together until well combined. Use a whisk to mix in the sugar and salt. Continue to whisk for about 4 minutes until the sugar and salt dissolves. Then mix in the vanilla extract, lime juice, and kiwi puree.
4. Pour the ingredients into your ice cream maker, and let it churn for 25 minutes.
5. Put the ice cream in an airtight container and place in the freezer for around 2 hours. Allow the ice cream to thaw for 15 minutes before serving.

### 39. Blackberry Lemon Coconut Vegan Frozen Yogurt

Servings: 1 Quart
Cooking Time: 2 Hours 35 Minutes
**Ingredients:**
- 2 cups coconut yogurt
- 1/4 cup sugar or maple syrup
- 1/2 teaspoon vanilla extract
- 1/4 cup shredded coconut
- ½ cup blackberries
- 1 lemon

**Directions:**
1. NOTE: Freeze your ice cream bowl for at least 24hrs prior to starting!
2. Puree the blackberries and lemon in a food processor or blender.
3. Place the yogurt in a bowl. Use a whisk to mix in the sugar. Continue to whisk for about 4 minutes until the sugar dissolves. Then mix in the vanilla extract, and blackberry puree.
4. Pour the ingredients into your ice cream maker, and let it churn for 25 minutes. About 5 minutes before the ice cream is done churning add the shredded coconut to your ice cream maker.

5. Put the frozen yogurt in an airtight container and place in the freezer for at least 2 hours, until desired consistency is reached.

### 40. Caramel Cookie Crunch Soft Serve Ice Cream

Servings: 6
Cooking Time: 35 Minutes
**Ingredients:**
- 2 cups heavy cream
- 1 cup milk
- 3/4 cup sugar
- 1 Tbs. vanilla extract
- 1 ½ cups chopped mini 1 Twix bar

**Directions:**
1. NOTE: Freeze your ice cream bowl for at least 24hrs prior to starting!
2. Place the milk and cream in a bowl, and mix them together until well combined. Use a whisk to mix in the sugar. Continue to whisk for about 4 minutes until the sugar dissolves. Mix in the vanilla extract.
3. Pour the ingredients into your ice cream maker, and let it churn for 25 minutes. About 5 minutes before the ice cream is done churning add the snickers to your ice cream maker.
4. Serve immediately.

### 41. Grapelicious Ice Cream

Servings: 6
Cooking Time: 2 Hours 50 Minutes
**Ingredients:**
- 2 cups heavy cream
- 1 cup milk
- 3/4 cup sugar
- 1 teaspoon vanilla extract
- 2 cans (12 ounces) frozen grape juice concentrate
- juice of 3 lemons

**Directions:**
1. Refer to note at the beginning of the chapter about freezing bowl.
2. Place the milk and cream in a bowl, and mix them together until well combined. Use a whisk to mix in the sugar. Continue to whisk for about 4 minutes until the sugar dissolves. Then mix in the vanilla extract, grape juice, and lemon juice.
3. Pour the ingredients into your ice cream maker, and let it churn for 25 minutes.
4. Put the ice cream in an airtight container and place in the freezer for around 2 hours. Allow the ice cream to thaw for 15 minutes before serving.

### 42. "bursting" Blueberry Maple Syrup Soft Serve Ice Cream

Servings: 6
Cooking Time: 35 Minutes
**Ingredients:**
- 2 cups heavy cream
- 1 cup milk
- 3/4 cup sugar
- 1 Tbs. vanilla extract
- 1 cup blueberries
- ¼ cup maple syrup

**Directions:**
1. Refer to note at the beginning of the chapter about freezing bowl.
2. Puree the blueberries in a food processor or blender.
3. Place the milk and cream in a bowl, and mix them together until well combined. Use a whisk to mix in the sugar. Continue to whisk for about 4 minutes until the sugar dissolves. Then mix in the vanilla extract. Then mix in the blueberries, and maple syrup.
4. Pour the ingredients into your ice cream maker, and let it churn for 25 minutes.
5. Serve immediately.

### 43. Chunky Cherry Sorbet

Servings: 6
Cooking Time: 2 Hours 40 Minutes
**Ingredients:**
- 6 cups frozen pitted cherries
- 1/4 cup sugar
- Juice of one lemon

**Directions:**
1. Refer to note at the beginning of the chapter about freezing bowl.
2. Puree the sugar and cherries in a food processor or blender until smooth.

Put in the lemon juice and pulse a few times to mix the ingredients.
3. Pour the ingredients into your ice cream maker, and let it churn for 25-30 minutes.
4. Place in an airtight container for up to 2 hours, until desired consistency is reached.

### 44. Blueberry Chocolate Vegan Soft Serve Ice Cream

Servings: 9
Cooking Time: 10 Minutes
**Ingredients:**
- 3/4 cup water
- 1 1/4 cups full fat coconut milk or coconut cream (as thick as possible)
- 2/3 cup organic cane sugar
- 2/3 cup unsweetened cocoa powder
- 1/4 tsp sea salt
- 6 ounces vegan dark chocolate, finely chopped
- 1/2 tsp pure vanilla extract
- 1/2 cup blueberries

**Directions:**
1. NOTE: Freeze your ice cream bowl for at least 24hrs prior to starting!
2. Put the first 5 ingredients in a large saucepan, and heat it on medium-high heat. Mix the ingredients together using a whisk. Allow the mixture to come to a low boil. Continue to whisk often, and remain cooking on a low boil for 1 minute.
3. Take the pan off the heat, and mix in the chocolate and vanilla extract using the whisk. Continue to mix until the chocolate is melted.
4. Place the mixture in a blender with the blueberries, and blend on high speed for about 30 seconds or until the blueberries are pureed.
5. Allow the mixture to cool
6. Pour the ingredients into your ice cream maker, and let it churn for 25 minutes.
7. Serve immediately.

### 45. Vanilla Apple Cinnamon Ice Cream

Servings: 6
Cooking Time: 2 Hours 50 Minutes
**Ingredients:**
- 2 cups heavy cream
- 1 cup milk
- 3/4 cup sugar
- 1 teaspoon vanilla extract
- 1 teaspoon ground cinnamon
- 2 large apples peeled, cored, and sliced
- 1/4 cup chopped walnuts

**Directions:**
1. Refer to note at the beginning of the chapter about freezing bowl.
2. Puree the apples in a food processor or blender.
3. Place the milk and cream in a bowl, and mix them together until well combined. Use a whisk to mix in the sugar. Continue to whisk for about 4 minutes until the sugar dissolves. Then mix in the vanilla extract, cinnamon, and apple puree.
4. Pour the ingredients into your ice cream maker, and let it churn for 25 minutes. About 5 minutes before the ice cream is finished churning, add in the walnuts and several drops of vanilla!.
5. Put the ice cream in an airtight container and place in the freezer for around 2 hours. Allow the ice cream to thaw for 15 minutes before serving.

### 46. Carob Chip Mint Soy Vanilla Vegan Ice Cream

Servings: Makes 1 Quart
Cooking Time: 35 Minutes
**Ingredients:**
- 1 pound silken tofu
- ½ cup plus 2 tablespoons organic or granulated sugar
- ½ teaspoon kosher salt
- 1 vanilla bean, split lengthwise
- ¾ cup virgin coconut oil, melted, ½ cooled
- 1 cup vegan carob chips
- ¼ cup mint (pulverized)

**Directions:**
1. NOTE: Freeze your ice cream bowl for at least 24hrs prior to starting!
2. Put the first 3 ingredients in a blender. Then add in the vanilla bean seeds. Puree the mixture until its

smooth, around 15 seconds. Turn the blender to medium speed, and slowly drizzle in the coconut oil. Blend the mixture until its thick, but don't over blend it.
3. Pour the ingredients into your ice cream maker, and let it churn for 25 minutes. About 5 minutes before the ice cream is done churning add the carob chips and mint to your ice cream maker.
4. Put the ice cream in an airtight container and place in the freezer for around 2 hours. Allow the ice cream to thaw for 15 minutes before serving.

### 47. Peanut Butter White Chocolate Soft Serve Ice Cream

Servings: 6
Cooking Time: 40 Minutes
**Ingredients:**
- 2 cups heavy cream
- 1 cup milk
- 3/4 cup sugar
- 1 Tbs. vanilla extract
- 1/2 cup peanut butter slightly melted
- 2 ounces semi-sweet chocolate

**Directions:**
1. NOTE: Freeze your ice cream bowl for at least 24hrs prior to starting!
2. Melt the chocolate in a medium sauce pan on low heat. Allow the chocolate to cool a bit.
3. While the chocolate is cooling, place the milk and cream in a bowl, and mix them together until well combined. Use a whisk to mix in the sugar. Continue to whisk for about 4 minutes until the sugar dissolves. Mix in the vanilla extract. Then whisk in the peanut butter, and then the chocolate.
4. Pour the ingredients into your ice cream maker, and let it churn for 25 minutes.
5. Serve immediately.

### 48. Sassy Strawberry Lime Sorbet

Servings: 4
Cooking Time: 3 Hours
**Ingredients:**
- 2 cups water
- 3 pounds chilled strawberries
- 2 ½ cup sugar
- 5 chilled limes

**Directions:**
1. Refer to note at the beginning of the chapter about freezing bowl.
2. Mix together the water and sugar in a large sauce pan on medium heat. Allow the mixture to come to a boil. Then lower to low heat, and let the mixture simmer until the sugar dissolve. Allow the mixture to cool completely.
3. Puree the strawberries in a food processor or blender until smooth. Then add the zest of 3 limes, juice of 5 limes, and the cooled syrup. Blend until all ingredients are mixed.
4. Mix the lime juice and zest with the cooled mixture.
5. Pour the ingredients into your ice cream maker, and let it churn for 25-30 minutes.
6. Place in an airtight container for up to 2 hours, until desired consistency is reached.

### 49. Rosemary Soft Serve Ice Cream

Servings: 6
Cooking Time: 35 Minutes
**Ingredients:**
- 2 cups heavy cream
- 1 cup milk
- 3/4 cup sugar
- 1 Tbs. vanilla extract
- 1 ½ cups packed rosemary

**Directions:**
1. NOTE: Freeze your ice cream bowl for at least 24hrs prior to starting!
2. Place the milk and cream in a bowl, and mix them together until well combined. Use a whisk to mix in the sugar. Continue to whisk for about 4 minutes until the sugar dissolves. Mix in the vanilla extract.
3. Pulverize the rosemary in a blender or food processor.
4. Place all the ingredients in a food processor or blender, and puree.

5. Pour the ingredients into your ice cream maker, and let it churn for 25 minutes.
6. Serve immediately.

### 50. Bursting Banana Nut Gelato

Servings: 4-6
Cooking Time: 2 Hours 35 Minutes
**Ingredients:**
- 1/2 cup heavy cream
- 2 cups milk
- 3/4 cup sugar
- 1 tablespoon vanilla extract
- 1 cup sliced banana
- ½ cup chopped walnuts

**Directions:**
1. Refer to note at the beginning of the chapter about freezing bowl.
2. Puree the bananas in a food processor or blender.
3. Place the milk and cream in a bowl, and mix them together until well combined. Use a whisk to mix in the sugar. Continue to whisk for about 4 minutes until the sugar dissolves. Then mix in the vanilla extract and banana puree.
4. Pour the ingredients into your ice cream maker, and let it churn for 25 minutes. About 5 minutes before the ice cream is done churning add the walnuts to your ice cream maker.
5. Put the gelato in an airtight container and place in the freezer for up to 2 hours, until desired consistency is reached.

### 51. Lemon Lime Milkshake

Servings: 6
Cooking Time: 25 Minutes
**Ingredients:**
- 2 cups heavy cream
- 1 cup milk
- 3/4 cup sugar
- 1 teaspoon vanilla extract
- ¼ cup lime juice
- ¼ cup lemon juice
- Zest of one lemon
- Zest of one lime

**Directions:**
1. Refer to note at the beginning of the chapter about freezing bowl.
2. Place the milk and cream in a bowl, and mix them together until well combined. Use a whisk to mix in the sugar. Continue to whisk for about 4 minutes until the sugar dissolves. Then mix in the vanilla extract, juice, and zest.
3. Pour the ingredients into your ice cream maker, and let it churn for 10-15 minutes, until desired consistency is reached.
4. Serve immediately.

### 52. Peaches And Cream Soft Serve Ice Cream

Servings: 6
Cooking Time: 35 Minutes
**Ingredients:**
- 2 cups heavy cream
- 1 cup milk
- 3/4 cup sugar
- 1 Tbs. vanilla extract
- 1 cup sliced peaches

**Directions:**
1. Refer to note at the beginning of the chapter about freezing bowl.
2. Puree the peaches in a food processor or blender.
3. Place the milk and cream in a bowl, and mix them together until well combined. Use a whisk to mix in the sugar. Continue to whisk for about 4 minutes until the sugar dissolves. Then mix in the vanilla extract. Then mix in the peaches.
4. Pour the ingredients into your ice cream maker, and let it churn for 25 minutes.
5. Serve immediately.

### 53. Mango Madness Coconut Raspberry Sorbet

Cooking Time: 5 Hours 35 Minutes
Servings: 11
**Ingredients:**
- 3 cups packed, cubed mango
- 1 cup fresh raspberries
- 1 cup full-fat coconut milk
- 1 cup sugar

- Pinch of salt
- 1 teaspoon lime juice

**Directions:**
1. Refer to note at the beginning of the chapter about freezing bowl.
2. Puree all the ingredients in a food processor or blender. Then transfer the mixture to a bowl, and refrigerate covered for 3-4 hours.
3. Pour the ingredients into your ice cream maker, and let it churn for 25-30 minutes.
4. Place in an airtight container for up to 2 hours, until desired consistency is reached.

## 54. Lemon Chocolate Blueberry Vegan Gelato

Servings: Makes 3 Cups
Cooking Time: 2 Hours 35 Minutes
**Ingredients:**
- 1 ½ cup refrigerated coconut cream
- 1 cup cut up lemons
- 3 tablespoons cocoa powder
- 1/2 teaspoon salt
- ½ cup blueberries

**Directions:**
1. NOTE: Freeze your ice cream bowl for at least 24hrs prior to starting!
2. Place all ingredients EXCEPT the blueberries in a blender. Blend on high speed until smooth.
3. Pour the mixture into your ice cream maker, and let it churn for 25 minutes. About 5 minutes before the ice cream is done churning add the blueberries to your ice cream maker.
4. Put the gelato in an airtight container and place in the freezer for up to 2 hours, until desired consistency is reached.

## 55. Double Cherry Chocolate Milkshake

Servings: 6
Cooking Time: 25 Minutes
**Ingredients:**
- 2 cups heavy cream
- 1 cup milk
- 3/4 cup sugar
- 1 teaspoon vanilla extract
- 1 cup cherry juice
- ¼ cup semi-sweet chocolate chips

**Directions:**
1. Refer to note at the beginning of the chapter about freezing bowl.
2. Place the milk and cream in a bowl, and mix them together until well combined. Use a whisk to mix in the sugar. Continue to whisk for about 4 minutes until the sugar dissolves. Then mix in the vanilla extract, and cherry juice.
3. Pour the ingredients into your ice cream maker, and let it churn for 10-15 minutes, until desired consistency is reached. About 5 minutes before the ice cream is finished churning, add in the chocolate chips.
4. Serve immediately.

## 56. Caribbean Pineapple Sorbet

Servings: 9
Cooking Time: 2 Hours 40 Minutes
**Ingredients:**
- 1 diced, peeled, and cored small pineapple
- 2 tablespoons lemon juice
- 1 cup plus 2 tablespoons sugar

**Directions:**
1. Refer to note at the beginning of the chapter about freezing bowl.
2. Puree the pineapple and lemon juice in a food processor or blender. Then add in the sugar and puree until the sugar dissolves.
3. Pour the ingredients into your ice cream maker, and let it churn for 25-30 minutes.
4. Place in an airtight container for up to 2 hours, until desired consistency is reached.

## 57. Astounding Apricot Almond Ice Cream

Servings: 6
Cooking Time: 2 Hours 50 Minutes
**Ingredients:**
- 2 cups heavy cream
- 1 cup milk
- 3/4 cup sugar
- 1 teaspoon vanilla extract
- 1 cup sliced apricots

- ½ cup chopped almonds

**Directions:**
1. Refer to note at the beginning of the chapter about freezing bowl.
2. Puree the apricots in a food processor or blender.
3. Place the milk and cream in a bowl, and mix them together until well combined. Use a whisk to mix in the sugar. Continue to whisk for about 4 minutes until the sugar dissolves. Then mix in the vanilla extract, and apricot puree.
4. Pour the ingredients into your ice cream maker, and let it churn for 25 minutes. About 5 minutes before the ice cream is finished churning, add in the almonds.
5. Put the ice cream in an airtight container and place in the freezer for around 2 hours. Allow the ice cream to thaw for 15 minutes before serving.

### 58. Tropical Mango Soft Serve Ice Cream

Servings: 6
Cooking Time: 35 Minutes
**Ingredients:**
- 2 cups heavy cream
- 1 cup milk
- 3/4 cup sugar
- 1 Tbs. vanilla extract
- 1 cup pureed mango (about 2.5 mangos)
- Juice of 1 lime

**Directions:**
1. Refer to note at the beginning of the chapter about freezing bowl.
2. Puree the mangos with the lime juice in a food processor or blender.
3. Place the milk and cream in a bowl, and mix them together until well combined. Use a whisk to mix in the sugar. Continue to whisk for about 4 minutes until the sugar dissolves. Then mix in the vanilla extract. Then mix in the mango puree.
4. Pour the ingredients into your ice cream maker, and let it churn for 25 minutes.
5. Serve immediately.

### 59. Apricot Honey Gelato

Servings: 4-6
Cooking Time: 2 Hours 35 Minutes
**Ingredients:**
- 1/2 cup heavy cream
- 2 cups milk
- 3/4 cup sugar
- 1 tablespoon vanilla extract
- 1 cup sliced apricot
- 1/4 cup honey

**Directions:**
1. Refer to note at the beginning of the chapter about freezing bowl.
2. Puree the apricots in a food processor or blender.
3. Place the milk and cream in a bowl, and mix them together until well combined. Use a whisk to mix in the sugar. Continue to whisk for about 4 minutes until the sugar dissolves. Then mix in the vanilla extract honey and apricot puree.
4. Pour the ingredients into your ice cream maker, and let it churn for 25 minutes.
5. Put the gelato in an airtight container and place in the freezer for up to 2 hours, until desired consistency is reached.

### 60. Basil Chocolate Vegan Soft Serve Ice Cream

Servings: 9
Cooking Time: 10 Minutes
**Ingredients:**
- 3/4 cup water
- 1 1/4 cups full fat coconut milk or coconut cream (as thick as possible)
- 2/3 cup organic cane sugar
- 2/3 cup unsweetened cocoa powder
- 1/4 tsp sea salt
- 6 ounces vegan dark chocolate, finely chopped
- 1/2 tsp pure vanilla extract
- ¼ cup basil (pulverized)

**Directions:**
1. NOTE: Freeze your ice cream bowl for at least 24hrs prior to starting!
2. Put the first 5 ingredients in a large saucepan, and heat it on medium-high heat. Mix the ingredients

together using a whisk. Allow the mixture to come to a low boil. Continue to whisk often, and remain cooking on a low boil for 1 minute.
3. Take the pan off the heat, and mix in the chocolate and vanilla extract using the whisk. Continue to mix until the chocolate is melted then add the basil.
4. Place the mixture in a blender, and blend on high speed for about 30 seconds.
5. Allow the mixture to cool
6. Pour the ingredients into your ice cream maker, and let it churn for 25 minutes.
7. Serve immediately.

### 61. Raspberry Pumpkin Spice Vegan Soy Frozen Yogurt

Servings: 1 Quart
Cooking Time: 2 Hours 30 Minutes
**Ingredients:**
- 2 ¾ cups unsweetened plain soy yogurt
- 1 ¼ raspberry jam
- 1 tbsp. pumpkin spice

**Directions:**
1. NOTE: Freeze your ice cream bowl for at least 24hrs prior to starting!
2. Place the yogurt in a bowl and mix in the jam. Use a hand mixer to beat the mixture for 5 minutes.
3. Pour the ingredients into your ice cream maker, and let it churn for 25 minutes.
4. Put the frozen yogurt in an airtight container and place in the freezer for at least 2 hours, until desired consistency is reached.

### 62. Chocolate Cherry Cocoa Banana Vegan Milkshake

Servings: 9
Cooking Time: 10 Minutes
**Ingredients:**
- 3/4 cup water
- 1 1/4 cups full fat coconut milk or coconut cream (as thick as possible)
- 2/3 cup organic cane sugar
- 2/3 cup unsweetened cocoa powder
- 1/4 tsp sea salt
- 6 oz. vegan dark chocolate, finely chopped
- 1/2 tsp pure vanilla extract
- ¼ cup sliced frozen bananas
- ¼ cup cherries (cut up fine)
- 1 tbsp. cinnamon

**Directions:**
1. NOTE: Freeze your ice cream bowl for at least 24hrs prior to starting!
2. Put the first 5 ingredients in a large saucepan, and heat it on medium-high heat. Mix the ingredients together using a whisk. Allow the mixture to come to a low boil. Continue to whisk often, and remain cooking on a low boil for 1 minute.
3. Take the pan off the heat, and mix in the chocolate and vanilla extract using the whisk. Continue to mix until the chocolate is melted. Add cherries and cinnamon.
4. Place the mixture in a blender with the bananas, and blend on high speed for about 30 seconds, then allow the mixture to cool
5. Pour the ingredients into your ice cream maker, and let it churn for 10-15 minutes, until desired consistency is reached and serve immediately.

### 63. Pulsating Pomegranate Mint Frozen Yogurt

Servings: 1 Quart
Cooking Time: 2 Hours 35 Minutes
**Ingredients:**
- 1 quart container full-fat plain yogurt
- ¼ teaspoon salt
- 1 cup sugar
- 1 tablespoon mint extract
- 1 cup 100% pomegranate juice
- 1/2 cup semi-sweet chocolate chips

**Directions:**
1. Refer to note at the beginning of the chapter about freezing bowl.
2. Place the yogurt in a bowl. Use a whisk to mix in the sugar and salt. Continue to whisk for about 4 minutes until the sugar dissolves. Then mix in the mint extract, and pomegranate juice.

3. Pour the ingredients into your ice cream maker, and let it churn for 25 minutes. About 5 minutes before the ice cream is done churning add the chocolate chips to your ice cream maker.

4. Put the frozen yogurt in an airtight container and place in the freezer for at least 2 hours, until desired consistency is reached.

# THE CLASSICS ICE CREAM

### 64. Mint Cookies 'n Cream "silkshake"

Servings: 6
Cooking Time: 25 Minutes
**Ingredients:**
- 2 cups heavy cream
- 1 cup milk
- 3/4 cup sugar
- 1 teaspoon vanilla extract
- 1 ½ teaspoons mint extract
- 10 chocolate sandwich cookies

**Directions:**
1. Refer to note at the beginning of the chapter about freezing bowl.
2. Place the milk and cream in a bowl, and mix them together until well combined. Use a whisk to mix in the sugar. Continue to whisk for about 4 minutes until the sugar dissolves. Then mix in the vanilla and mint extract.
3. Place the sandwich cookies in a food processor, and process until the cookies are no bigger than chocolate chips. If you don't have a food processor place the cookies in a large resealable plastic bag, and seal it shut. Use your hands, a mallet, or a rolling pin to crush the cookies.
4. Pour the ingredients into your ice cream maker, and let it churn for 10-15 minutes, until desired consistency is reached. About 5 minutes before the ice cream is done churning add the cookies to your ice cream maker.
5. Serve immediately.

### 65. Daiquiri Lime Soda Frozen Yogurt

Servings: 1 Quart
Cooking Time: 2 Hours 35 Minutes
**Ingredients:**
- 1 quart container full-fat plain yogurt
- ¼ teaspoon salt
- 1 cup sugar
- 1/4 cup lime juice
- ¼ cup sprite
- 4 tablespoons rum

**Directions:**
1. NOTE: Freeze your ice cream bowl for at least 24hrs prior to starting!
2. Place the yogurt in a bowl. Use a whisk to mix in the sugar and salt. Continue to whisk for about 4 minutes until the sugar dissolves. Then mix in the rum, and lime juice.
3. Pour the ingredients into your ice cream maker, and let it churn for 25 minutes.
4. Put the frozen yogurt in an airtight container and place in the freezer for at least 2 hours, until desired consistency is reached.

### 66. The Guinness Chocolate Milkshake

Servings: 6
Cooking Time: 25 Minutes
**Ingredients:**
- 2 cups heavy cream
- 1 cup milk
- 3/4 cup sugar
- 3 tablespoons Guinness beer
- 4 ounces chopped semi-sweet chocolate

**Directions:**
1. Refer to note at the beginning of the chapter about freezing bowl.
2. Melt the chocolate, and let it cool for a bit.
3. Place the milk and cream in a bowl, and mix them together until well combined. Use a whisk to mix in the sugar. Continue to whisk for about 4 minutes until the sugar dissolves. Then mix in the chocolate and Guinness.
4. Pour the ingredients into your ice cream maker, and let it churn for 10-15 minutes, until desired consistency is reached. About 5 minutes before the ice cream is done churning add the peanut butter cup to your ice cream maker.
5. Serve immediately.

### 67. Chocolate Chip Cookie Dough Frozen Yogurt

Servings: 1 Quart
Cooking Time: 2 Hours 35 Minutes
**Ingredients:**
- 1 quart container full-fat plain yogurt

- ¼ teaspoon salt
- 1 cup sugar
- 1 tablespoon vanilla extract
- ½ cup prepackaged cookie dough cut into small chunks

**Directions:**
1. Refer to note at the beginning of the chapter about freezing bowl.
2. Place the yogurt in a bowl. Use a whisk to mix in the sugar and salt. Continue to whisk for about 4 minutes until the sugar dissolves. Then mix in the vanilla extract.
3. Pour the ingredients into your ice cream maker, and let it churn for 25 minutes. About 5 minutes before the ice cream is done churning add the cookie dough to your ice cream maker.
4. Put the frozen yogurt in an airtight container and place in the freezer for at least 2 hours, until desired consistency is reached.

### 68. "tasty" Tequila Sunrise Gelato

Servings: 4-6
Cooking Time: 2 Hours 35 Minutes
**Ingredients:**
- 1/2 cup heavy cream
- 2 cups milk
- 3/4 cup sugar
- 1/2 cup orange juice
- 1 teaspoon vanilla extract
- 3 tablespoons tequila
- ½ tablespoon grenadi

**Directions:**
1. Refer to note at the beginning of the chapter about freezing bowl.
2. Place the milk and cream in a bowl, and mix them together until well combined. Use a whisk to mix in the sugar. Continue to whisk for about 4 minutes until the sugar dissolves. Then mix in the vanilla extract, orange juice, tequila and grenadine.
3. Pour the ingredients into your ice cream maker, and let it churn for 25 minutes.
4. Put the gelato in an airtight container and place in the freezer for up to 2 hours, until desired consistency is reached.

### 69. Lemon Tequila "sunset" Gelato

Servings: 4-6
Cooking Time: 2 Hours 35 Minutes
**Ingredients:**
- 1/2 cup heavy cream
- 2 cups milk
- 3/4 cup sugar
- 1/2 cup lemon juice
- 1 teaspoon vanilla extract
- 3 tablespoons tequila
- ½ tablespoon grenadine

**Directions:**
1. NOTE: Freeze your ice cream bowl for at least 24hrs prior to starting!
2. Place the milk and cream in a bowl, and mix them together until well combined. Use a whisk to mix in the sugar. Continue to whisk for about 4 minutes until the sugar dissolves. Then mix in the vanilla extract, lemon juice, tequila and grenadine.
3. Pour the ingredients into your ice cream maker, and let it churn for 25 minutes.
4. Put the gelato in an airtight container and place in the freezer for up to 2 hours, until desired consistency is reached.

### 70. Strawberry Cinnamon Margarita Soft Serve Ice Cream

Servings: 6
Cooking Time: 35 Minutes
**Ingredients:**
- 2 cups heavy cream
- 1 cup milk
- 3/4 cup sugar
- 1 Tbs. vanilla extract
- 3 tablespoons tequila
- 1 tablespoon cinnamon
- 1/2 cup lime juice
- ¼ cup strawberries (mashed up)
- 2 tablespoons orange liqueur

**Directions:**
1. NOTE: Freeze your ice cream bowl for at least 24hrs prior to starting!
2. Place the milk and cream in a bowl, and mix them together until well

combined. Use a whisk to mix in the sugar and cinnamon. Continue to whisk for about 4 minutes until the sugar dissolves. Mix the vanilla extract and whisk in the lime juice, strawberries, tequila, and liqueur.
3. Pour the ingredients into your ice cream maker, and let it churn for 25 minutes.
4. Serve immediately.

## 71. Very Strawberry Gelato

Servings: 4-6
Cooking Time: 2 Hours 35 Minutes
**Ingredients:**
- 1/2 cup heavy cream
- 2 cups milk
- 3/4 cup sugar
- 1 cup sliced strawberries
- 1 tablespoon vanilla extract

**Directions:**
1. Refer to note at the beginning of the chapter about freezing bowl.
2. Puree the strawberries in a food processor or blender.
3. Place the milk and cream in a bowl, and mix them together until well combined. Use a whisk to mix in the sugar. Continue to whisk for about 4 minutes until the sugar dissolves. Then mix in the vanilla extract and strawberry puree.
4. Pour the ingredients into your ice cream maker, and let it churn for 25 minutes.
5. Put the gelato in an airtight container and place in the freezer for up to 2 hours, until desired consistency is reached.

## 72. Grown Folks "old Fashioned" Ice Cream

Servings: 6
Cooking Time: 2 Hours 50 Minutes
**Ingredients:**
- 2 cups heavy cream
- 1 cup milk
- 3/4 cup sugar
- 1 tablespoon vanilla extract
- 3 tablespoons whiskey
- 1 dash of bitters

**Directions:**
1. NOTE: Freeze your ice cream bowl for at least 24hrs prior to starting!
2. Place the milk and cream in a bowl, and mix them together until well combined. Use a whisk to mix in the sugar. Continue to whisk for about 4 minutes until the sugar dissolves. Then mix in the vanilla extract, whiskey, and bitters.
3. Pour the ingredients into your ice cream maker, and let it churn for 25 minutes.
4. Put the ice cream in an airtight container and place in the freezer for around 2 hours. Allow the ice cream to thaw for 15 minutes before serving.

## 73. Miraculous Double Mint Chip Ice Cream

Servings: 6
Cooking Time: 2 Hours 50 Minutes
**Ingredients:**
- 2 cups heavy cream
- 1 cup milk
- 3/4 cup sugar
- 1 teaspoon vanilla extract
- 1 teaspoon peppermint extract
- 1 cup semi-sweet chocolate chips

**Directions:**
1. Refer to note at the beginning of the chapter about freezing bowl.
2. Place the milk and cream in a bowl, and mix them together until well combined. Use a whisk to mix in the sugar. Continue to whisk for about 4 minutes until the sugar dissolves. Then mix in the vanilla and peppermint extract.
3. Pour the ingredients into your ice cream maker, and let it churn for 25 minutes. About 5 minutes before the ice cream is finished churning, add in the chocolate chips.
4. Put the ice cream in an airtight container and place in the freezer for around 2 hours. Allow the ice cream to thaw for 15 minutes before serving.

## 74. Orange Tequila "sunrise" Gelato

Servings: 4-6
Cooking Time: 2 Hours 35 Minutes

**Ingredients:**
- 1/2 cup heavy cream
- 2 cups milk
- 3/4 cup sugar
- I/2 cup orange juice
- 1 teaspoon vanilla extract
- 3 tablespoons tequila
- ½ tablespoon grenadine

**Directions:**
1. NOTE: Freeze your ice cream bowl for at least 24hrs prior to starting!
2. Place the milk and cream in a bowl, and mix them together until well combined. Use a whisk to mix in the sugar. Continue to whisk for about 4 minutes until the sugar dissolves. Then mix in the vanilla extract, orange juice, tequila and grenadine.
3. Pour the ingredients into your ice cream maker, and let it churn for 25 minutes.
4. Put the gelato in an airtight container and place in the freezer for up to 2 hours, until desired consistency is reached.

### 75. "adults Old Fashioned" Ice Cream

Servings: 6
Cooking Time: 2 Hours 50 Minutes
**Ingredients:**
- 2 cups heavy cream
- 1 cup milk
- 3/4 cup sugar
- 1 tablespoon vanilla extract
- 3 tablespoons whiskey
- 1 dash of bitters

**Directions:**
1. Refer to note at the beginning of the chapter about freezing bowl.
2. Place the milk and cream in a bowl, and mix them together until well combined. Use a whisk to mix in the sugar. Continue to whisk for about 4 minutes until the sugar dissolves. Then mix in the vanilla extract, whiskey, and bitters.
3. Pour the ingredients into your ice cream maker, and let it churn for 25 minutes.
4. Put the ice cream in an airtight container and place in the freezer for around 2 hours. Allow the ice cream to thaw for 15 minutes before serving.

### 76. Sunrise Strawberry Daiquiri Milkshake

Servings: 6
Cooking Time: 25 Minutes
**Ingredients:**
- 2 cups heavy cream
- 1 cup milk
- 3/4 cup sugar
- 4 tablespoons rum
- 8 ounces strawberries

**Directions:**
1. Refer to note at the beginning of the chapter about freezing bowl.
2. Puree the strawberries in a food processor or blender.
3. Place the milk and cream in a bowl, and mix them together until well combined. Use a whisk to mix in the sugar. Continue to whisk for about 4 minutes until the sugar dissolves. Then mix in the rum, and strawberry puree.
4. Pour the ingredients into your ice cream maker, and let it churn for 10-15 minutes, until desired consistency is reached. About 5 minutes before the ice cream is done churning add the peanut butter cup to your ice cream maker.
5. Serve immediately.

### 77. Chunky Chocolate Chip Soft Serve Ice Cream

Servings: 6
Cooking Time: 35 Minutes
**Ingredients:**
- 2 cups heavy cream
- 1 cup milk
- 3/4 cup sugar
- 1 Tbs. vanilla extract
- 1 cup chocolate chips of your choice

**Directions:**
1. Refer to note at the beginning of the chapter about freezing bowl.
2. Place the milk and cream in a bowl, and mix them together until well combined. Use a whisk to mix in the sugar. Continue to whisk for about 4

minutes until the sugar dissolves. Then mix in the vanilla extract.
3. Pour the ingredients into your ice cream maker, and let it churn for 25 minutes. About 5 minutes before the ice cream is finished churning, add in the chocolate chips.
4. Serve immediately.

## 78. California Cookies-n-cream Soft Serve Ice Cream

Servings: 6
Cooking Time: 35 Minutes
**Ingredients:**
- 2 cups heavy cream
- 1 cup milk
- 3/4 cup sugar
- 1 Tbs. vanilla extract
- 20 chocolate sandwich cookies

**Directions:**
1. Refer to note at the beginning of the chapter about freezing bowl.
2. Place the milk and cream in a bowl, and mix them together until well combined. Use a whisk to mix in the sugar. Continue to whisk for about 4 minutes until the sugar dissolves. Then mix in the vanilla extract.
3. Place the sandwich cookies in a food processor, and process until the cookies are no bigger than chocolate chips. If you don't have a food processor place the cookies in a large resealable plastic bag, and seal it shut. Use your hands, a mallet, or a rolling pin to crush the cookies.
4. Pour the ingredients into your ice cream maker, and let it churn for 25 minutes. About 5 minutes before the ice cream is finished churning, add in the chocolate sandwich cookies.
5. Serve immediately.

## 79. Runnin' Rum And Coke Gelato

Servings: 4-6
Cooking Time: 2 Hours 50 Minutes
**Ingredients:**
- 1/2 cup heavy cream
- 2 cups milk
- 3/4 cup sugar
- 1 teaspoon vanilla extract
- 3 tablespoons rum
- 3 cups coca cola (2, 12 ounce cans)

**Directions:**
1. Refer to note at the beginning of the chapter about freezing bowl.
2. Pour the coke into a large skillet, and heat it on high heat until it comes to a boil. Allow the coke to cook for about another 15 or 20 minutes, until the coke reduces down to 1 cup of liquid. Let the liquid cool.
3. Place the milk and cream in a bowl, and mix them together until well combined. Use a whisk to mix in the sugar. Continue to whisk for about 4 minutes until the sugar dissolves. Then mix in the vanilla extract, coke reduction, and rum.
4. Pour the ingredients into your ice cream maker, and let it churn for 25 minutes.
5. Put the gelato in an airtight container and place in the freezer for up to 2 hours, until desired consistency is reached.

## 80. Lickin' Lime Daiquiri Frozen Yogurt

Servings: 1 Quart
Cooking Time: 2 Hours 35 Minutes
**Ingredients:**
- 1 quart container full-fat plain yogurt
- ¼ teaspoon salt
- 1 cup sugar
- 1/3 cup lime juice
- 4 tablespoons rum

**Directions:**
1. Refer to note at the beginning of the chapter about freezing bowl.
2. Place the yogurt in a bowl. Use a whisk to mix in the sugar and salt. Continue to whisk for about 4 minutes until the sugar dissolves. Then mix in the rum, and lime juice.
3. Pour the ingredients into your ice cream maker, and let it churn for 25 minutes.
4. Put the frozen yogurt in an airtight container and place in the freezer for at least 2 hours, until desired consistency is reached.

### 81. Cucumber Rosemary Honey Rum Sorbet

Servings: 8
Cooking Time: 2 Hours 35 Minutes
**Ingredients:**
- 4 cups chopped cucumbers
- ½ cup rosemary
- ½ cup honey
- 4 tablespoons rum

**Directions:**
1. NOTE: Freeze your ice cream bowl for at least 24hrs prior to starting!
2. Use a food processor or blender to puree all the ingredients until smooth.
3. Pour the ingredients into your ice cream maker, and let it churn for 25-30 minutes.
4. Place in an airtight container for up to 2 hours, until desired consistency is reached.

### 82. Margarita Madness Soft Serve Ice Cream

Servings: 6
Cooking Time: 35 Minutes
**Ingredients:**
- 2 cups heavy cream
- 1 cup milk
- 3/4 cup sugar
- 1 Tbs. vanilla extract
- 3 tablespoons tequila
- 1/2 cup lime juice
- 2 tablespoons orange liqueur

**Directions:**
1. Refer to note at the beginning of the chapter about freezing bowl.
2. Place the milk and cream in a bowl, and mix them together until well combined. Use a whisk to mix in the sugar. Continue to whisk for about 4 minutes until the sugar dissolves. Mix in the vanilla extract. Finally whisk in the lime juice, tequila, and liqueur.
3. Pour the ingredients into your ice cream maker, and let it churn for 25 minutes.
4. Serve immediately.

### 83. Kahlua & Pistachio Ice Cream

Servings: 6
Cooking Time: 2 Hours 50 Minutes
**Ingredients:**
- 2 cups heavy cream
- 1 cup milk
- 3/4 cup sugar
- 1 teaspoon vanilla extract
- 3 tablespoons Kahlua
- 3/4 cup chops almond

**Directions:**
1. NOTE: Freeze your ice cream bowl for at least 24hrs prior to starting!
2. Place the milk and cream in a bowl, and mix them together until well combined. Use a whisk to mix in the sugar. Continue to whisk for about 4 minutes until the sugar dissolves. Then mix in the vanilla extract, Kahlua.
3. Pour the ingredients into your ice cream maker, and let it churn for 25 minutes. About 5 minutes before the ice cream is done churning add the almonds to your ice cream maker.
4. Put the ice cream in an airtight container and place in the freezer for around 2 hours. Allow the ice cream to thaw for 15 minutes before serving.

### 84. Divine Coffee Frozen Yogurt

Servings: 1 Quart
Cooking Time: 2 Hours 35 Minutes
**Ingredients:**
- 1 quart container full-fat plain yogurt
- ¼ teaspoon salt
- 1 cup sugar
- 1 teaspoon vanilla extract
- 1 cup strong brewed coffee or espresso
- 1 tablespoon coffee grounds

**Directions:**
1. Refer to note at the beginning of the chapter about freezing bowl.
2. Place the yogurt in a bowl. Use a whisk to mix in the sugar and salt. Continue to whisk for about 4 minutes until the sugar dissolves. Then mix in the vanilla extract, coffee, and coffee grounds.
3. Pour the ingredients into your ice cream maker, and let it churn for 25 minutes.

4. Put the frozen yogurt in an airtight container and place in the freezer for at least 2 hours, until desired consistency is reached.

## 85. Pralines And "oh So Creamy" Milkshake

Servings: 6
Cooking Time: 25 Minutes
**Ingredients:**
- 2 cups heavy cream
- 1 cup milk
- 1 cup brown sugar
- 1 teaspoon vanilla extract
- 1/3 cup finely chopped pecans
- 1 tablespoon butter

**Directions:**
1. Refer to note at the beginning of the chapter about freezing bowl.
2. Melt the butter in a small skillet on medium heat. Add the pecans, and cook for about 5 minutes, until they become lightly browned.
3. Place the milk and cream in a bowl, and mix them together until well combined. Use a whisk to mix in the sugar. Continue to whisk for about 4 minutes until the sugar dissolves. Then mix in the vanilla extract.
4. Pour the ingredients into your ice cream maker, and let it churn for 10-15 minutes, until desired consistency is reached. About 5 minutes before the ice cream is done churning add the cookie dough to your ice cream maker.
5. Serve immediately.

## 86. Mango Strawberry Mint Daiquiri Milkshake

Servings: 6
Cooking Time: 25 Minutes
**Ingredients:**
- 2 cups heavy cream
- 1 cup milk
- 3/4 cup sugar
- 8 ounces strawberries
- ¼ cup mint
- ¼ cup mango
- 4 tablespoons rum

**Directions:**
1. NOTE: Freeze your ice cream bowl for at least 24hrs prior to starting!
2. Puree the strawberries, mango and mint in a food processor or blender.
3. Place the milk and cream in a bowl, and mix them together until well combined. Use a whisk to mix in the sugar. Continue to whisk for about 4 minutes until the sugar dissolves. Then mix in the rum, and strawberry puree.
4. Pour the ingredients into your ice cream maker, and let it churn for 10-15 minutes, until desired consistency is reached. About 5 minutes before the ice cream is done churning add the peanut butter cup to your ice cream maker.
5. Serve immediately.

## 87. Creamy Kahlua Almond Delight Ice Cream

Servings: 6
Cooking Time: 2 Hours 50 Minutes
**Ingredients:**
- 2 cups heavy cream
- 1 cup milk
- 3/4 cup sugar
- 1 teaspoon vanilla extract
- 3 tablespoons kahlua
- 3/4 cup chops almond

**Directions:**
1. Refer to note at the beginning of the chapter about freezing bowl.
2. Place the milk and cream in a bowl, and mix them together until well combined. Use a whisk to mix in the sugar. Continue to whisk for about 4 minutes until the sugar dissolves. Then mix in the vanilla extract, kahlua.
3. Pour the ingredients into your ice cream maker, and let it churn for 25 minutes. About 5 minutes before the ice cream is done churning add the almonds to your ice cream maker.
4. Put the ice cream in an airtight container and place in the freezer for around 2 hours. Allow the ice cream to thaw for 15 minutes before serving.

## 88. The Original "manhattan" Ice Cream

Servings: 6
Cooking Time: 2 Hours 50 Minutes
**Ingredients:**
- 2 cups heavy cream
- 1 cup milk
- 3/4 cup sugar
- 1 tablespoon vanilla extract
- 3 tablespoons whiskey
- 1 tablespoon vermouth
- 1 dash of bitters

**Directions:**
1. NOTE: Freeze your ice cream bowl for at least 24hrs prior to starting!
2. Place the milk and cream in a bowl, and mix them together until well combined. Use a whisk to mix in the sugar. Continue to whisk for about 4 minutes until the sugar dissolves. Then mix in the vanilla extract, whiskey, vermouth, and bitters.
3. Pour the ingredients into your ice cream maker, and let it churn for 25 minutes.
4. Put the ice cream in an airtight container and place in the freezer for around 2 hours. Allow the ice cream to thaw for 15 minutes before serving.

## 89. Double Gin And Juice Vanilla Soft Serve Ice Cream

Servings: 6
Cooking Time: 35 Minutes
**Ingredients:**
- 2 cups heavy cream
- 1 cup milk
- 3/4 cup sugar
- 1 Tbs. vanilla extract
- 4 tablespoons gin
- ½ cup orange juice
- ½ lime (peeled and cut up fine)

**Directions:**
1. NOTE: Freeze your ice cream bowl for at least 24hrs prior to starting!
2. Place the milk and cream in a bowl, and mix them together until well combined. Use a whisk to mix in the sugar. Continue to whisk for about 4 minutes until the sugar dissolves. Mix in the vanilla extract. Then whisk in the gin and orange juice and lime.
3. Pour the ingredients into your ice cream maker, and let it churn for 25 minutes.
4. Serve immediately.

## 90. Tropical Coconut Rum And Coke Gelato

Servings: 4-6
Cooking Time: 2 Hours 50 Minutes
**Ingredients:**
- 1/2 cup heavy cream
- 2 cups milk
- 3/4 cup sugar
- 1 teaspoon vanilla extract
- 3 tablespoons rum
- ¼ cup shaved coconut
- 3 cups coca cola (2, 12 ounce cans)

**Directions:**
1. NOTE: Freeze your ice cream bowl for at least 24hrs prior to starting!
2. Pour the coke into a large skillet, and heat it on high heat until it comes to a boil. Allow the coke to cook for about another 15 or 20 minutes, until the coke reduces down to 1 cup of liquid. Let the liquid cool.
3. Place the milk and cream in a bowl, and mix them together until well combined. Use a whisk to mix in the sugar. Continue to whisk for about 4 minutes until the sugar dissolves. Then mix in the vanilla extract, coke reduction, coconut chips and rum.
4. Pour the ingredients into your ice cream maker, and let it churn for 25 minutes.
5. Put the gelato in an airtight container and place in the freezer for up to 2 hours, until desired consistency is reached.

## 91. "the Big Stout" Almond Chocolate Milkshake

Servings: 6
Cooking Time: 25 Minutes
**Ingredients:**
- 2 cups heavy cream
- 1 cup milk
- 3/4 cup sugar
- 4 ounces chopped semi-sweet chocolate

- 3 tablespoons almonds
- 3 tablespoons Guinness beer

**Directions:**
1. NOTE: Freeze your ice cream bowl for at least 24hrs prior to starting!
2. Melt the chocolate, and let it cool for a bit.
3. Place the milk and cream in a bowl, and mix them together until well combined. Use a whisk to mix in the sugar. Continue to whisk for about 4 minutes until the sugar dissolves. Then mix in the chocolate and Guinness.
4. Pour the ingredients into your ice cream maker, and let it churn for 10-15 minutes, until desired consistency is reached. About 5 minutes before the ice cream is done churning add the almonds to your ice cream maker.
5. Serve immediately.

## 92. Double Gin And Tonic Soft Serve Ice Cream

Servings: 6
Cooking Time: 35 Minutes
**Ingredients:**
- 2 cups heavy cream
- 1 cup milk
- 3/4 cup sugar
- 1 Tbs. vanilla extract
- 4 tablespoons gin
- 125 ML tonic water

**Directions:**
1. Refer to note at the beginning of the chapter about freezing bowl.
2. Place the milk and cream in a bowl, and mix them together until well combined. Use a whisk to mix in the sugar. Continue to whisk for about 4 minutes until the sugar dissolves. Mix in the vanilla extract. Then whisk in the gin and tonic
3. Pour the ingredients into your ice cream maker, and let it churn for 25 minutes.
4. Serve immediately.

## 93. Power Punch Pistachio Ice Cream

Servings: 6
Cooking Time: 2 Hours 50 Minutes
**Ingredients:**
- 2 cups heavy cream
- 1 cup milk
- 3/4 cup sugar
- 1/4 teaspoon almond extract
- 1/2 cup chopped pistachios

**Directions:**
1. Refer to note at the beginning of the chapter about freezing bowl.
2. Place the milk and cream in a bowl, and mix them together until well combined. Use a whisk to mix in the sugar. Continue to whisk for about 4 minutes until the sugar dissolves. Then mix in the almond extract.
3. Pour the ingredients into your ice cream maker, and let it churn for 25 minutes. About 5 minutes before the ice cream is finished churning, add in the pistachios.
4. Put the ice cream in an airtight container and place in the freezer for around 2 hours. Allow the ice cream to thaw for 15 minutes before serving.

## 94. Tropical Piña Colada Frozen Yogurt

Servings: 1 Quart
Cooking Time: 2 Hours 35 Minutes
**Ingredients:**
- 1 quart container full-fat plain yogurt
- ¼ teaspoon salt
- 1 cup sugar
- ½ cup pineapple juice
- 1 drop coconut essence
- 2 teaspoons lime juice
- 1/4 cup shredded coconut
- 4 tablespoons rum

**Directions:**
1. Refer to note at the beginning of the chapter about freezing bowl.
2. Place the yogurt in a bowl. Use a whisk to mix in the sugar and salt. Continue to whisk for about 4 minutes until the sugar dissolves. Then mix in the rum, pineapple juice, lime juice, and coconut essence.
3. Pour the ingredients into your ice cream maker, and let it churn for 25 minutes. About 5 minutes before the ice cream is done churning add the shredded coconut to your ice cream maker.

4. Put the frozen yogurt in an airtight container and place in the freezer for at least 2 hours, until desired consistency is reached.

### 95. Classic Vanilla Soft-serve Ice Cream

Servings: 6
Cooking Time: 35 Minutes
**Ingredients:**
- 2 cups heavy cream
- 1 cup milk
- 3/4 cup sugar
- 1 Tbs. vanilla extract

**Directions:**
1. Refer to note at the beginning of the chapter about freezing bowl.
2. Place the milk and cream in a bowl, and mix them together until well combined. Use a whisk to mix in the sugar. Continue to whisk for about 4 minutes until the sugar dissolves. Then mix in the vanilla extract.
3. Pour the ingredients into your ice cream maker, and let it churn for 25 minutes.
4. Serve immediately.

### 96. Caribbean Colada Frozen Yogurt

Servings: 1 Quart
Cooking Time: 2 Hours 35 Minutes
**Ingredients:**
- 1 quart container full-fat plain yogurt
- ¼ teaspoon salt
- 1 cup sugar
- ½ cup pineapple juice
- 1 drop coconut essence
- 2 teaspoons lime juice
- 1/4 cup shredded coconut
- 4 tablespoons rum

**Directions:**
1. NOTE: Freeze your ice cream bowl for at least 24hrs prior to starting!
2. Place the yogurt in a bowl. Use a whisk to mix in the sugar and salt. Continue to whisk for about 4 minutes until the sugar dissolves. Then mix in the rum, pineapple juice, lime juice, and coconut essence.
3. Pour the ingredients into your ice cream maker, and let it churn for 25 minutes. About 5 minutes before the ice cream is done churning add the shredded coconut to your ice cream maker.
4. Put the frozen yogurt in an airtight container and place in the freezer for at least 2 hours, until desired consistency is reached.

### 97. Radical Rocky Road Ice Cream

Servings: 6
Cooking Time: 2 Hours 50 Minutes
**Ingredients:**
- 2 cups heavy cream
- 1 cup milk
- 3/4 cup sugar
- 1 Tbs. vanilla extract
- ½ cup unsweetened cocoa powder
- ½ cup chopped pecans
- 1 cup mini marshmallows

**Directions:**
1. Refer to note at the beginning of the chapter about freezing bowl.
2. Place the milk and cream in a bowl, and mix them together until well combined. Use a whisk to mix in the sugar. Continue to whisk for about 4 minutes until the sugar dissolves. Then whisk in cocoa powder until all lumps are gone, and well mixed. Then mix in the vanilla extract.
3. Pour the ingredients into your ice cream maker, and let it churn for 25 minutes. About 5 minutes before the ice cream is finished churning, add in the pecans and marshmallows.
4. Put the ice cream in an airtight container and place in the freezer for around 2 hours. Allow the ice cream to thaw for 15 minutes before serving.

### 98. Tropical Watermelon Lemon/lime Sorbet

Servings: Makes 1 Quart
Cooking Time: 2 Hours 40 Minutes
**Ingredients:**
- 3 1/2 cups sliced seedless watermelon
- 6-ounce chilled pineapple juice
- 3/4 cup chilled ginger ale
- ½ cup fresh lime juice
- 1/3 cup grenadine

**Directions:**
1. NOTE: Freeze your ice cream bowl for at least 24hrs prior to starting!
2. Puree all ingredients in a food processor or blender.
3. Pour the ingredients into your ice cream maker, and let it churn for 25-30 minutes.
4. Place in an airtight container for up to 2 hours, until desired consistency is reached.

### 99. Chocolate Screwdriver Soft Serve Ice Cream

Servings: 6
Cooking Time: 35 Minutes
**Ingredients:**
- 2 cups heavy cream
- 1 cup milk
- 3/4 cup sugar
- 1 Tbs. vanilla extract
- 1 tbsp. coco powder
- ½ cup orange juice
- 3 tablespoons vodka

**Directions:**
1. NOTE: Freeze your ice cream bowl for at least 24hrs prior to starting!
2. Place the milk and cream in a bowl, and mix them together until well combined. Use a whisk to mix in the sugar. Continue to whisk for about 4 minutes until the sugar dissolves. Mix in the vanilla extract and coco powder. Then mix in the orange juice. Finally whisk in the vodka.
3. Pour the ingredients into your ice cream maker, and let it churn for 25 minutes.
4. Serve immediately.

### 100. Double Dark Chocolate Gelato

Servings: 4-6
Cooking Time: 2 Hours 35 Minutes
**Ingredients:**
- 12 cup heavy cream
- 2 cups milk
- 34 cup sugar
- 14 teaspoon salt
- 7 ounces high quality dark chocolate
- 1 teaspoon vanilla extract

**Directions:**
1. Refer to note at the beginning of the chapter about freezing bowl.
2. Melt the chocolate, and allow it to cool a little bit.
3. Place the milk and cream in a bowl, and mix them together until well combined. Use a whisk to mix in the sugar and salt. Continue to whisk for about 4 minutes until the sugar and salt dissolve. Then mix in the vanilla extract. Finally mix in the chocolate until well combined.
4. Pour the ingredients into your ice cream maker, and let it churn for 25 minutes.
5. Put the gelato in an airtight container and place in the freezer for up to 2 hours, until desired consistency is reached.

### 101. Vanilla Screwdriver Soft Serve Ice Cream

Servings: 6
Cooking Time: 35 Minutes
**Ingredients:**
- 2 cups heavy cream
- 1 cup milk
- 3/4 cup sugar
- 1 Tbs. vanilla extract
- ½ cup orange juice
- 3 tablespoons vodka

**Directions:**
1. Refer to note at the beginning of the chapter about freezing bowl.
2. Place the milk and cream in a bowl, and mix them together until well combined. Use a whisk to mix in the sugar. Continue to whisk for about 4 minutes until the sugar dissolves. Mix in the vanilla extract. Then mix in the orange juice. Finally whisk in the vodka.
3. Pour the ingredients into your ice cream maker, and let it churn for 25 minutes.
4. Serve immediately.

### 102. "new York" Manhattan Ice Cream

Servings: 6
Cooking Time: 2 Hours 50 Minutes
**Ingredients:**
- 2 cups heavy cream

- 1 cup milk
- 3/4 cup sugar
- 1 tablespoon vanilla extract
- 3 tablespoons whiskey
- 1 tablespoon vermouth
- 1 dash of bitters

**Directions:**
1. Refer to note at the beginning of the chapter about freezing bowl.
2. Place the milk and cream in a bowl, and mix them together until well combined. Use a whisk to mix in the sugar. Continue to whisk for about 4 minutes until the sugar dissolves. Then mix in the vanilla extract, whiskey, vermouth, and bitters.
3. Pour the ingredients into your ice cream maker, and let it churn for 25 minutes.
4. Put the ice cream in an airtight container and place in the freezer for around 2 hours. Allow the ice cream to thaw for 15 minutes before serving.

### 103. Cuddling Cucumber Basil Rum Sorbet

Servings: 8
Cooking Time: 2 Hours 35 Minutes
**Ingredients:**
- 4 cups chopped cucumbers
- ½ cup basil
- ½ cup honey
- 4 tablespoons rum

**Directions:**
1. Refer to note at the beginning of the chapter about freezing bowl.
2. Use a food processor or blender to puree all the ingredients until smooth.
3. Pour the ingredients into your ice cream maker, and let it churn for 25-30 minutes.
4. Place in an airtight container for up to 2 hours, until desired consistency is reached.

# SIMPLE ICE CREAM

## 104. Basic Custard Ice Cream With Sea Salt

Servings: 10
Cooking Time: 30 Minutes
**Ingredients:**
- 3 cups whole milk
- 1 cup sugar
- 8 egg yolks
- 1 teaspoon vanilla
- A pinch of coarse sea salt

**Directions:**
1. Add the milk and sugar in a saucepan and heat over medium low flame. Simmer for 3 minutes or until the sugar dissolves. Remove from the heat.
2. In a bowl, whisk in the egg yolks. Drizzle ½ cup of the warm milk into the egg yolks while whisking constantly to form a smooth mixture. Whisk the egg mixture back into the pot.
3. Turn on the heat to medium low and cook until the mixture starts to thicken. Constantly stir while cooking.
4. Turn off the heat and strain the mixture to remove lumps. Allow the milk to cool at room temperature. Place in the fridge to chill for 2 hours.
5. Turn on the Cuisinart and pour the mixture in. Churn for 15 minutes.
6. Transfer to an airtight container and sprinkle with sea salt on top.
7. Place in the fridge to completely cool.

**Nutrition Info:** Calories per serving: 50; Protein: 1.42g; Carbs: 6.7g; Fat: 2g Sugar: 5g

## 105. All-american Double Vanilla Soft-serve Ice Cream

Servings: 6
Cooking Time: 35 Minutes
**Ingredients:**
- 2 cups heavy cream
- 1 cup milk
- 3/4 cup sugar
- 2 Tbs. vanilla extract

**Directions:**
1. NOTE: Freeze your ice cream bowl for at least 24hrs prior to starting!
2. Place the milk and cream in a bowl, and mix them together until well combined. Use a whisk to mix in the sugar. Continue to whisk for about 4 minutes until the sugar dissolves. Then mix in the vanilla extract.
3. Pour the ingredients into your ice cream maker, and let it churn for 25 minutes.
4. Serve immediately.

## 106. Orange Cola Soft Serve Ice Cream

Servings: 6
Cooking Time: 55 Minutes
**Ingredients:**
- 2 cups heavy cream
- 1 cup milk
- 3/4 cup sugar
- 1 tbsp. orange extract
- 1 tbs. vanilla extract
- 3 cups coca cola (2, 12 ounce cans)

**Directions:**
1. NOTE: Freeze your ice cream bowl for at least 24hrs prior to starting!
2. Pour the coke into a large skillet, and heat it on high heat until it comes to a boil. Allow the coke to cook for about another 15 or 20 minutes, until the coke reduces down to 1 cup of liquid. Let the liquid cool.
3. Place the milk and cream in a bowl, and mix them together until well combined. Use a whisk to mix in the sugar. Continue to whisk for about 4 minutes until the sugar dissolves. Mix in the vanilla and orange extract, then the coca cola.
4. Pour the ingredients into your ice cream maker, and let it churn for 25 minutes.
5. Serve immediately.

## 107. Crazy Cotton Candy Milkshake

Servings: 6
Cooking Time: 25 Minutes
**Ingredients:**
- 2 cups heavy cream
- 1 cup milk
- 3/4 cup sugar
- 1 teaspoon vanilla extract

- 1/2 cup cotton candy syrup
- 1 tablespoon plus 1 teaspoon pink or blue food coloring

**Directions:**
1. Refer to note at the beginning of the chapter about freezing bowl.
2. Place the milk and cream in a bowl, and mix them together until well combined. Use a whisk to mix in the sugar. Continue to whisk for about 4 minutes until the sugar dissolves. Then mix in the vanilla extract, syrup, and food coloring.
3. Pour the ingredients into your ice cream maker, and let it churn for 10-15 minutes, until desired consistency is reached.
4. Serve immediately.

### 108. Chocolate Chip Turmeric Peppermint Chip Ice Cream

Servings: 6
Cooking Time: 2 Hours 50 Minutes
**Ingredients:**
- 2 cups heavy cream
- 1 cup milk
- 3/4 cup sugar
- 1 teaspoon vanilla extract
- 1 teaspoon peppermint extract
- 1 cup semi-sweet chocolate chips
- 2 teaspoons turmeric

**Directions:**
1. NOTE: Freeze your ice cream bowl for at least 24hrs prior to starting!
2. Place the milk and cream in a bowl, and mix them together until well combined. Use a whisk to mix in the sugar. Continue to whisk for about 4 minutes until the sugar dissolves. Then mix in the vanilla, turmeric and peppermint extract.
3. Pour the ingredients into your ice cream maker, and let it churn for 25 minutes. About 5 minutes before the ice cream is finished churning, add in the chocolate chips.
4. Put the ice cream in an airtight container and place in the freezer for around 2 hours. Allow the ice cream to thaw for 15 minutes before serving.

### 109. Rocky Road Frozen Custard Ice Cream

Servings: 12
Cooking Time: 30 Minutes
**Ingredients:**
- 1 cup whole milk
- 2 cups heavy cream
- ¾ cup sugar
- ½ teaspoon salt
- 2 tablespoons unsweetened cocoa powder
- ½ teaspoon ground cinnamon
- 3 egg yolks
- 2 ounces chocolate bar, chopped
- 1 cup mini marshmallows
- ½ cup toasted pecans

**Directions:**
1. Add the milk, cream, sugar, and salt in a saucepan and heat over medium low flame. Simmer for 3 minutes or until the sugar dissolves. Add the cocoa powder and cinnamon. Stir for another minute. Remove from the heat.
2. In a bowl, whisk in the egg yolks. Drizzle ½ cup of the warm milk into the egg yolks while whisking constantly to form a smooth mixture. Whisk the egg mixture back into the pot.
3. Turn on the heat to medium low and cook until the mixture starts to thicken. Constantly stir while cooking.
4. Turn off the heat and strain the mixture to remove lumps. Allow the milk to cool at room temperature. Place in the fridge to chill for 2 hours.
5. Turn on the Cuisinart and pour the mixture in. Churn for 15 minutes.
6. Five minutes before the time ends, add the chopped chocolate, marshmallows, and pecans.
7. Transfer to an airtight container.
8. Place in the fridge to completely cool.

**Nutrition Info:** Calories per serving: 189; Protein: 2.6g; Carbs: 13.8g; Fat: 14.4g Sugar: 11.3g

### 110. Dr. Pepper Ice Cream

Servings: 6
Cooking Time: 2 Hours 50 Minutes
**Ingredients:**

- 2 cups heavy cream
- 1 cup milk
- 3/4 cup sugar
- 1 tablespoon vanilla extract
- 3 cups (2, 12 ounce cans) dr. pepper

**Directions:**
1. Refer to note at the beginning of the chapter about freezing bowl.
2. Pour the dr. pepper into a large skillet, and heat it on high heat until it comes to a boil. Allow the coke to cook for about another 15 or 20 minutes, until the root beer reduces down to 1 cup of liquid. Let the liquid cool.
3. Place the milk and cream in a bowl, and mix them together until well combined. Use a whisk to mix in the sugar. Continue to whisk for about 4 minutes until the sugar dissolves. Then mix in the vanilla extract and dr. pepper reduction.
4. Pour the ingredients into your ice cream maker, and let it churn for 25 minutes. \
5. Put the ice cream in an airtight container and place in the freezer for around 2 hours. Allow the ice cream to thaw for 15 minutes before serving.

## 111. Strawberry Matcha Custard Ice Cream

Servings: 10
Cooking Time: 30 Minutes
**Ingredients:**
- 3 cups heavy cream
- 1 cup milk
- ¾ cup sugar
- A pinch of salt
- 1 vanilla bean, scraped
- 6 egg yolks
- ½ cup chopped strawberries
- 3 tablespoons matcha or green tea powder

**Directions:**
1. Add the cream, milk, sugar, and salt in a saucepan and heat over medium low flame. Simmer for 3 minutes or until the sugar dissolves. Stir in the vanilla bean paste. Remove from the stove.
2. In a bowl, whisk in the egg yolks. Drizzle ½ cup of the warm milk into the egg yolks while whisking constantly to form a smooth mixture. Whisk the egg mixture back into the pot.
3. Turn on the heat to medium low and cook until the mixture starts to thicken. Constantly stir while cooking.
4. Turn off the heat and strain the mixture to remove lumps. Allow to cool at room temperature. Place in the fridge to chill for 2 hours.
5. Turn on the Cuisinart and pour the mixture in. Add the chopped strawberries. Churn for 15 minutes.
6. Transfer to an airtight container. Sprinkle with matcha powder on top.
7. Place in the fridge to completely cool.

**Nutrition Info:** Calories per serving: 204 ; Protein: 3.2g; Carbs: 10.6g; Fat: 16.9g Sugar: 10g

## 112. Pineapple Ice Cream

Servings: 6
Cooking Time: 45 Minutes
**Ingredients:**
- 1 ½ cup pineapple juice
- 1 can crushed pineapple
- ½ cup heavy whipping cream

**Directions:**
1. Put ice water in a large mixing bowl. Place a small bowl on top of the large bowl with ice.
2. Place all ingredients in the small bowl. Whisk until well combined.
3. Turn on the Cuisinart and pour the mixture in. Freeze for 45 minutes.
4. Transfer into air-tight containers.
5. Freeze overnight.

**Nutrition Info:** Calories per serving: 136; Protein: 1g; Carbs: 26g; Fat: 3.8g Sugar: 24g

## 113. Three Musketeer Gelato

Servings: 4-6
Cooking Time: 2 Hours 35 Minutes
**Ingredients:**
- 1/2 cup heavy cream
- 2 cups milk
- 3/4 cup sugar
- 1 tablespoon vanilla extract
- 1 ½ cups chopped mini three musketeers bars

**Directions:**
1. Refer to note at the beginning of the chapter about freezing bowl.
2. Place the milk and cream in a bowl, and mix them together until well combined. Use a whisk to mix in the sugar. Continue to whisk for about 4 minutes until the sugar dissolves. Then mix in the vanilla extract.
3. Pour the ingredients into your ice cream maker, and let it churn for 25 minutes. About 5 minutes before the ice cream is done churning add the three musketeers to your ice cream maker.
4. Put the gelato in an airtight container and place in the freezer for up to 2 hours, until desired consistency is reached.

### 114. Kiwi Lime Strawberry Ice Cream

Servings: 6
Cooking Time: 2 Hours 50 Minutes
**Ingredients:**
- 2 cups heavy cream
- 1 cup milk
- 3/4 cup sugar
- 1/2 teaspoon vanilla extract
- ½ teaspoon salt
- 1 kiwi, peeled
- 5 large strawberries chopped
- Juice of one and a half limes

**Directions:**
1. NOTE: Freeze your ice cream bowl for at least 24hrs prior to starting!
2. Puree the kiwi and strawberries in a food processor or blender.
3. Place the milk and cream in a bowl, and mix them together until well combined. Use a whisk to mix in the sugar and salt. Continue to whisk for about 4 minutes until the sugar and salt dissolves. Then mix in the vanilla extract, lime juice, and kiwi strawberry puree.
4. Pour the ingredients into your ice cream maker, and let it churn for 25 minutes.
5. Put the ice cream in an airtight container and place in the freezer for around 2 hours. Allow the ice cream to thaw for 15 minutes before serving.

### 115. Double Bubble Gum Soft Serve Ice Cream

Servings: 6
Cooking Time: 35 Minutes
**Ingredients:**
- 2 cups heavy cream
- 1 cup milk
- 3/4 cup sugar
- 1 Tbs. vanilla extract
- 1 dram bubble gum flavoring
- ½ cup mini gum balls

**Directions:**
1. Refer to note at the beginning of the chapter about freezing bowl.
2. Place the milk and cream in a bowl, and mix them together until well combined. Use a whisk to mix in the sugar. Continue to whisk for about 4 minutes until the sugar dissolves. Mix in the vanilla extract, and then the bubble gum flavoring.
3. Pour the ingredients into your ice cream maker, and let it churn for 25 minutes. About 5 minutes before the churning is done add the gum balls to your ice cream maker.
4. Serve immediately.

### 116. Chocolate Pistachio Ice Cream

Servings: 6
Cooking Time: 2 Hours 50 Minutes
**Ingredients:**
- 2 cups heavy cream
- 1 cup milk
- 3/4 cup sugar
- 1/4 teaspoon almond extract
- 1/2 cup chopped pistachios
- 1 cup semi-sweet chocolate chips

**Directions:**
1. NOTE: Freeze your ice cream bowl for at least 24hrs prior to starting!
2. Place the milk and cream in a bowl, and mix them together until well combined. Use a whisk to mix in the sugar. Continue to whisk for about 4 minutes until the sugar dissolves. Then mix in the almond extract.

3. Pour the ingredients into your ice cream maker, and let it churn for 25 minutes. About 5 minutes before the ice cream is finished churning, add in the pistachios and chocolate chips.
4. Put the ice cream in an airtight container and place in the freezer for around 2 hours. Allow the ice cream to thaw for 15 minutes before serving.

### 117. Blackberry Ice Cream

Servings: 10
Cooking Time: 45 Minutes
**Ingredients:**
- 1 ½ cups blackberries, frozen or fresh
- ¾ cup ice cold whole milk
- ½ cup sugar
- A pinch of salt
- 1 ½ cup heavy cream, ice cold
- 1 ½ teaspoon vanilla

**Directions:**
1. Clean the blackberries by removing the stem and seeds. Mash to release the juice and pass through a sieve. Save the juice and set aside.
2. Put ice water in a large mixing bowl. Place a small bowl on top of the large bowl with ice.
3. Place the whole milk, sugar, and salt. Whisk to combine everything. Add the cream, vanilla, and blackberry juice. Stir to combined.
4. Turn on the Cuisinart and pour the mixture in. Freeze for 45 minutes.
5. Transfer into air-tight containers.
6. Freeze overnight.

**Nutrition Info:** Calories per serving: 151; Protein: 3g; Carbs: 15g; Fat: 9.1g Sugar: 13.1g

### 118. Coffee Toffee Ice Cream

Servings: 10
Cooking Time: 45 Minutes
**Ingredients:**
- 1 ½ cups ice cold whole milk
- 1 1/8 cups granulated sugar
- 3 cups ice cold heavy cream
- 1 ½ tablespoons vanilla extract
- 4 tablespoons Instant Espresso Powder
- 12 ounces min chocolate bars, chopped

**Directions:**
1. Put ice water in a large mixing bowl. Place a small bowl on top of the large bowl with ice.
2. Place the milk and sugar in the bowl. Whisk to dissolve the sugar. Add the cream, vanilla extract, and espresso powder. Stir to combine everything.
3. Turn on the Cuisinart and pour the mixture in. Freeze for 45 minutes. Five minutes before the time, add the chopped chocolate bars.
4. Transfer into air-tight containers. Freeze overnight.

**Nutrition Info:** Calories per serving: 358; Protein: 6.6g; Carbs: 37.4g; Fat: 21.6g Sugar: 21g

### 119. Apricot Ice Cream

Servings: 10
Cooking Time: 45 Minutes
**Ingredients:**
- 1 ½ tablespoons lemon zest
- ½ cup apricot, mashed
- 1 cup sugar
- 1 ½ cups ice cold whole milk
- 1 ½ cups cold whipping cream

**Directions:**
1. Put ice water in a large mixing bowl. Place a small bowl on top of the large bowl with ice.
2. To the small bowl, whisk together the lemon zest, mashed apricot, sugar, and milk. Whisk until well combined.
3. Add the whipping cream then whisk again to incorporate all ingredients.
4. Turn on the Cuisinart and pour the mixture in. Freeze for 45 minutes.
5. Transfer into air-tight containers and freeze overnight.

**Nutrition Info:** Calories per serving: 143; Protein: 4.7g; Carbs: 16.5g; Fat: 6.8g Sugar: 14.2g

### 120. Chocolate Ice Cream

Servings: 10
Cooking Time: 25 Minutes
**Ingredients:**
- 1 cup whole milk
- ½ cup granulated sugar

- 8 ounces semi-sweet chocolate, chopped into small chunks
- 2 cups ice cold heavy cream
- 1 teaspoon pure vanilla extract

**Directions:**
1. Warm milk in a stovetop under low heat until the temperature reads at 1750F. Stir in the sugar and chocolate until dissolved. Turn off the heat and set aside in the fridge to cool.
2. Put ice water in a large mixing bowl. Place a small bowl on top of the large bowl with ice. Pour the milk chocolate mixture into the small bowl and add heavy cream and vanilla.
3. Turn on the Cuisinart and pour the mixture in. Freeze for 25 minutes before transferring into an air-tight container.
4. Freeze inside the fridge overnight before serving.

**Nutrition Info:** Calories per serving:240 ; Protein: 2.1g; Carbs: 22.6g; Fat: 17g Sugar: 20.4g

### 121. Custard Cantaloupe Ice Cream

Servings: 10
Cooking Time: 30 Minutes
**Ingredients:**
- 3 cups whole milk
- 1 cup sugar
- 8 egg yolks
- A pinch of salt
- 1 cup cantaloupe, seeds removed and mashed

**Directions:**
1. Add the milk and sugar in a saucepan and heat over medium low flame. Simmer for 3 minutes or until the sugar dissolves. Remove from the heat.
2. In a bowl, whisk in the egg yolks. Drizzle ½ cup of the warm milk into the egg yolks while whisking constantly to form a smooth mixture. Whisk the egg mixture back into the pot. Add the salt.
3. Turn on the heat to medium low and cook until the mixture starts to thicken. Constantly stir while cooking.
4. Turn off the heat and strain the mixture to remove lumps. Allow the milk to cool at room temperature. Place in the fridge to chill for 2 hours.
5. Turn on the Cuisinart and pour the mixture in. Churn for 15 minutes.
6. Five minutes before the time ends, add the mashed cantaloupe.
7. Transfer to an airtight container.
8. Place in the fridge to completely cool.

**Nutrition Info:** Calories per serving:155 ; Protein: 4.5g; Carbs: 21.4g; Fat: 5.9g Sugar: 20.1g

### 122. Butter Toffee Popcorn Soft Serve Ice Cream

Servings: 6
Cooking Time: 35 Minutes
**Ingredients:**
- 2 cups heavy cream
- 1 cup milk
- 3/4 cup sugar
- 1 Tbs. vanilla extract
- 2 cup butter toffee popcorn

**Directions:**
1. NOTE: Freeze your ice cream bowl for at least 24hrs prior to starting!
2. Place the milk and cream in a bowl, and mix them together until well combined. Use a whisk to mix in the sugar. Continue to whisk for about 4 minutes until the sugar dissolves. Mix in the vanilla extract. Place the mixture in a blender or food processor with 1 cup of the caramel corn, and puree.
3. Put the remaining caramel corn in a resealable plastic bag, and seal it. Crush the caramel corn using your hands, or a mallet.
4. Pour the ingredients into your ice cream maker, and let it churn for 25 minutes. About 5 minutes before the churning is finished add in the crushed caramel corn.
5. Serve immediately.

### 123. Barbados Custard Ice Cream

Servings: 12
Cooking Time: 30 Minutes
**Ingredients:**
- 2 cups whole milk

- ½ cup sugar
- ¼ cup light brown sugar
- A pinch of salt
- 1 vanilla pod, scraped
- 6 egg yolks
- ½ cup crème fraiche
- 1 tablespoon dark rum

**Directions:**
1. Add the milk, sugar, and salt in a saucepan and heat over medium low flame. Simmer for 3 minutes or until the sugar dissolves. Remove from the stove.
2. In a bowl, whisk in the egg yolks. Drizzle ½ cup of the warm milk into the egg yolks while whisking constantly to form a smooth mixture. Whisk the egg mixture back into the pot. Add the vanilla, crème fraiche, and rum.
3. Turn on the heat to medium low and cook until the mixture starts to thicken. Constantly stir while cooking.
4. Turn off the heat and strain the mixture to remove lumps. Allow to cool at room temperature. Place in the fridge to chill for 2 hours.
5. Turn on the Cuisinart and pour the mixture in. Churn for 15 minutes.
6. Transfer to an airtight container.
7. Place in the fridge to completely cool.

**Nutrition Info:** Calories per serving: 103; Protein: 2.7g; Carbs: 10.2g; Fat: 5.5g Sugar: 9.6g

### 124. Thermomix Licorice Ice Cream

Servings: 12
Cooking Time: 30 Minutes
**Ingredients:**
- 3 cups heavy cream
- 2 cups whole milk
- ½ cup sugar
- A pinch of salt
- 6 egg yolks
- ½ teaspoon black food coloring
- ¼ cup soft licorice, chopped

**Directions:**
1. Add the cream, milk, sugar, and salt in a saucepan and heat over medium low flame. Simmer for 3 minutes or until the sugar dissolves. Remove from the stove.
2. In a bowl, whisk in the egg yolks. Drizzle ½ cup of the warm milk into the egg yolks while whisking constantly to form a smooth mixture. Whisk the egg mixture back into the pot. Add the black food coloring and licorice.
3. Turn on the heat to medium low and cook until the mixture starts to thicken. Constantly stir while cooking.
4. Turn off the heat and strain the mixture to remove lumps. Allow the milk to cool at room temperature. Place in the fridge to chill for 2 hours.
5. Turn on the Cuisinart and pour the mixture in. Churn for 15 minutes.
6. Transfer to an airtight container.
7. Place in the fridge to completely cool.

**Nutrition Info:** Calories per serving 342 ; Protein 3g; Carbs 32g; Fat 22g Sugar 22g

### 125. Pumpkin Custard Ice Cream

Servings: 6
Cooking Time: 30 Minutes
**Ingredients:**
- 2 cups heavy cream
- 2 cups milk
- ¼ cup granulated sugar
- ¾ cup brown sugar
- 1/8 teaspoon salt
- 3 egg yolk
- 1 teaspoon cinnamon
- ¼ teaspoon grated nutmeg
- 1/8 teaspoon ground cloves
- 1/8 teaspoon ground ginger
- 1 tablespoon vanilla extract
- 1 cup canned pumpkin, mashed

**Directions:**
1. Add the cream, milk, sugar, and salt in a saucepan and heat over medium low flame. Simmer for 3 minutes or until the sugar dissolves. Remove from the stove.
2. In a bowl, whisk in the egg yolks. Drizzle ½ cup of the warm milk into the egg yolks while whisking constantly to form a smooth mixture. Whisk the egg mixture back into the

pot. Add the cinnamon, nutmeg, cloves, ginger, and vanilla.
3. Turn on the heat to medium low and cook until the mixture starts to thicken. Constantly stir while cooking.
4. Turn off the heat and strain the mixture to remove lumps. Allow the milk to cool at room temperature. Place in the fridge to chill for 2 hours.
5. Turn on the Cuisinart and pour the mixture in. Add the mashed pumpkin. Churn for 15 minutes.
6. Transfer to an airtight container.
7. Place in the fridge to completely cool.

**Nutrition Info:** Calories per serving:457 ; Protein: 10.7g; Carbs: 40g; Fat: 29g Sugar: 47g

### 126. "cool" Cake Batter Soft Serve Ice Cream

Servings: 6
Cooking Time: 35 Minutes
**Ingredients:**
- 2 cups heavy cream
- 1 cup milk
- 3/4 cup sugar
- 1 Tbs. vanilla extract
- 2/3 cup cake mix

**Directions:**
1. Refer to note at the beginning of the chapter about freezing bowl.
2. Place the milk and cream in a bowl, and mix them together until well combined. Use a whisk to mix in the sugar. Continue to whisk for about 4 minutes until the sugar dissolves. Mix in the vanilla extract, and then the 2/3 cup cake mix.
3. Pour the ingredients into your ice cream maker, and let it churn for 25 minutes.
4. Serve immediately.

### 127. Banana Custard Ice Cream

Servings: 8
Cooking Time: 30 Minutes
**Ingredients:**
- 2 cups heavy cream
- 2 cups half and half
- 5 tablespoons evaporated milk
- 1 ¼ cups granulated sugar
- ¼ teaspoon salt
- 4 egg yolks, beaten
- 1 cup mashed ripe bananas
- 2 tablespoons roasted peanuts, chopped

**Directions:**
1. Add the cream, half and half, milk, sugar, and salt in a saucepan and heat over medium low flame. Simmer for 3 minutes or until the sugar dissolves. Remove from the stove.
2. In a bowl, whisk in the egg yolks. Drizzle ½ cup of the warm milk into the egg yolks while whisking constantly to form a smooth mixture. Whisk the egg mixture back into the pot.
3. Turn on the heat to medium low and cook until the mixture starts to thicken. Constantly stir while cooking.
4. Turn off the heat and strain the mixture to remove lumps. Allow to cool at room temperature. Place in the fridge to chill for 2 hours.
5. Turn on the Cuisinart and pour the mixture in. Add the mashed bananas. Churn for 15 minutes.
6. Five minutes before the time ends, add the roasted peanuts.
7. Transfer to an airtight container.
8. Place in the fridge to completely cool.

**Nutrition Info:** Calories per serving: 298; Protein: 5.4g; Carbs: 35g; Fat:16.2 g Sugar: 26g

### 128. Gummy Worm Cotton Candy Ice Cream

Servings: 6
Cooking Time: 2 Hours 50 Minutes
**Ingredients:**
- 2 cups heavy cream
- 1 cup milk
- 3/4 cup sugar
- 1 tablespoon vanilla extract
- 1 tablespoon cotton candy extract
- 1 ½ cups gummy worm candy

**Directions:**
1. NOTE: Freeze your ice cream bowl for at least 24hrs prior to starting!
2. Place the milk and cream in a bowl, and mix them together until well

combined. Use a whisk to mix in the sugar. Continue to whisk for about 4 minutes until the sugar dissolves. Then mix in the vanilla extract.
3. Pour the ingredients into your ice cream maker, and let it churn for 25 minutes. About 5 minutes before the ice cream is done churning add the M&Ms to your ice cream maker.
4. Put the ice cream in an airtight container and place in the freezer for around 2 hours. Allow the ice cream to thaw for 15 minutes before serving.

### 129. Mocha Ice Cream

Servings: 10
Cooking Time: 25 Minutes
**Ingredients:**
- 1 cup ice cold whole milk
- ¼ cup granulated sugar
- 2 cups heavy cream
- 1 teaspoon vanilla extract
- 2 tablespoons instant coffee, dissolved in 3 tablespoons hot water

**Directions:**
1. Put ice water in a large mixing bowl. Place a small bowl on top of the large bowl with ice.
2. Pour the milk in the small bowl and add the sugar. Whisk until well-combined and the sugar dissolves. Add the rest of the ingredients and whisk.
3. Turn on the Cuisinart and pour the mixture in. Freeze for 25 minutes.
4. Transfer into air-tight containers and freeze overnight.

**Nutrition Info:** Calories per serving:139 ; Protein: 3.4g; Carbs: 4.4g; Fat: 12.1g Sugar: 3.2g

### 130. Classic Root Beer Lemon Gelato

Servings: 4-6
Cooking Time: 2 Hours 50 Minutes
**Ingredients:**
- 1/2 cup heavy cream
- 2 cups milk
- 3/4 cup sugar
- 1 teaspoon vanilla extract
- 3 cups (2, 12 ounce cans) root beer
- 2 tablespoons lemon juice

**Directions:**
1. NOTE: Freeze your ice cream bowl for at least 24hrs prior to starting!
2. Pour the root beer into a large skillet, and heat it on high heat until it comes to a boil. Allow the coke to cook for about another 15 or 20 minutes, until the root beer reduces down to 1 cup of liquid. Let the liquid cool.
3. Place the milk and cream in a bowl, and mix them together until well combined. Use a whisk to mix in the sugar. Continue to whisk for about 4 minutes until the sugar dissolves. Then mix in the vanilla extract and root beer reduction and lemon juice.
4. Pour the ingredients into your ice cream maker, and let it churn for 25 minutes. About 5 minutes before the ice cream is done churning add the chocolate to your ice cream maker.
5. Put the gelato in an airtight container and place in the freezer for up to 2 hours, until desired consistency is reached.

### 131. Peanut Butter Cup Milkshake

Servings: 6
Cooking Time: 25 Minutes
**Ingredients:**
- 2 cups heavy cream
- 1 cup milk
- 3/4 cup sugar
- 1 tablespoon vanilla extract
- 1 1/2 cups chopped mini peanut butter cups
- ½ cup maple syrup

**Directions:**
1. Refer to note at the beginning of the chapter about freezing bowl.
2. Place the milk and cream in a bowl, and mix them together until well combined. Use a whisk to mix in the sugar. Continue to whisk for about 4 minutes until the sugar dissolves. Then mix in the vanilla extract.
3. Pour the ingredients into your ice cream maker, and let it churn for 10-15 minutes, until desired consistency is reached. About 5 minutes before the ice cream is done churning add

the peanut butter cup to your ice cream maker.
4. Serve immediately.

### 132. Circus Cotton Candy Milkshake

Servings: 6
Cooking Time: 25 Minutes
**Ingredients:**
- 2 cups heavy cream
- 1 cup milk
- 3/4 cup sugar
- 1 teaspoon vanilla extract
- 1/2 cup cotton candy syrup
- 1 tablespoon plus 1 teaspoon pink or blue food coloring

**Directions:**
1. NOTE: Freeze your ice cream bowl for at least 24hrs prior to starting!
2. Place the milk and cream in a bowl, and mix them together until well combined. Use a whisk to mix in the sugar. Continue to whisk for about 4 minutes until the sugar dissolves. Then mix in the vanilla extract, syrup, and food coloring.
3. Pour the ingredients into your ice cream maker, and let it churn for 10-15 minutes, until desired consistency is reached.
4. Serve immediately.

### 133. Mango Ice Cream

Servings: 10
Cooking Time: 15 Minutes
**Ingredients:**
- 3 cups whole milk
- 1 cup sugar
- 8 egg yolks
- A pinch of salt
- ¼ cup mango puree
- 3 tablespoons dried mango, chopped

**Directions:**
1. Add the milk and sugar in a saucepan and heat over medium low flame. Simmer for 3 minutes or until the sugar dissolves. Remove from the heat.
2. In a bowl, whisk in the egg yolks. Drizzle ½ cup of the warm milk into the egg yolks while whisking constantly to form a smooth mixture. Whisk the egg mixture back into the pot. Add the salt.
3. Turn on the heat to medium low and cook until the mixture starts to thicken. Constantly stir while cooking. Add the mango puree last.
4. Turn off the heat and strain the mixture to remove lumps. Allow the milk to cool at room temperature. Place in the fridge to chill for 2 hours.
5. Turn on the Cuisinart and pour the mixture in. Churn for 15 minutes.
6. Five minutes before the time ends, add the dried mango.
7. Transfer to an airtight container.
8. Place in the fridge to completely cool.

**Nutrition Info:** Calories per serving:154 ; Protein: 4.3g; Carbs: 21.2g; Fat: 5.8g Sugar: 20.4g

### 134. Tangerine Soda Ice Cream

Servings: 6
Cooking Time: 2 Hours 50 Minutes
**Ingredients:**
- 2 cups heavy cream
- 1 cup milk
- 3/4 cup sugar
- 1 teaspoon vanilla extract
- 20 ounces of your favorite orange soda
- orange extract (just a few drops)

**Directions:**
1. NOTE: Freeze your ice cream bowl for at least 24hrs prior to starting!
2. Place the milk and cream in a bowl, and mix them together until well combined. Use a whisk to mix in the sugar. Continue to whisk for about 4 minutes until the sugar dissolves. Then mix in the vanilla extract, orange soda and the few drops of orange extract.
3. Pour the ingredients into your ice cream maker, and let it churn for 25 minutes.
4. Put the ice cream in an airtight container and place in the freezer for around 2 hours. Allow the ice cream to thaw for 15 minutes before serving.

### 135. Turmeric Ice Cream

Servings: 10

Cooking Time: 30 Minutes
**Ingredients:**
- 3 cups whole milk
- 1 cup sugar
- 2 tablespoons turmeric powder
- 8 egg yolks
- A pinch of salt

**Directions:**
1. Add the milk, sugar, and turmeric powder in a saucepan and heat over medium low flame. Simmer for 3 minutes or until the sugar dissolves. Remove from the heat.
2. In a bowl, whisk in the egg yolks. Drizzle ½ cup of the warm milk into the egg yolks while whisking constantly to form a smooth mixture. Whisk the egg mixture back into the pot. Add the salt.
3. Turn on the heat to medium low and cook until the mixture starts to thicken. Constantly stir while cooking.
4. Turn off the heat and strain the mixture to remove lumps. Allow the milk to cool at room temperature. Place in the fridge to chill for 2 hours.
5. Turn on the Cuisinart and pour the mixture in. Churn for 15 minutes.
6. Transfer to an airtight container.
7. Place in the fridge to completely cool.

**Nutrition Info:** Calories per serving: 155; Protein: 5g; Carbs: 22g; Fat: 5g Sugar: 19g

### 136. Vegan Ice Cream

Servings: 12
Cooking Time: 45 Minutes
**Ingredients:**
- 2 13.5-ounce cans full-fat coconut milk
- ½ cup raw sugar
- 1 teaspoon vanilla extract
- 1 pinch xanthan gum
- ½ cup dark chocolate chips
- 1/3 cup roasted salted peanuts

**Directions:**
1. Pour in the coconut milk and sugar in a saucepan and whisk until well-combined. Add the vanilla and xanthan gum. Bring to a boil and whisk for 5 minutes.
2. Turn off the heat and allow to cool in the fridge for at least 6 hours.
3. Turn on the Cuisinart and pour the mixture in. Freeze for 45 minutes.
4. Add the chocolate chips and peanuts into the mixture 5 minutes before stopping the machine.
5. Transfer into air-tight containers and freeze overnight.

**Nutrition Info:** Calories per serving: 361; Protein: 4.1g; Carbs: 27.3g; Fat: 28.6g Sugar: 23.4g

### 137. Island Coconut Banana Sorbet

Servings: 4-8
Cooking Time: 2 Hours 40 Minutes
**Ingredients:**
- 3 peeled, mashed bananas
- 2-4 tablespoons honey to taste
- 1 1/2 cups light coconut milk
- 1 teaspoon vanilla extract

**Directions:**
1. Refer to note at the beginning of the chapter about freezing bowl.
2. Puree all ingredients in a food processor or blender. Taste, and add more honey if desired.
3. Pour the ingredients into your ice cream maker, and let it churn for 25-30 minutes.
4. Place in an airtight container for up to 2 hours, until desired consistency is reached.

### 138. Blueberry Honey Cake Batter Soft Serve Ice Cream

Servings: 6
Cooking Time: 35 Minutes
**Ingredients:**
- 2 cups heavy cream
- 1 cup milk
- 3/4 cup sugar
- 1 Tbs. vanilla extract
- 2/3 cup cake mix
- ½ cup blueberries
- 2 tablespoons honey

**Directions:**
1. NOTE: Freeze your ice cream bowl for at least 24hrs prior to starting!
2. Place the milk and cream in a bowl, and mix them together until well

combined. Use a whisk to mix in the sugar. Continue to whisk for about 4 minutes until the sugar dissolves. Mix in the vanilla extract, and then the 2/3 cup cake mix honey and blueberries.
3. Pour the ingredients into your ice cream maker, and let it churn for 25 minutes.
4. Serve immediately.

### 139. Butter Pecan Ice Cream

Servings: 10
Cooking Time: 25 Minutes
**Ingredients:**
- ½ cup unsalted butter
- 1 cup chopped pecan
- 1 teaspoon salt
- 1 cup ice cold whole milk
- ¾ cup granulated sugar
- 2 cups ice cold heavy cream
- 1 teaspoon pure vanilla extract

**Directions:**
1. Melt the butter in skillet and add the nuts and salt. Sauté over medium heat until the nuts are golden. Remove and strain the nuts. Reserve the butter for another use. Set aside the nuts. Allow the nuts to cool at least to room temperature.
2. Put ice water in a large mixing bowl. Place a small bowl on top of the large bowl with ice. Whisk in the milk and sugar until the sugar dissolves. Add the heavy cream and vanilla. Stir until combined.
3. Turn on the Cuisinart and pour the mixture in. Freeze for 25 minutes and add the nuts five minutes before the time ends.
4. Place the ice cream into a container and freeze overnight.

**Nutrition Info:** Calories per serving: 281; Protein: 4.6g; Carbs:10.2 g; Fat: 25.4g Sugar: 9g

### 140. Chilled Cherry Soda Frozen Yogurt

Servings: 1 Quart
Cooking Time: 2 Hours 50 Minutes
**Ingredients:**
- 1 quart container full-fat plain yogurt
- ¼ teaspoon salt
- 1 cup sugar
- 1 teaspoon vanilla extract
- 3 cups (2, 12 ounce cans) cherry soda

**Directions:**
1. Refer to note at the beginning of the chapter about freezing bowl.
2. Pour the cherry soda into a large skillet, and heat it on high heat until it comes to a boil. Allow the coke to cook for about another 15 or 20 minutes, until the root beer reduces down to 1 cup of liquid. Let the liquid cool.
3. Place the yogurt in a bowl. Use a whisk to mix in the sugar and salt. Continue to whisk for about 4 minutes until the sugar dissolves. Then mix in the vanilla extract, and reduced cherry soda.
4. Pour the ingredients into your ice cream maker, and let it churn for 25 minutes.
5. Put the frozen yogurt in an airtight container and place in the freezer for at least 2 hours, until desired consistency is reached.

### 141. My Delicious M&m Ice Cream

Servings: 6
Cooking Time: 2 Hours 50 Minutes
**Ingredients:**
- 2 cups heavy cream
- 1 cup milk
- 3/4 cup sugar
- 1 tablespoon vanilla extract
- 1 ½ cups M&Ms candy

**Directions:**
1. Refer to note at the beginning of the chapter about freezing bowl.
2. Place the milk and cream in a bowl, and mix them together until well combined. Use a whisk to mix in the sugar. Continue to whisk for about 4 minutes until the sugar dissolves. Then mix in the vanilla extract.
3. Pour the ingredients into your ice cream maker, and let it churn for 25 minutes. About 5 minutes before the ice cream is done churning add the M&Ms to your ice cream maker.

4. Put the ice cream in an airtight container and place in the freezer for around 2 hours. Allow the ice cream to thaw for 15 minutes before serving.

### 142. California Mango Lime Soft Serve Ice Cream

Servings: 6
Cooking Time: 35 Minutes
**Ingredients:**
- 2 cups heavy cream
- 1 cup milk
- 3/4 cup sugar
- 1 Tbs. vanilla extract
- 1 cup pureed mango (about 2.5 mangos)
- Juice of 1 lime

**Directions:**
1. NOTE: Freeze your ice cream bowl for at least 24hrs prior to starting!
2. Puree the mangos with the lime juice in a food processor or blender.
3. Place the milk and cream in a bowl, and mix them together until well combined. Use a whisk to mix in the sugar. Continue to whisk for about 4 minutes until the sugar dissolves. Then mix in the vanilla extract. Then mix in the mango lime puree.
4. Pour the ingredients into your ice cream maker, and let it churn for 25 minutes.
5. Serve immediately.

### 143. Vanilla Frozen Custard

Servings: 6
Cooking Time: 30 Minutes
**Ingredients:**
- 2 cups heavy cream
- 1 cup whole milk
- 2/3 cup granulated sugar
- A pinch of salt
- 6 large egg yolks
- 2 teaspoons vanilla extract

**Directions:**
1. Add the cream, milk, sugar, and salt in a saucepan and heat over medium low flame. Simmer for 3 minutes or until the sugar dissolves.
2. Remove from the heat.
3. In a bowl, whisk in the egg yolks. Drizzle ½ cup of the warm milk into the egg yolks while whisking constantly to form a smooth mixture. Whisk the egg mixture back into the pot and add vanilla.
4. Turn on the heat to medium low and cook until the mixture starts to thicken. Constantly stir while cooking.
5. Turn off the heat and strain the mixture to remove lumps. Allow the milk to cool at room temperature. Place in the fridge to chill for 2 hours.
6. Turn on the Cuisinart and pour the mixture in. Churn for 15 minutes.
7. Transfer to an airtight container and place in the fridge to completely cool.

**Nutrition Info:** Calories per serving: 443; Protein: 5g; Carbs: 27 g; Fat: 35g Sugar: 24g

### 144. Purple Taro Ice Cream

Servings: 10
Cooking Time: 1 Hour 15 Minutes
**Ingredients:**
- 1 cup purple taro, peeled and cubed
- 1 cup ice cold whole milk
- ¾ cup sugar
- 1 ½ cup ice cold heavy cream
- 2 tablespoons vanilla extract

**Directions:**
1. Place the purple taro in a saucepan and add enough water to cover the taro. Bring to a boil for 35 minutes or until soft. Drain to remove excess water. Mash the purple taro using fork and remove big lumps. Set aside to cool.
2. Put ice water in a large mixing bowl. Place a small bowl on top of the large bowl with ice.
3. Place the milk and sugar in the bowl and stir to dissolve the sugar. Add the mashed and cooled taro in the mixture. Add the heavy cream and vanilla. Stir to combine.
4. Turn on the Cuisinart and pour the mixture in. Freeze for 45 minutes.
5. Transfer into air-tight containers.
6. Freeze overnight.

**Nutrition Info:** Calories per serving: 154; Protein: 3.3g; Carbs: 11.8 g; Fat: 9.9g Sugar: 8.3g

### 145. Butterfinger Cinnamon Crunch Gelato

Servings: 4-6
Cooking Time: 2 Hours 35 Minutes
**Ingredients:**
- 1/2 cup heavy cream
- 2 cups milk
- 3/4 cup sugar
- 1 teaspoon vanilla extract
- 1 ½ cups chopped mini Butterfinger bars
- 2 teaspoons ground cinnamon

**Directions:**
1. NOTE: Freeze your ice cream bowl for at least 24hrs prior to starting!
2. Place the milk and cream in a bowl, and mix them together until well combined. Use a whisk to mix in the sugar. Continue to whisk for about 4 minutes until the sugar dissolves. Then mix in the vanilla extract and cinnamon.
3. Pour the ingredients into your ice cream maker, and let it churn for 25 minutes. About 5 minutes before the ice cream is done churning add the Butterfinger to your ice cream maker.
4. Put the gelato in an airtight container and place in the freezer for up to 2 hours, until desired consistency is reached.

### 146. Banana Pudding Ice Cream

Servings: 8
Cooking Time: 25 Minutes
**Ingredients:**
- 1 ½ cups half and half
- ½ cup packed brown sugar
- ½ cup white sugar
- 1/8 teaspoon salt
- 1 cup heavy whipping cream
- 1 ½ teaspoon vanilla extract
- 2 ripe bananas, mashed
- 1 cup crushed wafers, any brand

**Directions:**
1. Place the half and half, brown sugar, white sugar, and salt in a saucepan. Bring to a boil until the sugar dissolves. Turn off the heat and place in the fridge to cool.
2. Put ice water in a large mixing bowl. Place a small bowl on top of the large bowl with ice.
3. Place the cooled milk mixture in the bowl and add the whipping cream, vanilla extract, and bananas. Whisk to combine everything.
4. Turn on the Cuisinart and pour the mixture in. Freeze for 25 minutes. Five minutes before the time, add the wafers.
5. Transfer into air-tight containers. Freeze overnight.

**Nutrition Info:** Calories per serving:196 ; Protein: 2.6g; Carbs: 28.4g; Fat: 8.8g Sugar: 22.1g

### 147. Blueberry Mint Soft Serve Ice Cream

Servings: 6
Cooking Time: 35 Minutes
**Ingredients:**
- 2 cups heavy cream
- 1 cup milk
- 3/4 cup sugar
- ½ cup blueberries
- 1 Tbs. vanilla extract
- 1 cup sliced peaches
- 1 hand full of mint leaves

**Directions:**
1. NOTE: Freeze your ice cream bowl for at least 24hrs prior to starting!
2. Puree the peaches and mint in a food processor or blender.
3. Place the milk and cream in a bowl, and mix them together until well combined. Use a whisk to mix in the sugar. Continue to whisk for about 4 minutes until the sugar dissolves. Then mix in the vanilla extract, blueberries and mint.
4. Pour the ingredients into your ice cream maker, and let it churn for 25 minutes.
5. Serve immediately.

### 148. Cookies And Cream Ice Cream

Servings: 10
Cooking Time: 30 Minutes
**Ingredients:**
- 2 cups heavy cream

- 1 cup whole milk
- ¾ cup sugar
- 2 teaspoons vanilla extract
- A pinch of salt
- 6 egg yolks
- 1 cup Oreo cookies, chopped

**Directions:**
1. Add the cream, milk, sugar, vanilla extract, and salt in a saucepan and heat over medium low flame. Simmer for 3 minutes or until the sugar dissolves. Remove from the stove.
2. In a bowl, whisk in the egg yolks. Drizzle ½ cup of the warm milk into the egg yolks while whisking constantly to form a smooth mixture. Whisk the egg mixture back into the pot.
3. Turn on the heat to medium low and cook until the mixture starts to thicken. Constantly stir while cooking.
4. Turn off the heat and strain the mixture to remove lumps. Allow to cool at room temperature. Place in the fridge to chill for 2 hours.
5. Turn on the Cuisinart and pour the mixture in. Churn for 15 minutes.
6. Five minutes before the time ends, add the chopped Oreo cookies.
7. Transfer to an airtight container.
8. Place in the fridge to completely cool.

**Nutrition Info:** Calories per serving:219 ; Protein: 4g; Carbs: 20 g; Fat: 13.9g Sugar: 15.5g

### 149.Nutella Ice Cream

Servings: 10
Cooking Time: 30 Minutes
**Ingredients:**
- 2 cups heavy cream
- 1 cup whole milk
- 2/3 cup granulated sugar
- 1 teaspoon salt
- 6 egg yolks
- ½ cup Nutella
- 1 teaspoon vanilla extract

**Directions:**
1. Add the cream, milk, sugar, and salt in a saucepan and heat over medium low flame. Simmer for 3 minutes. Remove from the stove.
2. In a bowl, whisk in the egg yolks. Drizzle ½ cup of the warm milk into the egg yolks while whisking constantly to form a smooth mixture. Whisk the egg mixture back into the pot.
3. Turn on the heat to medium low and cook until the mixture starts to thicken. Constantly stir while cooking. Add Nutella and vanilla.
4. Turn off the heat and strain the mixture to remove lumps. Allow to cool at room temperature. Place in the fridge to chill for 2 hours.
5. Turn on the Cuisinart and pour the mixture in. Churn for 15 minutes.
6. Transfer to an airtight container.
7. Place in the fridge to completely cool.

**Nutrition Info:** Calories per serving: 219; Protein: 3.4g; Carbs: 17.4g; Fat: 15.3g Sugar: 15.8g

### 150.Crunchy Cinnamon Butterfinger Gelato

Servings: 4-6
Cooking Time: 2 Hours 35 Minutes
**Ingredients:**
- 1/2 cup heavy cream
- 2 cups milk
- 3/4 cup sugar
- 1 teaspoon vanilla extract
- 1 ½ cups chopped mini butterfinger bars
- 2 teaspoons ground cinnamon

**Directions:**
1. Refer to note at the beginning of the chapter about freezing bowl.
2. Place the milk and cream in a bowl, and mix them together until well combined. Use a whisk to mix in the sugar. Continue to whisk for about 4 minutes until the sugar dissolves. Then mix in the vanilla extract and cinnamon.
3. Pour the ingredients into your ice cream maker, and let it churn for 25 minutes. About 5 minutes before the ice cream is done churning add the butterfinger to your ice cream maker.
4. Put the gelato in an airtight container and place in the freezer for up to 2

hours, until desired consistency is reached.

### 151. Mocha Madness Ice Cream

Servings: 10
Cooking Time: 45 Minutes
**Ingredients:**
- 2 tablespoons unsweetened cocoa
- 2 tablespoons espresso powder
- 1 cup ice cold whole milk
- ¾ cup sugar
- 2 cups ice cold heavy cream
- 8 Oreo cookies, broken into small pieces

**Directions:**
1. Place cocoa, espresso powder, half of the milk and sugar in a pan. Bring to a simmer until everything dissolves. Turn off the heat and set aside in the fridge to cool.
2. Put ice water in a large mixing bowl. Place a small bowl on top of the large bowl with ice.
3. Pour in milk, sugar, espresso powder, and cocoa in the chilled bowl. Whisk until well combined.
4. Turn on the Cuisinart and pour the mixture in. Freeze for 45 minutes.
5. Transfer into air-tight containers and freeze overnight.

**Nutrition Info:** Calories per serving: 213; Protein: 4.2g; Carbs: 17.4g; Fat: 14.8g Sugar: 11.6g

### 152. Cinnamon Ice Cream

Servings: 10
Cooking Time: 45 Minutes
**Ingredients:**
- 2 cups heavy cream
- 1 cup half and half
- ½ cup sugar
- ¼ cup brown sugar
- 1 teaspoon vanilla extract
- 1 tablespoon cinnamon
- A pinch of salt

**Directions:**
1. Put ice water in a large mixing bowl. Place a small bowl on top of the large bowl with ice.
2. Pour all ingredients in the bowl. Whisk until well-combined.
3. Turn on the Cuisinart and pour the mixture in. Freeze for 45 minutes.
4. Transfer into air-tight containers. Freeze overnight.

**Nutrition Info:** Calories per serving: 140; Protein: 1.1g; Carbs: 13.8 g; Fat: 9.2g Sugar: 12.1g

### 153. "give Me More" S'mores Frozen Yogurt

Servings: 1 Quart
Cooking Time: 2 Hours 35 Minutes
**Ingredients:**
- 1 quart container full-fat plain yogurt
- ¼ teaspoon salt
- 1 cup sugar
- 1 teaspoon vanilla extract
- 3 large graham crackers
- 4 ounces chopped semi-sweet chocolate
- ½ cup mini marshmallows

**Directions:**
1. Refer to note at the beginning of the chapter about freezing bowl.
2. Place the yogurt in a bowl. Use a whisk to mix in the sugar and salt. Continue to whisk for about 4 minutes until the sugar dissolves. Then mix in the vanilla extract.
3. Place the graham crackers in a food processor, and process until the crackers are no bigger than chocolate chips. If you don't have a food processor place the crackers in a large resealable plastic bag, and seal it shut. Use your hands, a mallet, or a rolling pin to crush the cookies.
4. Pour the ingredients into your ice cream maker, and let it churn for 25 minutes. About 5 minutes before the ice cream is done churning add the chocolate, graham crackers, and marshmallows to your ice cream maker.
5. Put the frozen yogurt in an airtight container and place in the freezer for at least 2 hours, until desired consistency is reached.

### 154. Double Espresso Ice Cream

Servings: 10
Cooking Time: 30 Minutes

**Ingredients:**
- 2 cups half and half
- 1 ½ cups heavy cream
- 14 ounces sweetened condensed milk
- 2 tablespoons espresso powder
- 6 egg yolks
- ¼ cup chocolate-covered espresso beans, chopped

**Directions:**
1. Add the half and half, cream, condensed milk, and espresso powder in a saucepan and heat over medium low flame. Simmer for 3 minutes. Remove from the stove.
2. In a bowl, whisk in the egg yolks. Drizzle ½ cup of the warm milk into the egg yolks while whisking constantly to form a smooth mixture. Whisk the egg mixture back into the pot.
3. Turn on the heat to medium low and cook until the mixture starts to thicken. Constantly stir while cooking.
4. Turn off the heat and strain the mixture to remove lumps. Allow to cool at room temperature. Place in the fridge to chill for 2 hours.
5. Turn on the Cuisinart and pour the mixture in. Churn for 15 minutes.
6. Five minutes before the time ends, add the chocolate-covered espresso beans.
7. Transfer to an airtight container.
8. Place in the fridge to completely cool.

**Nutrition Info:** Calories per serving:166 ; Protein: 4.8g; Carbs: 9.2g; Fat: 12.4g Sugar: 5.6g

### 155. Rhubarb Swirl Ice Cream

Servings: 10
Cooking Time: 45 Minutes
**Ingredients:**
- 4 stalks rhubarb, cut into ½ inch pieces
- 1 cup water
- ¾ cup sugar
- 1 cup ice cold whole milk
- ¾ cup sugar
- 1 ½ teaspoon pure vanilla extract
- A pinch of salt
- 2 cups cold heavy cream

**Directions:**
1. Place the rhubarb, water, and sugar in a saucepan and heat over high flame. Bring to a boil and cook while stirring constantly until the rhubarb will break down and turns into a jelly-like consistency. Set aside to cool.
2. Put ice water in a large mixing bowl. Place a small bowl on top of the large bowl with ice.
3. To the chilled small bowl, add the milk, sugar, vanilla, and salt. Whisk until well combined. Whisk in the heavy cream.
4. Turn on the Cuisinart and pour the mixture in. Freeze for 45 minutes.
5. Transfer into air-tight containers. Drizzle with the cooled rhubarb jelly and stir again.
6. Freeze overnight.

**Nutrition Info:** Calories per serving: 190; Protein: 3.5g; Carbs: 17.4g; Fat: 12.1g Sugar: 15.7g

### 156. "georgia Peach" Maple Syrup Soft Serve Ice Cream

Servings: 6
Cooking Time: 35 Minutes
**Ingredients:**
- 2 cups heavy cream
- 1 cup milk
- 3/4 cup sugar
- 1 Tbs. vanilla extract
- 1 cup peaches
- ¼ cup maple syrup

**Directions:**
1. NOTE: Freeze your ice cream bowl for at least 24hrs prior to starting!
2. Puree the peaches in a food processor or blender.
3. Place the milk and cream in a bowl, and mix them together until well combined. Use a whisk to mix in the sugar. Continue to whisk for about 4 minutes until the sugar dissolves. Then mix in the vanilla extract. Then mix in the blueberries, and maple syrup.

4. Pour the ingredients into your ice cream maker, and let it churn for 25 minutes.
5. Serve immediately.

### 157. Cinnamon Blackberry Pineapple Ice Cream

Servings: 6
Cooking Time: 2 Hours 50 Minutes
**Ingredients:**
- 2 cups heavy cream
- 1 cup milk
- 3/4 cup sugar
- 1 teaspoon vanilla extract
- ½ cup pineapples
- ¼ cup of blackberries
- 1 tsp. cinnamon
- juice of 1/2 lemon

**Directions:**
1. NOTE: Freeze your ice cream bowl for at least 24hrs prior to starting!
2. Place the milk and cream in a bowl, and mix them together until well combined. Use a whisk to mix in the sugar. Continue to whisk for about 4 minutes until the sugar dissolves. Then mix in the vanilla extract, pineapples, blackberries lemon juice, and cinnamon.
3. Pour the ingredients into your ice cream maker, and let it churn for 25 minutes.
4. Put the ice cream in an airtight container and place in the freezer for around 2 hours. Allow the ice cream to thaw for 15 minutes before serving.

### 158. Cookies 'n Cream Rice Crispy Treat Frozen Yogurt

Servings: 1 Quart
Cooking Time: 2 Hours 35 Minutes
**Ingredients:**
- 1 quart container full-fat plain yogurt
- ¼ teaspoon salt
- 1 cup sugar
- 1 teaspoon vanilla extract
- 10 chocolate sandwich cookies
- 1/2 cup rice crispy treats

**Directions:**
1. Refer to note at the beginning of the chapter about freezing bowl.
2. Place the yogurt in a bowl. Use a whisk to mix in the sugar and salt. Continue to whisk for about 4 minutes until the sugar dissolves. Then mix in the vanilla extract.
3. Place the sandwich cookies in a food processor, and process until the cookies are no bigger than chocolate chips. If you don't have a food processor place the cookies in a large resealable plastic bag, and seal it shut. Use your hands, a mallet, or a rolling pin to crush the cookies.
4. Pour the ingredients into your ice cream maker, and let it churn for 25 minutes. About 5 minutes before the ice cream is done churning add the cookies, and small chunks of the rice crispy treats to your ice cream maker.
5. Put the frozen yogurt in an airtight container and place in the freezer for at least 2 hours, until desired consistency is reached.

### 159. Cinnamon Chocolate Chip Soft Serve Ice Cream

Servings: 6
Cooking Time: 35 Minutes
**Ingredients:**
- 2 cups heavy cream
- 1 cup milk
- 3/4 cup sugar
- 1 Tbs. vanilla extract
- 1 cup chocolate chips of your choice
- 2 tsps. cinnamon

**Directions:**
1. NOTE: Freeze your ice cream bowl for at least 24hrs prior to starting!
2. Place the milk and cream in a bowl, and mix them together until well combined. Use a whisk to mix in the sugar. Continue to whisk for about 4 minutes until the sugar dissolves. Then mix in the vanilla extract.
3. Pour the ingredients into your ice cream maker, and let it churn for 25 minutes. About 5 minutes before the ice cream is finished churning, add in the chocolate chips.
4. Serve immediately.

## 160. Peach Ice Cream

Servings: 10
Cooking Time: 45 Minutes
**Ingredients:**
- 2 ripe peaches, peeled, pitted, and sliced
- 1 ½ cups ice cold whole milk
- 1 cup ice cold whipping cream
- 4 ounces cubed cream cheese, room temperature
- ½ cup sugar
- 2 tablespoons honey
- ½ teaspoon vanilla extract
- 1/8 teaspoon salt

**Directions:**
1. Put ice water in a large mixing bowl. Place a small bowl on top of the large bowl with ice.
2. Place the peaches in a blender and pulse until smooth.
3. Pour the peaches in the chilled bowl and add the milk, whipping cream, cream cheese, and sugar. Whisk until well combined and smooth. Add the honey, vanilla extract, and salt.
4. Turn on the Cuisinart and pour the mixture in. Freeze for 45 minutes.
5. Transfer into air-tight containers and freeze overnight.

**Nutrition Info:** Calories per serving:176 ; Protein: 5.6g; Carbs: 17.6 g; Fat: 9.7g Sugar: 14.2g

## 161. Red Velvet Raspberry Milkshake

Servings: 6
Cooking Time: 25 Minutes
**Ingredients:**
- 2 cups heavy cream
- 1 cup milk
- 3/4 cup sugar
- 1 teaspoons vanilla extract
- 1 - 8-ounce package cream cheese, softened
- 1 tablespoon cocoa powder
- 1 tablespoon & 1 teaspoon red food coloring
- ¼ cup raspberries

**Directions:**
1. NOTE: Freeze your ice cream bowl for at least 24hrs prior to starting!
2. Place the milk and cream in a bowl, and mix them together until well combined. Use a whisk to mix in the sugar. Continue to whisk for about 4 minutes until the sugar dissolves. Put all the ingredients in a blender and pulse for around 30 seconds until well mixed.
3. Pour the ingredients into your ice cream maker, and let it churn for 10-15 minutes, until desired consistency is reached.
4. Serve immediately.

## 162. Red Velvet Milkshake

Servings: 6
Cooking Time: 25 Minutes
**Ingredients:**
- 2 cups heavy cream
- 1 cup milk
- 3/4 cup sugar
- 1 teaspoons vanilla extract
- 1 8 ounce package cream cheese, softened
- 1 tablespoon cocoa powder
- 1 tablespoon plus 1 teaspoon red food coloring

**Directions:**
1. Refer to note at the beginning of the chapter about freezing bowl.
2. Place the milk and cream in a bowl, and mix them together until well combined. Use a whisk to mix in the sugar. Continue to whisk for about 4 minutes until the sugar dissolves. Put all the ingredients in a blender and pulse for around 30 seconds until well mixed.
3. Pour the ingredients into your ice cream maker, and let it churn for 10-15 minutes, until desired consistency is reached.
4. Serve immediately.

## 163. Caramel Corn Soft Serve Ice Cream

Servings: 6
Cooking Time: 35 Minutes
**Ingredients:**
- 2 cups heavy cream
- 1 cup milk
- 3/4 cup sugar

- 1 Tbs. vanilla extract
- 2 cup caramel corn

**Directions:**
1. Refer to note at the beginning of the chapter about freezing bowl.
2. Place the milk and cream in a bowl, and mix them together until well combined. Use a whisk to mix in the sugar. Continue to whisk for about 4 minutes until the sugar dissolves. Mix in the vanilla extract. Place the mixture in a blender or food processor with 1 cup of the caramel corn, and puree.
3. Put the remaining caramel corn in a resealable plastic bag, and seal it. Crush the caramel corn using your hands, or a mallet.
4. Pour the ingredients into your ice cream maker, and let it churn for 25 minutes. About 5 minutes before the churning is finished add in the crushed caramel corn.
5. Serve immediately.

### 164. Dark Chocolate Cheery Custard Ice Cream

Servings: 12
Cooking Time: 30 Minutes
**Ingredients:**
- 1 cup whole milk
- 2 cups heavy cream
- 1 cup granulated sugar
- A pinch of salt
- 6 egg yolks
- 2 teaspoons vanilla extract
- ½ cup cherries, pitted and chopped
- ½ cup dark chocolate chips, shaved

**Directions:**
1. Add the milk, cream, sugar, and salt in a saucepan and heat over medium low flame. Simmer for 3 minutes. Remove from the stove.
2. In a bowl, whisk in the egg yolks. Drizzle ½ cup of the warm milk into the egg yolks while whisking constantly to form a smooth mixture. Whisk the egg mixture back into the pot. Add the vanilla extract.
3. Turn on the heat to medium low and cook until the mixture starts to thicken. Constantly stir while cooking.
4. Turn off the heat and strain the mixture to remove lumps. Allow to cool at room temperature. Place in the fridge to chill for 2 hours.
5. Turn on the Cuisinart and pour the mixture in. Churn for 15 minutes.
6. Before the churning time ends, add the cherries and chocolate shavings.
7. Transfer to an airtight container.
8. Place in the fridge to completely cool.

**Nutrition Info:** Calories per serving:196 ; Protein: 2.8g; Carbs: 18.1g; Fat: 12.6g Sugar: 14.8g

### 165. Custard Chocolate Ice Cream

Servings: 10
Cooking Time: 30 Minutes
**Ingredients:**
- 1/3 cup unsweetened cocoa powder
- 2 cups heavy whipping cream
- 1 cup whole milk
- ¾ cup sugar
- 6 large egg yolks
- A pinch of salt
- 1 ½ teaspoons vanilla extract

**Directions:**
1. Add the coca powder, cream, milk and sugar in a saucepan and heat over medium low flame. Simmer for 3 minutes or until the sugar dissolves. Remove from the heat.
2. In a bowl, whisk in the egg yolks. Drizzle ½ cup of the warm milk into the egg yolks while whisking constantly to form a smooth mixture. Whisk the egg mixture back into the pot. Add the salt and vanilla.
3. Turn on the heat to medium low and cook until the mixture starts to thicken. Constantly stir while cooking.
4. Turn off the heat and strain the mixture to remove lumps. Allow the milk to cool at room temperature. Place in the fridge to chill for 2 hours.
5. Turn on the Cuisinart and pour the mixture in. Churn for 15 minutes.
6. Transfer to an airtight container.
7. Place in the fridge to completely cool.

**Nutrition Info:** Calories per serving: 175; Protein: 3.5g; Carbs: 13.4g; Fat: 12.7g Sugar: 11.3g

### 166. Key Lime Ice Cream

Servings: 12
Cooking Time: 25 Minutes
**Ingredients:**
- 1 ½ cups ice cold whole milk, divided
- 2/3 cup sugar
- 1 ¼ cups ice cold heavy whipping cream
- ½ cup key lime juice, freshly squeezed
- 2 tablespoons light corn syrup
- ¼ tablespoon salt

**Directions:**
1. Put ice water in a large mixing bowl. Place a small bowl on top of the large bowl with ice.
2. Pour in the milk and sugar until well-combined. Add the cream and whip until well combined.
3. Stir in the rest of the ingredients while whipping constantly.
4. Turn on the Cuisinart and pour the mixture in. Freeze for 25 minutes.
5. Transfer into air-tight containers and freeze overnight.

**Nutrition Info:** Calories per serving: 96; Protein: 1.4g; Carbs: 11g; Fat: 5.6g Sugar: 10.2g

### 167. Green Apple Musketeer Gelato

Servings: 4-6
Cooking Time: 2 Hours 35 Minutes
**Ingredients:**
- 1/2 cup heavy cream
- 2 cups milk
- 3/4 cup sugar
- 1 tablespoon vanilla extract
- 1 ½ cups chopped mini Musketeers bars
- ¼ cup green apples

**Directions:**
1. NOTE: Freeze your ice cream bowl for at least 24hrs prior to starting!
2. Place the milk and cream in a bowl, and mix them together until well combined. Use a whisk to mix in the sugar. Continue to whisk for about 4 minutes until the sugar dissolves. Then mix in the vanilla extract.
3. Pour the ingredients into your ice cream maker, and let it churn for 25 minutes. About 5 minutes before the ice cream is done churning add the three musketeers and green apples to your ice cream maker.
4. Put the gelato in an airtight container and place in the freezer for up to 2 hours, until desired consistency is reached.

### 168. Radical Root Beer Gelato

Servings: 4-6
Cooking Time: 2 Hours 50 Minutes
**Ingredients:**
- 1/2 cup heavy cream
- 2 cups milk
- 3/4 cup sugar
- 1 teaspoon vanilla extract
- 3 cups (2, 12 ounce cans) root beer

**Directions:**
1. Refer to note at the beginning of the chapter about freezing bowl.
2. Pour the root beer into a large skillet, and heat it on high heat until it comes to a boil. Allow the coke to cook for about another 15 or 20 minutes, until the root beer reduces down to 1 cup of liquid. Let the liquid cool.
3. Place the milk and cream in a bowl, and mix them together until well combined. Use a whisk to mix in the sugar. Continue to whisk for about 4 minutes until the sugar dissolves. Then mix in the vanilla extract and root beer reduction.
4. Pour the ingredients into your ice cream maker, and let it churn for 25 minutes. About 5 minutes before the ice cream is done churning add the chocolate to your ice cream maker.
5. Put the gelato in an airtight container and place in the freezer for up to 2 hours, until desired consistency is reached.

### 169. Dr. Pepper Cherry Lime Ice Cream

Servings: 6
Cooking Time: 2 Hours 50 Minutes
**Ingredients:**

- 2 cups heavy cream
- 1 cup milk
- 3/4 cup sugar
- 1 tablespoon vanilla extract
- 3 cups (2, 12 ounce cans) Dr. Pepper
- ½ cup mashed up cherries
- 1 tablespoon lime juice

**Directions:**
1. NOTE: Freeze your ice cream bowl for at least 24hrs prior to starting!
2. Pour the dr. pepper into a large skillet, and heat it on high heat until it comes to a boil. Allow the coke to cook for about another 15 or 20 minutes, until the root beer reduces down to 1 cup of liquid. Let the liquid cool.
3. Place the milk and cream in a bowl, and mix them together until well combined. Use a whisk to mix in the sugar. Continue to whisk for about 4 minutes until the sugar dissolves. Then mix in the vanilla extract, lime juice Dr. pepper reduction and cherries.
4. Pour the ingredients into your ice cream maker, and let it churn for 25 minutes. \
5. Put the ice cream in an airtight container and place in the freezer for around 2 hours. Allow the ice cream to thaw for 15 minutes before serving.

### 170. Kiddo's Coca Cola Soft Serve Ice Cream

Servings: 6
Cooking Time: 55 Minutes
**Ingredients:**
- 2 cups heavy cream
- 1 cup milk
- 3/4 cup sugar
- 1 Tbs. vanilla extract
- 3 cups coca cola (2, 12 ounce cans)

**Directions:**
1. Refer to note at the beginning of the chapter about freezing bowl.
2. Pour the coke into a large skillet, and heat it on high heat until it comes to a boil. Allow the coke to cook for about another 15 or 20 minutes, until the coke reduces down to 1 cup of liquid. Let the liquid cool.
3. Place the milk and cream in a bowl, and mix them together until well combined. Use a whisk to mix in the sugar. Continue to whisk for about 4 minutes until the sugar dissolves. Mix in the vanilla extract, and then the reduced coca cola.
4. Pour the ingredients into your ice cream maker, and let it churn for 25 minutes.
5. Serve immediately.

### 171. Bubble Gum Cola Soft Serve Ice Cream

Servings: 6
Cooking Time: 35 Minutes
**Ingredients:**
- 2 cups heavy cream
- 1 cup milk
- 3/4 cup sugar
- 1 Tbs. vanilla extract
- 1 gram bubble gum flavoring
- ½ cup mini gum balls
- ½ cup coca cola

**Directions:**
1. NOTE: Freeze your ice cream bowl for at least 24hrs prior to starting!
2. Place the milk and cream in a bowl, and mix them together until well combined. Use a whisk to mix in the sugar. Continue to whisk for about 4 minutes until the sugar dissolves. Mix in the vanilla extract, coca cola and then the bubble gum flavoring.
3. Pour the ingredients into your ice cream maker, and let it churn for 25 minutes. About 5 minutes before the churning is done add the gum balls to your ice cream maker.
4. Serve immediately.

### 172. Chocolate Cookie Rice Crispy Treat Frozen Yogurt

Servings: 1 Quart
Cooking Time: 2 Hours 35 Minutes
**Ingredients:**
- 1 quart container full-fat plain yogurt
- ¼ teaspoon salt
- 1 cup sugar
- 1 teaspoon vanilla extract
- 10 chocolate sandwich cookies
- 1/2 cup rice crispy treats

- ¼ cup milk chocolate (chopped fine)

**Directions:**
1. NOTE: Freeze your ice cream bowl for at least 24hrs prior to starting!
2. Place the yogurt in a bowl. Use a whisk to mix in the sugar and salt. Continue to whisk for about 4 minutes until the sugar dissolves. Then mix in the vanilla extract.
3. Place the sandwich cookies in a food processor, and process until the cookies are no bigger than chocolate chips. If you don't have a food processor place the cookies in a large resealable plastic bag, and seal it shut. Use your hands, a mallet, or a rolling pin to crush the cookies.
4. Pour the ingredients into your ice cream maker, and let it churn for 25 minutes. About 5 minutes before the ice cream is done churning add the cookies, and small chunks of the rice crispy treats to your ice cream maker.
5. Put the frozen yogurt in an airtight container and place in the freezer for at least 2 hours, until desired consistency is reached.

## 173. Honey Ice Cream

Servings: 12
Cooking Time: 30 Minutes
**Ingredients:**
- 1 ½ cups heavy cream
- 1 ½ cups whole milk
- ½ cup honey
- ½ teaspoon salt
- 4 large egg yolks
- 1 ½ teaspoon vanilla extract

**Directions:**
1. Add the cream, milk, honey, and salt in a saucepan and heat over medium low flame. Simmer for 3 minutes or until the sugar dissolves.
2. In a bowl, whisk in the egg yolks. Drizzle ½ cup of the warm milk into the egg yolks while whisking constantly to form a smooth mixture. Whisk the egg mixture back into the pot.
3. Turn on the heat to medium low and cook until the mixture starts to thicken. Constantly stir while cooking.
4. Turn off the heat and strain the mixture to remove lumps. Allow the milk to cool at room temperature. Place in the fridge to chill for 2 hours.
5. Turn on the Cuisinart and pour the mixture in. Churn for 15 minutes.
6. Transfer to an airtight container.
7. Place in the fridge to completely cool.

**Nutrition Info:** Calories per serving:142 ; Protein: 2.2g; Carbs: 16.3g; Fat: 8g Sugar: 16g

## 174. Graham Cracker Peanut Butter Cup Milkshake

Servings: 6
Cooking Time: 25 Minutes
**Ingredients:**
- 2 cups heavy cream
- 1 cup milk
- 3/4 cup sugar
- 1 tablespoon vanilla extract
- 1 1/2 cups chopped mini peanut butter cups
- ½ cup maple syrup
- 4 graham crackers

**Directions:**
1. NOTE: Freeze your ice cream bowl for at least 24hrs prior to starting!
2. Place the milk and cream in a bowl, and mix them together until well combined. Use a whisk to mix in the sugar. Continue to whisk for about 4 minutes until the sugar dissolves. Then mix in the vanilla extract.
3. Pour the ingredients into your ice cream maker, and let it churn for 10-15 minutes, until desired consistency is reached. About 5 minutes before the ice cream is done churning add the peanut butter cup and the graham crackers to your ice cream maker.
4. Serve immediately.

## 175. Cherry Blueberry Lime Soda Frozen Yogurt

Servings: 1 Quart
Cooking Time: 2 Hours 50 Minutes
**Ingredients:**
- 1 quart container full-fat plain yogurt

- ¼ teaspoon salt
- 1 cup sugar
- ½ lime (peeled and cut up fine)
- 1/2 cup blueberries
- 1 teaspoon vanilla extract
- 3 cups (2, 12 ounce cans) cherry soda

**Directions:**
1. NOTE: Freeze your ice cream bowl for at least 24hrs prior to starting!
2. Pour the cherry soda into a large skillet, and heat it on high heat until it comes to a boil. Allow the coke to cook for about another 15 or 20 minutes, until the root beer reduces down to 1 cup of liquid. Let the liquid cool.
3. Place the yogurt in a bowl. Use a whisk to mix in the sugar and salt. Continue to whisk for about 4 minutes until the sugar dissolves. Then mix in the vanilla extract, blueberries, lime and reduced cherry soda.
4. Pour the ingredients into your ice cream maker, and let it churn for 25 minutes.
5. Put the frozen yogurt in an airtight container and place in the freezer for at least 2 hours, until desired consistency is reached.

## 176. Tropical Coconut Banana Animal Cracker Sorbet

Servings: 4-8
Cooking Time: 2 Hours 40 Minutes
**Ingredients:**
- 3 peeled, mashed bananas
- 2-4 tablespoons honey to taste
- 1 1/2 cups light coconut milk
- 1 teaspoon vanilla extract
- 10 animal crackers

**Directions:**
1. NOTE: Freeze your ice cream bowl for at least 24hrs prior to starting!
2. Puree all ingredients in a food processor or blender. Taste, and add more honey if desired.
3. Pour the ingredients into your ice cream maker, and let it churn for 25-30 minutes. Mix in the animal crackers about 5 minutes before sorbet is complete.
4. Place in an airtight container for up to 2 hours, until desired consistency is reached.

## 177. Sour Patch Chocolate Ice Cream

Servings: 6
Cooking Time: 2 Hours 50 Minutes
**Ingredients:**
- 2 cups heavy cream
- 1 cup milk
- 3/4 cup sugar
- 1 tablespoon vanilla extract
- 1 cups chopped sour patch
- ½ cup chocolate (chopped fine)

**Directions:**
1. NOTE: Freeze your ice cream bowl for at least 24hrs prior to starting!
2. Place the milk and cream in a bowl, and mix them together until well combined. Use a whisk to mix in the sugar. Continue to whisk for about 4 minutes until the sugar dissolves. Then mix in the vanilla extract.
3. Pour the ingredients into your ice cream maker, and let it churn for 25 minutes. About 5 minutes before the ice cream is done churning add the sour patch and chocolate to your ice cream maker.
4. Put the ice cream in an airtight container and place in the freezer for around 2 hours. Allow the ice cream to thaw for 15 minutes before serving.

## 178. Chicago Style Cookies-n-cream Soft Serve Ice Cream

Servings: 6
Cooking Time: 35 Minutes
**Ingredients:**
- 2 cups heavy cream
- 1 cup milk
- 3/4 cup sugar
- 1 Tbs. vanilla extract
- 20 chocolate sandwich cookies

**Directions:**
1. NOTE: Freeze your ice cream bowl for at least 24hrs prior to starting!
2. Place the milk and cream in a bowl, and mix them together until well

combined. Use a whisk to mix in the sugar. Continue to whisk for about 4 minutes until the sugar dissolves. Then mix in the vanilla extract.
3. Place the sandwich cookies in a food processor, and process until the cookies are no bigger than chocolate chips. If you don't have a food processor place the cookies in a large resealable plastic bag, and seal it shut. Use your hands, a mallet, or a rolling pin to crush the cookies.
4. Pour the ingredients into your ice cream maker, and let it churn for 25 minutes. About 5 minutes before the ice cream is finished churning, add in the chocolate sandwich cookies.
5. Serve immediately.

### 179. Eggless Pistachio Ice Cream

Servings: 10
Cooking Time: 45 Minutes
**Ingredients:**
- 1 cup ice cold whole milk
- 1 cup sugar
- 2 cups ice cold heavy cream
- ½ teaspoon vanilla extract
- 1 cup pistachio nuts, chopped

**Directions:**
1. Put ice water in a large mixing bowl. Place a small bowl on top of the large bowl with ice.
2. Place the milk and sugar in the bowl and whisk to dissolve the sugar. Add the cream and vanilla extract.
3. Turn on the Cuisinart and pour the mixture in. Freeze for 45 minutes. Five minutes before the time, add the pistachio nuts.
4. Transfer into air-tight containers. Freeze overnight.

**Nutrition Info:** Calories per serving: 235 ; Protein: 5.8g; Carbs: 15.8g; Fat: 17.7g Sugar: 11.5 g

### 180. Malted Milk Chocolate Ice Cream

Servings: 8
Cooking Time: 25 Minutes
**Ingredients:**
- 1 ¾ cups heavy cream
- 1 cup whole milk
- 2/3 cup malted milk powder
- ½ cup sugar
- A pinch of salt
- 6 egg yolks
- 6 ounces milk chocolate, chopped
- ½ cup mini Cadbury eggs, chopped

**Directions:**
1. Add the cream, milk, sugar, and salt in a saucepan and heat over medium low flame. Simmer for 3 minutes. Remove from the stove.
2. In a bowl, whisk in the egg yolks. Drizzle ½ cup of the warm milk into the egg yolks while whisking constantly to form a smooth mixture. Whisk the egg mixture back into the pot.
3. Turn on the heat to medium low and cook until the mixture starts to thicken. Constantly stir while cooking.
4. Turn off the heat and strain the mixture to remove lumps. Allow to cool at room temperature. Place in the fridge to chill for 2 hours.
5. Turn on the Cuisinart and pour the mixture in. Churn for 15 minutes.
6. Before the churning time ends, add the chopped milk chocolate and Cadbury eggs.
7. Transfer to an airtight container.
8. Place in the fridge to completely cool.

**Nutrition Info:** Calories per serving: 210; Protein: 5g; Carbs: 22g; Fat: 12g Sugar: 17g

### 181. Orange Creamsicle Ice Cream

Servings: 10
Cooking Time: 45 Minutes
**Ingredients:**
- ¼ cup water
- Zest from 1 orange
- ½ cup orange juice
- 1 tablespoon arrowroot powder
- 1 cup ice cold whole milk
- ¾ cup granulated sugar
- 2 cups heavy cream
- A pinch of salt

**Directions:**
1. Place half of the ¼ cup water orange zest, orange juice, and arrowroot powder in a saucepan. Stir to combine everything. Bring to a boil

until the mixture thickens. Set aside to cool.
2. Put ice water in a large mixing bowl. Place a small bowl on top of the large bowl with ice.
3. Add the milk and sugar. Whisk until well combined. Stir in the cooled orange mixture and whisk until well incorporated and the lumps are dissolved. Add the rest of the ingredients.
4. Turn on the Cuisinart and pour the mixture in. Freeze for 45 minutes.
5. Transfer into air-tight containers.
6. Freeze overnight.

**Nutrition Info:** Calories per serving:164 ; Protein: 3.4g; Carbs: 11.1g; Fat: 12.1g Sugar: 9.1g

## 182. Peppermint Hibiscus Tea Ice Cream

Servings: 6
Cooking Time: 2 Hours 50 Minutes
**Ingredients:**
- 2 cups heavy cream
- 1 cup milk
- 3/4 cup sugar
- 1 teaspoon vanilla extract
- 2 tablespoons peppermint tea
- 2 tablespoons hibiscus tea

**Directions:**
1. NOTE: Freeze your ice cream bowl for at least 24hrs prior to starting!
2. Put the milk in a pan and bring it to a simmer. Add in the tea, take the pot off the heat, and allow to seep for 5 minutes. Discard the tea, and allow milk to cool.
3. Place the milk and cream in a bowl, and mix them together until well combined. Use a whisk to mix in the sugar. Continue to whisk for about 4 minutes until the sugar dissolves. Then mix in the vanilla extract.
4. Pour the ingredients into your ice cream maker, and let it churn for 25 minutes.
5. Put the ice cream in an airtight container and place in the freezer for around 2 hours. Allow the ice cream to thaw for 15 minutes before serving.

## 183. Custard Cream Gelato

Servings: 20
Cooking Time: 30 Minutes
**Ingredients:**
- 6 cups whole milk
- 1 1/3 cups sugar
- 12 egg yolks
- 1 medium lemon juice

**Directions:**
1. Add the milk and sugar in a saucepan and heat over medium low flame. Simmer for 3 minutes or until the sugar dissolves. Remove from the stove.
2. In a bowl, whisk in the egg yolks. Drizzle ½ cup of the warm milk into the egg yolks while whisking constantly to form a smooth mixture. Whisk the egg mixture back into the pot. Add the lemon juice while stirring constantly.
3. Turn on the heat to medium low and cook until the mixture starts to thicken. Constantly stir while cooking.
4. Turn off the heat and strain the mixture to remove lumps. Allow the milk to cool at room temperature. Place in the fridge to chill for 2 hours.
5. Turn on the Cuisinart and pour the mixture in. Churn for 15 minutes.
6. Transfer to an airtight container.
7. Place in the fridge to completely cool.

**Nutrition Info:** Calories per serving:125 ; Protein: 3.8g; Carbs: 16.6g; Fat: 4.9g Sugar: 16g

## 184. Pralines And Cream Custard Ice Cream

Servings: 8
Cooking Time: 30 Minutes
**Ingredients:**
- 2 cups heavy cream
- 1 ½ cups half and half
- ¾ cup sugar
- 1 teaspoon vanilla extract
- ¼ teaspoon salt
- 4 egg yolks
- 1 cup caramel sauce
- 1 cup praline pecans

**Directions:**

1. Add the cream, milk, sugar, vanilla extract, and salt in a saucepan and heat over medium low flame. Simmer for 3 minutes or until the sugar dissolves. Remove from the stove.
2. In a bowl, whisk in the egg yolks. Drizzle ½ cup of the warm milk into the egg yolks while whisking constantly to form a smooth mixture. Whisk the egg mixture back into the pot.
3. Turn on the heat to medium low and cook until the mixture starts to thicken. Constantly stir while cooking.
4. Turn off the heat and strain the mixture to remove lumps. Allow to cool at room temperature. Place in the fridge to chill for 2 hours.
5. Turn on the Cuisinart and pour the mixture in. Churn for 15 minutes.
6. Five minutes before the time ends, add the caramel sauce and pecans.
7. Transfer to an airtight container.
8. Place in the fridge to completely cool.

**Nutrition Info:** Calories per serving: 474; Protein: 4g; Carbs: 46g; Fat: 32g Sugar: 24g

### 185. Honey Matcha Tea Extreme Ice Cream

Servings: 6
Cooking Time: 2 Hours 50 Minutes
**Ingredients:**
- 2 cups heavy cream
- 1 cup milk
- 3/4 cup sugar
- 1 teaspoon vanilla extract
- 1 tablespoon Matcha
- 3 tablespoons organic honey

**Directions:**
1. NOTE: Freeze your ice cream bowl for at least 24hrs prior to starting!
2. Place the milk and cream in a bowl, and mix them together until well combined. Use a whisk to mix in the sugar. Continue to whisk for about 4 minutes until the sugar dissolves. Then mix in the vanilla extract. Finally whisk in the Matcha until well mixed.
3. Pour the ingredients into your ice cream maker, and let it churn for 25 minutes.
4. Put the ice cream in an airtight container and place in the freezer for around 2 hours. Allow the ice cream to thaw for 15 minutes before serving.

### 186. "crispy" Caramel Graham Cracker Ice Cream

Servings: 6
Cooking Time: 2 Hours 50 Minutes
**Ingredients:**
- 2 cups heavy cream
- 1 cup milk
- 3/4 cup sugar
- 1 tablespoon vanilla extract
- 1 ½ cups chopped mini Kit Kats
- 2 oz. caramel

**Directions:**
1. NOTE: Freeze your ice cream bowl for at least 24hrs prior to starting!
2. Place the milk and cream in a bowl, and mix them together until well combined. Use a whisk to mix in the sugar. Continue to whisk for about 4 minutes until the sugar dissolves. Then mix in the vanilla extract.
3. Warm up the caramel to add to the ice cream maker towards the end of the process.
4. Pour the ingredients into your ice cream maker, and let it churn for 25 minutes. About 5 minutes before the ice cream is done churning add the graham crackers and caramel to the machine.
5. Put the ice cream in an airtight container and place in the freezer for around 2 hours. Allow the ice cream to thaw for 15 minutes before serving.

### 187. Fresh Strawberry Ice Cream

Servings: 10
Cooking Time: 25 Minutes
**Ingredients:**
- 1-pint strawberries, hulled and sliced
- 3 tablespoons lemon juice
- 1 cup white sugar, divided
- 1 cup ice cold whole milk
- 2 cups ice cold heavy cream

- 1 teaspoon vanilla extract

**Directions:**
1. Place half of the strawberries, lemon juice, and half of the sugar in a bowl. Macerate then strain to reserve the juice.
2. Chop the remaining strawberries. Set aside.
3. Put ice water in a large mixing bowl. Place a small bowl on top of the large bowl with ice.
4. Whisk together the whole milk, half of the sugar, heavy cream, and vanilla extract. Add the strawberry juice.
5. Turn on the Cuisinart and pour the mixture in. Freeze for 25 minutes. Five minutes before turning off the machine, add the chopped strawberries.
6. Transfer into air-tight containers and freeze overnight.

**Nutrition Info:** Calories per serving: 178; Protein: 3.5g; Carbs: 14.5g; Fat: 12.2g Sugar: 12.4g

## 188. Screamin' Sour Patch Kids Ice Cream

Servings: 6
Cooking Time: 2 Hours 50 Minutes
**Ingredients:**
- 2 cups heavy cream
- 1 cup milk
- 3/4 cup sugar
- 1 tablespoon vanilla extract
- 1 cups chopped sour patch kids

**Directions:**
1. Refer to note at the beginning of the chapter about freezing bowl.
2. Place the milk and cream in a bowl, and mix them together until well combined. Use a whisk to mix in the sugar. Continue to whisk for about 4 minutes until the sugar dissolves. Then mix in the vanilla extract.
3. Pour the ingredients into your ice cream maker, and let it churn for 25 minutes. About 5 minutes before the ice cream is done churning add the sour patch kids to your ice cream maker.
4. Put the ice cream in an airtight container and place in the freezer for around 2 hours. Allow the ice cream to thaw for 15 minutes before serving.

## 189. Orange Almond Apricot Ice Cream

Servings: 6
Cooking Time: 2 Hours 50 Minutes
**Ingredients:**
- 2 cups heavy cream
- 1 cup milk
- 3/4 cup sugar
- 1 teaspoon vanilla extract
- 1 cup sliced apricots
- ½ cup chopped almonds
- orange extract (just a few drops will do)

**Directions:**
1. ⟩NOTE: Freeze your ice cream bowl for at least 24hrs prior to starting!
2. Puree the apricots in a food processor or blender.
3. Place the milk and cream in a bowl, and mix them together until well combined. Use a whisk to mix in the sugar. Continue to whisk for about 4 minutes until the sugar dissolves. Then mix in the vanilla extract, and apricot puree.
4. Pour the ingredients into your ice cream maker, and let it churn for 25 minutes. About 5 minutes before the ice cream is finished churning, add in the almonds and orange extract.
5. Put the ice cream in an airtight container and place in the freezer for around 2 hours. Allow the ice cream to thaw for 15 minutes before serving.

## 190. S'mores Camp Fire Frozen Yogurt

Servings: 1 Quart
Cooking Time: 2 Hours 35 Minutes
**Ingredients:**
- 1 quart container full-fat plain yogurt
- ¼ teaspoon salt
- 1 cup sugar
- 1 teaspoon vanilla extract
- 3 large graham crackers
- 4 ounces chopped semi-sweet chocolate
- ½ cup mini marshmallows
- 1 tsp smoke flavor extract

**Directions:**

1. NOTE: Freeze your ice cream bowl for at least 24hrs prior to starting!
2. Place the yogurt in a bowl. Use a whisk to mix in the sugar and salt. Continue to whisk for about 4 minutes until the sugar dissolves. Then mix in the vanilla and smoke flavored extract.
3. Place the graham crackers in a food processor, and process until the crackers are no bigger than chocolate chips. If you don't have a food processor place the crackers in a large resealable plastic bag, and seal it shut. Use your hands, a mallet, or a rolling pin to crush the cookies.
4. Pour the ingredients into your ice cream maker, and let it churn for 25 minutes. About 5 minutes before the ice cream is done churning add the chocolate, graham crackers, and marshmallows to your ice cream maker.
5. Put the frozen yogurt in an airtight container and place in the freezer for at least 2 hours, until desired consistency is reached.

# VANILLA ICE CREAM

### 191. Six Threes Ice Cream Recipe

**Ingredients:**
- 3 cups sugar
- 3 cups cream
- 3 cups milk
- 3 medium (7" to 7-7/8" long)s bananas, mashed
- 3 fruit, (2-5/8" dia, sphere)s oranges, juiced
- 3 fruit, without seeds lemons, juiced

**Directions:**
1. In a huge bowl, whisk together sugar and cream until sugar is dissolved. Mix in the milk, mashed bananas, and fruit drinks.
2. Pour mixture into ice cream maker. Freeze according to manufacturer's directions, about 45 minutes.

### 192. Caramel-apple Ice Cream

**Ingredients:**
- 2 tablespoons unsalted butter
- 2 granny smith apples—peeled, quartered and very thinly sliced
- 1 tablespoon sugar
- 1/8 teaspoon cinnamon
- 1/4 cup dulce de leche
- 2 pints vanilla ice cream
- chocolate shavings, for garnish
- crumbled gingersnaps, for garnish

**Directions:**
1. Melt the butter in a medium skillet. Add the apples and cook over moderate heat, stirring, until softened and browned, about five minutes. Add the sugar, cinnamon and 1/4 cup of water and cook for 2 minutes longer. Stir in the dulce de leche until melted. Scrape the mixture into a bowl and refrigerate until chilled.
2. Fold the apple mixture into softened vanilla ice cream and freeze until firm, about 4 hours. Scoop into bowls and garnish with chocolate shavings and crumbled gingersnaps.

### 193. Coconut Ice Cream

**Ingredients:**
- 1 cup milk
- 1 (14-ounce) can cream of coconut
- 1 1/2 cups heavy cream
- 1 1/2 cups sweetened flaked coconut

**Directions:**
1. Combine the milk and cream of coconut in the container of a food processor or blender, and mix thoroughly. Stir in cream and flaked coconut.
2. Pour in to the container of an ice cream maker, and freeze based on the manufacturer's instructions.

### 194. Root Beer Float Ice Cream Recipe

**Ingredients:**
- 2 large eggs
- 3/4 cup white sugar
- 2 cups heavy cream
- 1 cup whole milk
- 1 teaspoon vanilla extract
- 3/4 teaspoon root beer extract

**Directions:**
1. Whip eggs until foamy, then slowly pour in sugar while continuing to whip eggs until ribbony. Fold in cream, milk, vanilla extract, root beer extract until evenly mixed.
2. Freeze in ice cream maker according to manufacturer's directions, about 30 minutes.

### 195. Vanilla Ice Cream Vi Recipe

**Ingredients:**
- 4 large eggs
- 2 1/2 cups white sugar
- 1/2 teaspoon salt
- 6 cups milk
- 3 cups evaporated milk
- 2 tablespoons vanilla extract
- 1 cup water

**Directions:**
1. Beat eggs until foamy. Whisk in sugar until thickened. Gradually whisk in salt, 6 cups milk, evaporated milk, vanilla and water.
2. Pour into freezer canister of ice cream maker.
3. Fill to fill line with remaining milk if necessary.

4. Freeze according to manufacturers' directions.

### 196. Ice Cream In A Can Recipe
**Ingredients:**
- 1 pasteurized egg
- 1/2 cup white sugar
- 1 tablespoon instant vanilla pudding mixes
- 1 cup milk
- 1 cup half-and-half cream
- 1 teaspoon vanilla extract
- 1 cup rock salt
- 1 pound crushed ice

**Directions:**
1. In a medium bowl, whisk together the egg, sugar, instant pudding, milk, half and half and vanilla. Pour the mixture into a 12 ounce size coffee can. Cover the top with plastic wrap, and then the plastic lid. Place the filled coffee can into an empty 34.5 ounce coffee can (the big ones). Fill the empty space with crushed ice, sprinkle generously with rock salt, and cover with the plastic lid.
2. Roll the cans around on the floor for about 20 minutes. If the center of the ice cream is still soft, place the containers in the freezer to harden.

### 197. Peppermint Bark No-churn Ice Cream
**Ingredients:**
- 3 cups heavy cream
- 1 can sweetened condensed milk, 14 oz.
- 1 teaspoon pure vanilla extract
- 4 miniature candy canes, crushed
- 2/3 cup peppermint bark, crumbled
- 1/2 cup miniature semisweet chocolate chips

**Directions:**
1. Beat heavy cream using an electric mixer until stiff peaks form, about 3 minutes. Stir in sweetened condensed milk and vanilla until thoroughly combined.
2. Mix in candy cane pieces, mixing just enough so they start to leave pink streaks in the ice cream. Fold in peppermint bark and chocolate chips, setting aside a few to sprinkle along with the ice cream.
3. Pour the ice cream batter right into a loaf pan, add remaining chips and bark, and place in the freezer until firm, about 6 hours.

### 198. Vanilla Ice Cream I Recipe
**Ingredients:**
- 1 cup white sugar
- 1 cup milk
- 2 large eggs
- 2 cups heavy cream
- 1 1/2 teaspoons vanilla extract
- 1 tablespoon fresh lemon juice

**Directions:**
1. Combine the cream, milk, and sugar in a bowl. Stir before sugar is totally dissolved. Stir in the vanilla and almond extract.
2. Add the cherries. Pour the mixture into an ice cream maker and churn based on the manufacturer's instructions. Transfer to a freezer-safe container and freeze for at least 2 hours before serving

### 199. Fruited Ice Cream Recipe
**Ingredients:**
- 2 (14-ounce) cans sweetened condensed milk
- 5 cups milk
- 2 cups heavy cream
- 2 tablespoons vanilla extract
- 1/2 teaspoon salt
- 3 cups chopped strawberries

**Directions:**
1. Combine condensed milk, milk, cream, vanilla, salt and fruit in freezer canister of ice cream maker.
2. Freeze according to manufacturer's directions.

### 200. Tropical Avocado Ice Cream
**Ingredients:**
- 4 avocados, peeled and pitted
- 1 cup lime juice (about 4 juicy limes)
- zest of 2 lime
- 1 cup maple syrup
- 2 cans coconut cream
- 2 teaspoons vanilla extract

- 2 tablespoons coconut oils
- 1/2 teaspoon kosher salt
- 1/2 lime, thinly sliced into quarters, for garnish

**Directions:**
1. Combine all ingredients, except lime slices, in a blender. Blend on high until smooth.
2. Pour into loaf pan and garnish with lime slices. Freeze until firm, at least 3 hours or overnight.

## 201. Healthy Chunky Monkey Ice Cream Recipe

**Ingredients:**
- 2 eaches bananas, chopped
- 1 tablespoon 1% milk
- 1 tablespoon chunky peanut butter
- 1/2 ounce dark chocolate (such as ghiradelli®), chopped

**Directions:**
1. Place chopped bananas in freezer until frozen, 8 hours to overnight.
2. Blend frozen bananas, milk, peanut butter, and chocolate in a blender until smooth.

## 202. Ice Cream Recipe

**Ingredients:**
- 4 cups half-and-half
- 4 cups milk
- 1 (14-ounce) can sweetened condensed milk
- 4 medium (blank)s eggs
- 1 3/4 cups white sugar
- 1 teaspoon vanilla extract

**Directions:**
1. Beat half-an-half, milk, sweetened condensed milk, and eggs together in a bowl on low mixer speed; slowly add sugar while constantly beating, followed by vanilla extract.
2. Pour milk mixture into ice cream maker's container and freeze according to manufacturer's directions.

## 203. Easy Cherry-chocolate Chunk Ice Cream Recipe

**Ingredients:**
- 1 (12-ounce) package frozen sweet cherries
- 1 3/4 cups heavy cream
- 1 (14-ounce) can sweetened condensed milk
- 3/4 cup milk
- 1 teaspoon vanilla extract
- 1 (4-ounce) bar semisweet baking chocolate, broken into small chunks

**Directions:**
1. Place cherries in a food processor; process into small pieces.
2. Mix heavy cream, sweetened condensed milk, milk, and vanilla extract together until well combined. Pour into an ice cream maker and start. Add the chopped cherries while the machine is running; freeze until desired consistency is reached, about 20 minutes. Stir in chocolate chunks.

## 204. Italian Crema Ice Cream (gelato Alla Crema)

**Ingredients:**
- 2 cups whole milk
- 2/3 cup white sugar
- 1 tablespoon white sugar
- 5 large eggs yolks egg yolks
- 1 cup heavy cream
- 1 teaspoonkosher salt

**Directions:**
1. Pour milk right into a saucepan. Add 2/3 cup plus 1 tablespoon sugar and egg yolks. Whisk thoroughly. Cook over medium heat, stirring gently with a spatula, until custard is steaming-hot and thick enough to coat the back of a spoon, about 10 minutes. Stir in heavy cream and salt and remove from heat.
2. Pour custard through an excellent mesh strainer and refrigerate until completely chilled, 8 hours to overnight.
3. Pour mixture into an ice cream maker and churn according to manufacturer's instructions, about 20 minutes. Seal top with plastic wrap, cover with a lid, and freeze until firm, at least 4 hours.

## 205. Creamy Lemon Grass Ice Cream Recipe

**Ingredients:**
- 2 cups light cream
- 1 1/2 cups fat free sweetened condensed milk
- 3 stalks chopped lemons grass
- 2 large eggs yolks egg yolks

**Directions:**
1. Heat cream, condensed milk, lemon grass in a saucepan over medium heat until mixture steams. Remove from heat prior to the mixture boils and invite to steep for at least 30 minutes, up to 1 one hour and 30 minutes.
2. Reheat the cream mixture over medium heat until it begins to steam. Whisk egg yolks in a little bowl. Temper the egg yolks by pouring a little amount of the hot mixture in while whisking constantly in order to avoid scrambling the eggs.
3. Pour the warm egg mixture into the cream mixture. Continue steadily to cook and stir before mixture has the capacity to coat the back of a spoon. Strain mixture through a sieve to eliminate the bits of lemon grass. Refrigerate until cold.
4. Pour the chilled mixture into an ice cream maker and freeze according to manufacturer's directions until it reaches "soft-serve" consistency. Transfer ice cream to a one- or two-quart lidded plastic container; cover surface with plastic wrap and seal. For best results, ice cream should ripen in the freezer for at least 2 hours or overnight.

## 206. Fast And Easy Creamy Ice Cream Recipe

**Ingredients:**
- 1 quart half-and-half
- 1 (3.5 ounce) package instant pudding mix, any flavor

**Directions:**
1. Place the bowl of an ice cream maker in the freezer until completely chilled, at least one hour.
2. Chill half-and-half in the freezer, shaking every ten minutes, until chilled but not frozen, about 30 minutes.
3. Pour chilled half-and-half and pudding mix right into a bowl and mix well with a whisk.
4. Place frozen plate of ice cream maker into the ice cream maker; add the stirring component and lid. Turn on the machine so the bowl is rotating. Pour pudding mixture into the machine through the hole in the lid.
5. Allow ice cream to process in the ice cream maker until desired consistency is reached, about 30 minutes.

## 207. Vanilla Ice Cream

**Ingredients:**
- 3 cups half-and-half
- 1/2 cup + 2 tablespoons sugar
- 8 eggs yolks
- 1 vanilla bean, split lengthwise

**Directions:**
1. Scrape out seeds from vanilla bean with a sharp paring knife. Add seeds and pods to a medium, heavy saucepan.
2. Add the half-and-half, cream and sugar and bring to a simmer over moderate heat, stirring to dissolve the sugar. Cover and let steep off the heat for 30 minutes.
3. In a large stainless-steel bowl, whisk the egg yolks. Very gradually whisk in 1/2 cup of the hot half-and-half, then gradually whisk in the rest. Pour the mixture into the saucepan and cook over very low heat, stirring constantly, until the custard thickens, about 10 minutes. The custard should be thick enough to coat the back of a spoon.
4. Strain the custard into a large stainless-steel bowl set in an ice water bath and discard the vanilla pod. Stir occasionally until the custard is thoroughly chilled. Pour the custard in an ice cream maker, in batches, according to the manufacturer's instructions. Churn

until the ice cream is set but not rock hard. Store the ice cream in airtight containers in the freezer for up to 3 days.

## 208. Rosewater-and-saffron Ice Cream (bastani Irani)?

**Ingredients:**
- 6 large eggs yolks
- 1 1/2 cups heavy cream
- 1 1/2 cups whole milk
- 3/4 cup sugar
- 1/2 teaspoon kosher salt
- 1/2 teaspoon saffron, finely ground
- 1/4 cup pure rosewater, preferably sadaf brand (see note)
- 1/2 teaspoon pure vanilla extract
- dried roses, for garnish

**Directions:**
1. Set a medium bowl in a sizable plate of ice water. In another medium bowl, beat the egg yolks until pale, one to two 2 minutes.?
2. In a medium saucepan, whisk the cream with the milk, sugar, salt and saffron. Bring to a simmer over moderate heat, whisking, before sugar is totally dissolved. Very gradually whisk half of the hot cream mixture into the beaten egg yolks in a thin stream, then whisk this mixture back into the saucepan. Cook over moderately low heat, stirring constantly with a wooden spoon, before custard is thick enough to lightly coat the back of the spoon, about ?12 minutes; don't allow it boil.?
3. Strain the custard through a fine-mesh sieve into the bowl set in the ice water. ?Allow custard cool completely, stirring occasionally. Stir in the rosewater and vanilla extract. Press a bit of plastic wrap on the custard and refrigerate until well chilled, at least 4 hours.?
4. Pour the custard base into an ice cream maker and freeze based on the manufacturer's instructions. Transfer the ice cream to a chilled 9-by-4-inch metal loaf pan, cover and freeze until firm, at least ?4 hours.
5. Serve the ice cream in bowls, garnished with dried rose

## 209. Lavender Honey Ice Cream Recipe

**Ingredients:**
- 2 cups heavy whipping cream
- 1 cup half-and-half
- 2/3 cup honey
- 2 tablespoons dried lavender flowers
- 2 large eggs
- teaspoon ? salt

**Directions:**
1. Heat heavy cream, half-and-half, honey, and lavender flowers in a heavy 2-quart saucepan, stirring occasionally, until cream just starts to bubble. Remove from heat and cover; let steep for thirty minutes.
2. Strain cream mixture right into a bowl utilizing a fine-mesh sieve. Discard lavender flowers. Clean saucepan and pour strained cream mixture back in. Heat over medium heat until hot, about five minutes.
3. Whisk eggs and salt together in a bowl. Whisk in 1 cup hot cream in a slow stream.
4. Pour egg mixture in to the remaining hot cream in the saucepan. Cook over medium-low heat, stirring constantly with a wooden spoon, until custard coats the trunk of the spoon and reads 175 degrees F (80 degrees C) on an instant-read thermometer, about five minutes.
5. Pour custard through a fine-mesh sieve into a bowl. Let cool completely, stirring occasionally, about a quarter-hour. Chill, covered, for at least 3 hours.
6. Freeze custard in an ice cream maker according to manufacturer's instructions, about 20 minutes. Transfer to an airtight container and place in the freezer to set.

## 210. Chocolate Snow Ice Cream Recipe

**Ingredients:**
- 2 cups milk
- 1 cup confectioners' sugar
- 1 tablespoon vanilla extract

- 1/4 cup unsweetened cocoa powder
- 1 teaspoon powdered instant coffee
- 1 gallon clean fresh snow

**Directions:**
1. In a bowl, whisk together the milk, confectioners' sugar, vanilla extract, cocoa powder, and instant coffee until the sugar has dissolved and the mixture is smooth.
2. Place the snow into a huge bowl, and pour the chocolate mixture over the snow. With a huge spoon, stir until the snow ice cream is thoroughly combined. Serve immediately.

### 211. Simple Mint Chocolate Chip Strawberry Ice Cream Recipe

**Ingredients:**
- 2 cups whipping cream heavy whipping cream
- 1 cup milk whole milk
- 1/2 cup sugar white sugar
- 1/2 teaspoon peppermint extract pure peppermint extract
- 2 ounces chocolate dark chocolate finely chopped
- 6 strawberries medium (1-1/4" dia)s fresh strawberries diced

**Directions:**
1. Mix heavy cream, whole milk, sugar, and peppermint extract in a bowl.
2. Pour mixture into an ice cream maker and freeze until slightly thickened, 25 to 30 minutes (time varies according to ice cream maker specifications). Stir chocolate and strawberries into ice cream mixture; allow to combine until thickened, 3 to 5 5 more minutes.

### 212. Salted Watermelon Ice Cream

**Ingredients:**
- 1 1/4 cups fresh or bottled watermelon juice (such as tsamma)
- 1 cup granulated sugar
- 3/4 teaspoon kosher salt
- 1 (13.66-ounce) can unsweetened coconut milk, well-shaken and stirred
- 1/2 cup sweetened condensed milk
- 1/2 cup heavy cream
- 1 1/2 teaspoons lime zest plus 1 tablespoon fresh lime juice (from 1 lime), divided, plus more zest for garnish
- chopped fresh watermelon and flaky sea salt, for garnish

**Directions:**
1. Stir together watermelon juice, sugar, and kosher salt in a little saucepan. Cook over medium, whisking often, until sugar has fully dissolved, three to four 4 minutes. (Usually do not simmer.) Remove from heat, and whisk in coconut milk, sweetened condensed milk, heavy cream, and lime juice until fully incorporated.
2. Pour mixture into freezer container of a 1 1/2-quart ice cream maker, and proceed according to manufacturer's instructions until ice cream gets the texture of soft serve, about one hour. (Instructions and times can vary greatly.) Stir in lime zest.
3. Quickly transfer ice cream to a freezer-safe container; press parchment paper directly onto surface. Cover container, and freeze until firm, at least 6 hours. Ice cream can be stored in freezer up to three months. To serve, garnish with fresh watermelon, flaky sea salt, and lime zest.

### 213. Peanut Butter Cup Ice Cream Recipe

**Ingredients:**
- 1/4 cup sugar
- 3 large eggs
- 1 cup whole milk
- 3/4 cup peanut butter
- 3/4 cup sweetened condensed milk
- 1/2 cup half-and-half cream
- 2 teaspoons vanilla extract
- 12 eaches miniature peanut butter cups, chopped

**Directions:**
1. In a medium bowl, beat the sugar and eggs with an electric mixer until thick, about three minutes. Set aside. Pour milk into a small saucepan, and bring to a simmer over low heat. Gradually drizzle the hot milk into the eggs

while whisking vigorously. Then pour the whole mixture into the saucepan. Cook over low heat, stirring constantly, until thick enough to coat the back of a metal spoon. Usually do not boil.
2. Remove from heat, and whisk in peanut butter. Allow to cool slightly, then whisk in the sweetened condensed milk, half-and-half and vanilla. Cover and refrigerate until chilled.
3. Pour the mixture into an ice cream maker, and freeze based on the manufacturer's instructions. Fold in peanut butter cups when mixture continues to be soft, then transfer to a container, and freeze until solid.

### 214. Cherry Cheesecake Ice Cream
**Ingredients:**
- 3 cups cold heavy cream
- 1 14 cans -oz. sweetened condensed milk
- 1 teaspoon pure vanilla extract
- 1 cup hand crushed graham crackers (about 4 whole crackers), plus more for garnish
- 1 cup cherry pie filling

**Directions:**
1. In a sizable bowl utilizing a hand mixer, beat cream until stiff peaks form, 2-3 three minutes. Fold in sweetened condensed milk and vanilla until fully incorporated, then fold in crushed graham crackers.
2. Transfer half the mixture to a 9"-x-5" loaf pan. Dollop 1/2 cup pie filling over top, then swirl with a knife.
3. Add remaining cream mixture, then swirl in remaining 1/2 cup pie filling. Top with graham crackers. Freeze until firm, at least 8 hours, covering lightly with plastic wrap after 4 hours. Let soften ten minutes before scooping and serving.

### 215. Five Minute Ice Cream
**Ingredients:**
- 1 (10-ounce) package frozen sliced strawberries
- 1/2 cup sugar
- 2/3 cup heavy cream

**Directions:**
1. Combine the frozen strawberries and sugar in a food processor or blender.
2. Process until the fruit is roughly chopped. With the processor running, slowly pour in the heavy cream until fully incorporated. Serve immediately or freeze for up to one week.

### 216. Mocha Coconut Ice Cream Recipe
**Ingredients:**
- 10 ounces dark chocolate, broken into pieces
- 2 (14-ounce) cans coconut milk
- 3 tablespoons strong brewed coffee
- 1 teaspoon vanilla extract
- 1 pinch salt

**Directions:**
1. Place chocolate into a little heatproof bowl; place bowl over warm water. Stir chocolate occasionally until melted and smooth, about five minutes.
2. Whisk coconut milk, coffee, vanilla extract, and salt together in a bowl; whisk in melted chocolate until smooth. Place coconut milk mixture in refrigerator until cool, about thirty minutes.
3. Freeze in ice cream maker according to manufacturer's instructions.

### 217. Creamy Banana Ice Cream Recipe
**Ingredients:**
- 4 eaches bananas, sliced
- 1/2 cup milk
- 1/2 cup heavy whipping cream

**Directions:**
1. Line a baking sheet with parchment paper. Arrange banana slices in some recoverable format and freeze until solid, three to five 5 hours.
2. Peel bananas from the parchment paper and place in the blender.
3. Add milk and cream and blend until smooth; transfer to a sealable container and freeze until set, about 2 hours.

### 218. Lemon Ice Ii Recipe
**Ingredients:**

- 1 lemon, zested and juiced
- 1 lemon, juiced
- 2 cups cold milk, chilled
- 1 (14-ounce) can nonfat sweetened condensed milk, chilled

**Directions:**
1. In the freezer canister of an ice cream maker, combine lemon zest, lemon juice, milk and sweetened condensed milk. Freeze according to manufacturers' directions.

## 219. Tart Lemon Ice Cream Recipe

**Ingredients:**
- 1 large lemon, juiced and zested
- 1 cup white sugar
- 1 cup milk
- 1 cup heavy cream, chilled

**Directions:**
1. Combine the lemon zest and sugar in the container of a food processor. Blend before zest is very fine. In a medium bowl, stir together the sugar and milk until sugar has dissolved, then stir in the lemon juice. In another bowl, whip the heavy cream until stiff however, not grainy. Gently fold the whipped cream in to the lemon mixture until evenly blended.
2. Pour the mixture right into a 9x5 inch loaf pan, and cover with plastic wrap. Freeze for 3 hours, or until firm.

## 220. Coffee Ice Cream

**Ingredients:**
- 4 large eggs yolks
- 1/2 cup whole coffee beans
- 2 cups heavy cream
- 1 cup half-and-half
- 3/4 cup packed light brown sugar
- 1/4 teaspoon kosher salt
- 1 teaspoon pure vanilla extract

**Directions:**
1. Set a medium bowl in a sizable bowl of ice water. In another medium bowl, whisk the egg yolks until pale and slightly thickened, about 2 minutes.
2. In a spice grinder, pulse the coffees until coarsely chopped. In a medium saucepan, combine the coffee with the cream, half-and-half, sugar and salt. Bring to a simmer and cook over moderate heat, whisking occasionally, before sugar is totally dissolved and the cream mixture is steaming, about 7 minutes. Very gradually whisk half of the hot cream mixture into the beaten egg yolks in a thin stream, then whisk this mixture in to the saucepan. Cook over moderately low heat, stirring constantly with a rubber spatula, until the custard is thick enough to lightly coat the back of the spoon, about 7 minutes; don't allow it boil.
3. Transfer the custard to the bowl set in the ice water, stir in the vanilla and let cool for approximately thirty minutes, stirring occasionally. Pour the custard through a fine-mesh strainer into another medium bowl and refrigerate until very cold, about 1 hour.
4. Whisk the chilled custard several times, then scrape it into an ice cream maker. Freeze based on the manufacturer's instructions. Transfer the ice cream to a plastic container, cover and freeze until firm, at least 3 hours

## 221. Strawberry Ice Cream Recipe

**Ingredients:**
- 1 quart fresh strawberries, hulled
- 1 1/2 cups heavy cream, divided
- 3/4 cup white sugar
- 3 large eggs yolks egg yolks
- 3 tablespoons light corn syrup

**Directions:**
1. Place the berries into the container of a blender or food processor, and puree until smooth. Pour into a sizable bowl, and set aside.
2. Heat 1 1/4 cups of the cream in a saucepan over medium heat until it starts to bubble at the edge of the pan. In a huge bowl, whisk together the sugar, egg yolks, remaining 1/4 cup cream, and corn syrup. Gradually pour the hot cream in to the egg yolk mixture, whisking constantly. Return the mixture to the saucepan, and heat

before mixture is thick enough to coat the back of a metal spoon, about five minutes. Don't allow the mixture to boil. Strain custard in to the berry puree through a sieve, mix, and refrigerate until chilled.
3. Fill an ice cream maker with the mixture, and freeze according to the manufacturer's instructions.

## 222. Maplenut Ice Cream Recipe
**Ingredients:**
- 3 quarts milk
- 1 (14-ounce) can sweetened condensed milk
- 3 large eggs, beaten
- 2 cups white sugar
- 1 teaspoon vanilla extract
- 1 teaspoon maple flavored extract
- 1 cup wheat and barley nugget cereal (e.g. grape-nuts)

**Directions:**
1. Combine milk, condensed milk, eggs, sugar, vanilla, maple extract and cereal in the freezer canister of an ice cream maker. Freeze according to manufacturer's directions.

## 223. Mocha Espresso Ice Cream Recipe
**Ingredients:**
- 2 cups heavy whipping cream
- 1 1/2 cups whole milk
- 3/4 cup white sugar
- 1/2 cup brewed espresso, chilled
- 1/4 cup chocolate syrup
- 3/4 cup cocoa roast almonds, chopped
- 4 ounces dark chocolate, chopped

**Directions:**
1. Mix heavy cream, dairy, sugar, espresso, and chocolate syrup in a bowl until sugar is dissolved. Refrigerate until chilled.
2. Pour the chilled mixture into an ice cream maker and freeze according to manufacturer's directions until it reaches "soft-serve" consistency. Stir in almonds and chocolates. Serve soft ice cream or transfer ice cream to a one- or two-quart lidded plastic container; cover surface with plastic wrap and seal. For best results, ice cream should ripen in the freezer for at least 2 hours or overnight.

## 224. Cheesecake Ice Cream Recipe
**Ingredients:**
- 1 quart lowfat 1% milk
- 2 (8-ounce) packages reduced fat cream cheese, softened
- 1 1/2 cups white sugar
- 1/3 cup triple sec
- 1 tablespoon vanilla extract
- 1 pinch salt

**Directions:**
1. Place milk, cream cheese, sugar, triple sec, vanilla extract, and salt right into a blender; blend until smooth.
2. Freeze in the plate of an ice cream maker based on the manufacturer's instructions.

## 225. Peach-blueberry Ice Cream
**Ingredients:**
- 11 ounces fresh blueberries (about 2 cups)
- 3/4 cup granulated sugar, divided
- 1 tablespoon fresh lemon juice
- 1 pound fresh peaches, peeled and chopped (about 3 cups)
- 1 1/2 cups heavy cream
- 1 1/2 cups whole milk
- 1/4 cup light corn syrup
- 1/4 teaspoon kosher salt
- 5 large eggs yolks
- 1/2 teaspoon vanilla extract
- 1/4 cup (2 ounces) bourbon

**Directions:**
1. Cook blueberries, 1/4 cup sugar, and lemon juice in a medium-size, heavy-bottomed saucepan over medium-high, stirring occasionally, until berries to burst and liquid to thicken, 8 to 10 minutes Remove from heat, and let cool Transfer to a bowl. Cover and chill until completely cool, at least 1 hour or until repared to useto at least one 1 week.
2. Process chopped peaches in a food processor until almost smooth (applesauce consistency), leaving a

few chunky bits, about 30 seconds. Reserve.
3. Stir together heavy cream, dairy, corn syrup, salt, and remaining 1/2 cup sugar in a medium saucepan, and cook over medium, stirring occasionally, just until mixture starts to simmer (bubbles start to form around the exterior edge of pan), 5 to 6 minutes.
4. Meanwhile, whisk together egg yolks and vanilla in a huge a sizable bowl. While whisking yolk mixture constantly, carefully ladle about 1 cup hot cream mixture into yolk mixture; continue whisking until cream mixture is fully incorporated. Carefully whisk in remaining hot cream mixture.
5. Pour custard mixture back to saucepan, and cook over medium-high, whisking constantly, until mixture starts to thicken and coats the trunk of a spoon, six to eight minutes. Remove from heat, and let cool ten minutes.
6. Stir bourbon and pureed peaches into custard. Pour custard mixture right into a gallon-size ziplock plastic freezer bag. Seal bag, and place within an ice bath. Let stand until mixture is totally cool, about 30 minutes.
7. Pour mixture right into a 1 1/2-quart electric ice cream maker, and proceed according to manufacturer's instructions. (Instructions and times can vary greatly.) Transfer to an airtight, freezer-safe container; freeze until slightly firm, about thirty minutes. Dollop blueberry mixture over ice cream, and swirl with a spoon. Cover and freeze until firm, at least 4 hours or up to overnight.

## 226. Guinness Ice Cream With Chocolate-covered Pretzels

**Ingredients:**
- 2 cups guinness (16 ounces)
- 2 cups heavy cream
- 1 3/4 cups whole milk
- 15 large eggs yolks
- 1 cup granulated sugar
- chocolate-covered pretzels, for serving

**Directions:**
1. In a sizable saucepan, combine the Guinness with the cream and milk and bring to a simmer over moderately high temperature. In a huge bowl, whisk the egg yolks with the sugar. Gradually add the hot Guinness cream to the yolks, whisking constantly until well blended.
2. Pour the mixture in to the saucepan and cook over moderate heat, stirring constantly until it coats the trunk of a spoon, about 6 minutes; don't let it boil. Pour the custard into a medium bowl set in a large bowl filled up with ice water. Let stand before custard is cold, stirring occasionally, about thirty minutes.
3. Pour the custard into an ice cream maker and freeze based on the manufacturer's instructions (this may have to be done in 2 batches).
4. Pack the ice cream into an airtight container and freeze until firm, about 4 hours.
5. Spoon the ice cream into bowls and top with some Chocolate-Covered Pretzels. Serve simultaneously.

## 227. Strawberry Snow Ice Cream Recipe

**Ingredients:**
- 2 cups milk
- 1/2 cup strawberry-flavored milk powder (such as nesquik)
- 1 gallon clean fresh snow

**Directions:**
1. Whisk the milk and strawberry milk powder together in a sizable bowl until thoroughly combined.
2. Gradually stir in the snow, about 1 cup at a time, before mixture is creamy and holds soft peaks. Serve immediately.

## 228. Peach Ice Cream Recipe

**Ingredients:**
- 6 large eggs, beaten
- 3 1/2 cups white sugar

- 10 medium (2-1/2" dia) (approx 4 per lb)s fresh peaches, pitted and chopped
- 4 cups heavy cream
- 2 cups half-and-half cream
- 2 teaspoons vanilla extract
- 3/4 teaspoon salt

**Directions:**
1. In large bowl, mix together eggs and sugar until smooth; puree peaches in blender or food processor and stir 5 cups of puree into egg mixture. Stir in cream, half-and-half, vanilla and salt and mix well.
2. Pour mixture into freezer canister of ice cream maker and freeze according to manufacturer's instructions.

### 229. Vanilla Ice Cream With Brown Butter Crumble

**Ingredients:**
- 1 stick plus 6 tablespoons unsalted butter
- 1/2 cup granulated sugar
- 1 1/2 cups all-purpose flour
- 3/4 cup dark brown sugar
- 1/2 cup almond meal or almond flour
- 1 1/4 teaspoons fine sea salt
- vanilla ice cream, caramel sauce and chocolate sauce, for serving

**Directions:**
1. In a little saucepan, cook the butter over moderate heat, shaking the pan occasionally, before butter is nutty-smelling and golden and the foam subsides, about five minutes. Pour the brown butter into a heatproof bowl and stir in the granulated sugar. Let cool slightly.
2. Line a baking sheet with parchment paper. In a medium bowl, whisk the flour with the brown sugar, almond meal and salt. Stir in the brown butter mixture until evenly moistened crumbs form. Transfer to the prepared baking sheet and, using your hands, press the crumbs into a straight layer a scant inch thick. Cover with plastic wrap and refrigerate until well chilled, about 1 hour.
3. Preheat the oven to 350°. Break the dough into small chunks and bake for 20 minutes, until it really is golden and slightly dry. Let cool, then serve the crumble over vanilla ice cream with caramel and chocolate sauces.

### 230. Cherry Ice Cream Recipe

**Ingredients:**
- 1/4 cup cherry juice concentrate
- 1/2 cup fat free milk
- 1 cup vanilla low-fat yogurt
- 1 cup heavy cream
- 1/2 cup white sugar
- 1 pinch salt
- 1 cup frozen dark sweet cherries
- 2 teaspoons almond extract

**Directions:**
1. Place the cherry juice, milk, yogurt, and heavy cream into the plate of a blender. Add the sugar, salt, cherries, and almond extract. Puree until only small bits of the cherries remain.
2. Pour right into a 1 1/2 quart ice cream maker and freeze according to manufacturer's directions.

### 231. Snow Ice Cream I Recipe

**Ingredients:**
- 1 (12 fluid ounce) can evaporated milk
- 2 large eggs, beaten
- 1 1/2 teaspoons vanilla extract
- 3/4 cup white sugar
- 1 gallon snow

**Directions:**
1. In a sizable bowl, combine evaporated milk, eggs, vanilla and sugar until smooth.
2. Gradually stir in snow until mixture reaches desired consistency. Eat simultaneously

### 232. Homemade Soft Serve Ice Cream

**Ingredients:**
- 1/2 cup heavy cream
- 1 tablespoon powdered sugar
- 3 cups vanilla ice cream, softened
- 2 ice cream cones, for serving
- rainbow sprinkles, for topping

**Directions:**

1. In a sizable bowl utilizing a handheld electric mixer, beat cream until medium peaks form, 2 to 3 3 minutes. Add sugar and beat 30 seconds more.
2. Stir in ice cream until completely combined, then transfer mixture to a sizable resealable bag and freeze until firm, three to four 4 hours.
3. Remove ice cream from freezer and knead until soft, 1 minute. Snip a corner from the bag and pipe right into a cone. Top with sprinkles and serve immediately.

### 233. Vanilla Ice Cream Iii Recipe

**Ingredients:**
- 1 (14-ounce) can sweetened condensed milk
- 1 (12 fluid ounce) can evaporated milk
- 2 tablespoons vanilla extract
- 1 pinch salt
- 1 cup white sugar
- 6 cups milk , or as needed

**Directions:**
1. Combine condensed milk, evaporated milk, vanilla, salt and sugar in freezer canister of ice cream maker, and stir well.
2. Add enough milk to bring mixture to the fill line on canister. Freeze according to manufacturer's directions.

### 234. Lina And Jens' Delicious Vegan Chocolate Ice Cream Recipe

**Ingredients:**
- 7 ounces dark chocolate , chopped
- 1 1/4 cups aquafaba
- 1/2 teaspoon xanthan gum
- 1/2 cup confectioners' sugar
- 2 teaspoons vanilla sugar

**Directions:**
1. Melt chocolate in top of a double boiler over simmering water, stirring frequently and scraping down the sides with a rubber spatula in order to avoid scorching. Let cool slightly, about ten minutes.
2. Pour aquafaba in to the plate of a stand mixer fitted with a whisk attachment. Beat on high speed until fluffy and quadrupled in volume, about 1 minute. Add xanthan gum and beat for 30 seconds. Add confectioners' sugar and vanilla sugar; continue beating until foam is firm and glossy, about 2 minutes more.
3. Fold melted chocolate gently into whipped foam until thoroughly incorporated. Transfer to a lidded container.
4. Freeze until firm, 8 hours to overnight.

### 235. Easy Banana Ice Cream Recipe

**Ingredients:**
- 2 eaches peeled and chopped bananas, frozen
- 1/2 cup skim milk

**Directions:**
1. Combine frozen bananas and 1/4 cup skim milk in a blender; blend for 30 seconds.
2. Add remaining 1/4 cup milk and blend on high speed until smooth, about 30 seconds more.

### 236. Ice Cream Bonbon Pops

**Ingredients:**
- crushed popcorn
- 1 pint vanilla ice cream, or your favorite flavor
- about eighteen 4-inch lollipop sticks
- crushed candy , such as sno-caps, whoppers, skittles and m&m's

**Directions:**
1. Place 2 parchment paper-lined large plates in the freezer for quarter-hour. Disseminate crushed popcorn on a baking sheet.
2. Using an ice cream scoop and working quickly, scoop out 9 ice cream balls and place along with the popcorn. Return the pint of ice cream to the freezer so it doesn't melt. Roll the balls in the popcorn to coat, pressing to greatly help it adhere. Insert sticks into the centers of the balls, then transfer the bonbons to 1 of the frozen plates and transfer to the freezer.

3. Repeat with the candy and remaining ice cream and plate. Freeze the bonbons until they are completely firm, about thirty minutes.

## 237. Homemade Vanilla Ice Cream (plus 5 Delish Mix-ins)

**Ingredients:**
- 3 cups half and half
- 1/3 cup sugar
- 3 eggs yolks
- 2 vanilla bean pods, seeds scraped, or 1 tablespoon pure vanilla extract
- 1/4 cup bourbon
- 1/4 cup olive oil
- 1 teaspoon zested lemons
- 1/2 cup salted caramel
- 1/4 cup pistachio cream (available at specialty food stores)
- 1 teaspoon rose water
- 1/2 cup roughly chopped pistachios
- 3/4 cup smashed strawberries

**Directions:**
1. In large pot over medium heat, combine half and half and vanilla bean and bring to a simmer for at least quarter-hour.
2. Strain half and half mixture and reserve. In a huge bowl, whisk together egg yolks, sugar, and salt until smooth.
3. To temper eggs, carefully whisk about 1 cup of the hot half and half into egg mixture until smooth.
4. Then whisk egg mixture back into the half and half mixture in the pot. Go back to medium-low heat and cook to 170 degrees F, constantly stirring along bottom of pot to make sure even cooking.
5. Once temperature has already reached 170 degrees F, remove from heat and strain through fine-mesh strainer into bowl. In the same bowl, cool ice cream base to room temperature within an ice bath, then pop base into the fridge to fully chill, at least 2 hours.
6. Once base is chilled, process within an ice cream maker. When it's somewhere within soft serve and ice cream from the freezer, transfer ice cream to container and freeze until firm. Bourbon Ice Cream: Add 1/4 cup bourbon once you strain. Lemon ESSENTIAL OLIVE OIL Ice Cream: Add 1/4 cup olive oil and 1 teaspoon lemon zest to the sugar and eggs. Salted Caramel Ice Cream: Add 1/2 cup salted caramel to the half-and-half. (You might want to use less sugar so it is not too sweet.) Pistachio Rose: Add 1/4 cup pistachio cream to the sugar and eggs.
7. Add 1 teaspoon rosewater and 1/2 cup roughly chopped pistachios once you strain. Classic Strawberry: Add 3/4 cup smashed strawberries after you strain.

## 238. Easy And Delicious Strawberry Frozen Yogurt Recipe

**Ingredients:**
- 1 pound fresh strawberries
- 1/2 lemon, juiced
- 2 (7-ounce) containers greek yogurt (such as fag)
- 3/4 cup white sugar

**Directions:**
1. Blend strawberries and lemon juice together in a blender until smooth; refrigerate until cold, about one hour.
2. Stir yogurt and sugar into strawberry mixture until well blended and smooth; pour mixture into ice cream machine's container.
3. Freeze according to manufacturer's directions for a soft-serve consistency.

## 239. Death By Chocolate Ice Cream

**Ingredients:**
- 6 ounces chocolate (semisweet or dark)
- 1 1/2 cups. whole milk
- 1 1/2 cups. heavy cream
- 1/3 cup cocoa powder
- 3/4 cup granulated sugar
- 6 large eggs yolks
- 2 teaspoons pure vanilla extract
- 1/4 teaspoon kosher salt

**Directions:**

1. The day before you plan to churn, freeze the bowl of your ice cream maker. (As your ice cream base will need to chill as well, we suggest which makes it the night time before, too.)
2. Make ice cream base: Fill a sizable bowl with ice and water, reserve. Fill a medium saucepan with about 2" water and place over medium heat. Bring to a bare simmer, then place a big heatproof bowl on top.
3. Add chocolate and stir until melted. Let cool slightly. In a medium saucepan over medium heat, whisk together milk, cream, and cocoa powder.
4. When mixture starts to boil, remove from heat and set aside. In a sizable bowl, whisk sugar and egg yolks until pale and thick ribbons form, three to four 4 minutes. (You could also use a hand mixer.) Whisking constantly, steadily add hot milk mixture, one ladle at the same time, to warm through egg mixture.
5. Pour mixture into saucepan then whisk in melted chocolate and place over low heat. Cook, stirring frequently with a wooden spoon, until mixture thickens, making sure the mixture never comes up to a simmer, about 4 to five minutes. To check if the mixture is performed, coat the back of your wooden spoon with the mixture and swipe your finger through the mixture. If your finger leaves a clean line, your mixture is good to go-this will be at around 170°, if you are utilizing a candy thermometer. When the custard is adequately thickened, stir in vanilla and salt. Strain into a huge bowl and place in ice bath. Let cool to room temperature, then cover and chill 3 hours, up to overnight.
6. When your custard is chilled and your ice cream maker bowl is frozen, churn ice cream according to manufacturer's instructions.
7. When ice cream is soft-serve consistency, transfer to another container and freeze until hardened, 2-3 3 hours, up to overnight.

## 240. Vegan Blueberry Coconut Ice Cream Recipe

**Ingredients:**
- 2 tablespoons roasted flax seeds
- 2 (15-ounce) cans full-fat coconut milk, chilled
- 2 cups blueberries
- 1 tablespoon lemon juice
- 1 teaspoon vanilla extract
- 1 teaspoon coconut oils
- 1 teaspoon stevia powder
- 1/2 teaspoon xanthan gum, or more as desired
- 1/4 teaspoon himalayan black salt

**Directions:**
1. Pulse flax seeds in a coffee grinder until finely ground.
2. Combine 1 can coconut milk, blueberries, and lemon juice in a blender; puree until blueberry skins breakdown completely. Add ground flax seeds, remaining coconut milk, vanilla extract, coconut oil, stevia, xanthan gum, and salt; puree until very smooth.
3. Transfer blender container to the freezer to chill mixture briefly, about 15 minutes
4. Pour mixture into an ice cream maker and churn according to manufacturer's instructions, about 20 minutes. Transfer to a lidded container before serving.

## 241. Easy Mint Chocolate Chip Ice Cream Recipe

**Ingredients:**
- 2 cups 2% milk
- 2 cups heavy cream
- 1 cup sugar
- 1/2 teaspoon salt
- 1 teaspoon vanilla extract
- 1 teaspoon peppermint extract
- 3 drops green food coloring
- 1 cup miniature semisweet chocolate chips

**Directions:**
1. In a big bowl, stir together the milk, cream, sugar, salt, vanilla extract and peppermint extract before sugar has dissolved. Color to your liking with the green food coloring.
Advertisement
2. Pour the mixture into an ice cream maker, and freeze according to the manufacturer's instructions. After about ten minutes into the freezing, add the chocolate chips. Following the ice cream has thickened, about 30 minutes later, spoon right into a container, and freeze for 2 hours.

## 242. Super Lemon Ice Cream Recipe

**Ingredients:**
- 2 cups heavy whipping cream
- 1 cup half-and-half cream
- 1 ? cups white sugar
- 3 tablespoons grated lemon zest
- 5 large eggs yolks egg yolks
- 3/4 cup fresh lemon juice

**Directions:**
1. Combine heavy cream, half and half, sugar, and lemon zest in a saucepan; bring to a simmer over low heat. Cook and stir until sugar is dissolved, about five minutes. Remove from heat. Cover saucepan and invite the mixture to steep for 10 minutes.
2. Uncover pan and bring back to a simmer over low heat. Beat the egg yolks in a bowl. Gradually stir one glass of the hot cream mixture into the eggs, several tablespoons at the same time. This will bring the eggs up to temperature without scrambling them. Stir the egg mixture back to the cream mixture in the saucepan. Cook and stir over low heat before mixture just coats the back of a spoon, 5 to ten minutes. Transfer to a sizable bowl; cover. Refrigerate overnight.
3. Stir the lemon juice in to the cold ice cream mixture. Freeze in a 4 to 5 quart ice cream maker according to manufacturer's directions. Transfer ice cream to a lidded freezer container, and freeze for 4 hours to ripen flavors before serving.

## 243. Chocolate-hazelnut Soy Ice Cream Recipe

**Ingredients:**
- 1/2 (12-ounce) package extra-firm silken tofu
- 1 cup soy milk
- 1 tablespoon hazelnut flavored syrup
- 4 teaspoons instant espresso powder
- 1 teaspoon vanilla extract
- 2/3 cup semisweet chocolate chips, melted

**Directions:**
1. Place the tofu, soy milk, hazelnut syrup, espresso powder, and vanilla extract right into a blender. Cover, and puree until smooth.
2. Pour in the melted chocolate, and puree until evenly incorporated. Pour the mixture right into a bowl, cover, and refrigerate until cold, at least one hour.
3. Pour the chilled mixture into an ice cream maker and freeze according to the manufacturer's directions.
4. After the ice cream has thickened and is hard to stir, remove it from the ice cream maker and transfer it to a freezer container. Permit the ice cream to harden 4 hours to overnight before serving.

## 244. Homemade Mint Chocolate Chip Ice Cream Recipe

**Ingredients:**
- 2 cups heavy whipping cream
- 1 (14-ounce) can sweetened condensed milk
- 1 cup milk
- 1 teaspoon mint extract
- 1/2 teaspoon vanilla extract
- 1 (12-ounce) bag semisweet chocolate chips

**Directions:**
1. Stir heavy cream, sweetened condensed milk, milk, mint extract, vanilla extract, and chocolate chips in a bowl until evenly mixed.

2. Pour mixture into an ice cream maker and freeze according to manufacturer's directions until softly frozen. Transfer ice cream to a lidded container; cover surface with plastic wrap and seal. For best results, ice cream should ripen in the freezer for at least 2 hours to overnight.

### 245. Creamy Pomegranate Ice Cream Recipe
**Ingredients:**
- 1 cup heavy cream
- 1 cup white sugar
- 1 cup pomegranate juice
- 1 teaspoon vanilla extract
- 1 pinch salt

**Directions:**
1. The first step 1 Stir together the heavy cream and sugar. Stir in the pomegranate juice, vanilla extract, and salt.
2. Add the mixture to an ice cream maker and freeze predicated on the manufacturer's directions.

### 246. Dark Chocolate And Cinnamon Frozen Custard Recipe
**Ingredients:**
- 2 1/2 cups heavy whipping cream
- 1/2 cup milk
- 3/4 cup white sugar
- 2 tablespoons unsweetened dark cocoa powder
- 1 ounce high-quality dark chocolate (85%), finely chopped
- 5 large eggs yolks egg yolks
- 1 1/2 teaspoons ground cinnamon, plus more for dusting

**Directions:**
1. Whisk cream, milk, sugar, and cocoa powder in a saucepan over medium heat before mixture is thoroughly combined and the sugar has dissolved. Bring almost to a simmer and stir in chocolates until melted. Whisk egg yolks into the cream mixture and cook until batter is slightly thickened, 1 to 2 2 minutes. Transfer to a container, cover, and refrigerate until chilled, at least 6 hours.
2. Stir cinnamon into chilled custard batter and freeze within an ice cream machine following manufacturer's instructions. Sprinkle frozen custard with more cinnamon to serve.

### 247. Matcha Green Tea Ice Cream Recipe
**Ingredients:**
- 1 tablespoon matcha green tea powder, or more to taste
- 1 cup whole milk
- 2 cups heavy whipping cream
- 3/4 cup white sugar
- 2 large eggs

**Directions:**
1. Whisk matcha powder in a bowl to eliminate any lumps; add a splash of milk and whisk until matcha powder is totally dissolved. Gradually whisk remaining milk into matcha mixture.
2. Combine cream and matcha mixture in a pot over medium-low heat; cook, stirring occasionally, until heated through, about 5 minutes.
3. Whisk sugar and eggs together in a bowl. Pour 1/2 cup hot matcha mixture into egg mixture; mix thoroughly. Repeat with remaining matcha mixture. Pour mixture back into the pot.
4. Cook and stir matcha mixture over medium-low heat until heated through, about three minutes. Remove from heat and cool to room temperature. Refrigerate until chilled, at least 4 hours.
5. Pour cooled matcha mixture into an ice cream maker and freeze according to the manufacturer's instructions.

### 248. Easy Eggnog Ice Cream Recipe
**Ingredients:**
- 2 cups eggnog
- 1 cup heavy whipping cream
- 1 cup milk

**Directions:**
1. Mix the eggnog, whipping cream, and milk together in a bowl, and pour the mixture in to the freezer container of an ice cream maker.

2. Freeze according to manufacturer's directions. Once frozen, spoon the ice cream right into a container, and freeze 2 hours more.

### 249. Cookie Butter No-churn Ice Cream

**Ingredients:**
- 3 cups heavy whipping cream
- 1 14 ounces . can sweetened condensed milk
- 1/4 cup cookie butter, like biscoff
- 2 cups crumbled biscoff cookies, divided

**Directions:**
1. In a huge bowl, combine heavy whipping cream and condensed milk. Beat with a power mixer on high until stiff peaks form.
2. Slowly fold in cookie butter until well-combined. Sprinkle over 1 cup of crumbled cookies and fold in. Spoon mixture into loaf pan, and freeze for 4 hours or overnight until set.
3. Serve in glasses with remaining crumbled cookie garnish.

### 250. Dark Brownie Fudge Ice Cream Recipe

**Ingredients:**
- 1 cup heavy whipping cream
- 3/4 cup whole milk
- 1/4 teaspoon ground espresso beans
- 1/3 cup semi-sweet chocolate chips
- 1 cup packed dark brown sugar
- 2 tablespoons dutch dark cocoa powder
- 1/4 cup unsalted butter
- 1 tablespoon vanilla extract

**Directions:**
1. Combine whipping cream and milk in a little saucepan over medium heat. Cook for 2 minutes. Stir in ground espresso. Gently add chocolate chips and stir continuously until chocolate melts and is fully blended with the cream mixture, making sure nothing sticks to underneath of the pan.
2. Stir in brown sugar until dissolved, reducing heat to low when the mixture starts to boil. Mix in cocoa powder until incorporated. Add butter; stir until melted. Stir in vanilla extract. Continue stirring over low heat until mixture is dark brown and smooth.
3. Pass the mixture through an excellent strainer to remove espresso granules, then pour into an ice cream maker and freeze according to manufacturer's instructions, about 20 minutes. Transfer to an airtight container and freeze until firm, about 4 hours.

### 251. Tropical Ice Cream Sandwiches Recipe

**Ingredients:**
- 16 pieces (1/10 of cake)s slices pound cake
- 1 (16-ounce) container mango sorbet, softened
- 1/2 cup granular no-calorie sucralose sweetener (e.g., splenda )
- 1 lime, juiced
- 1 (10-ounce) can coconut milk
- 1 pint blueberries
- 1 mango, cubed
- 1 pint strawberries , hulled and quartered
- 2 eaches fresh peaches , sliced
- 8 tablespoons sweetened whipped cream
- 8 sprigs fresh mint for garnish

**Directions:**
1. Make 8 sandwiches, using 2 slices of pound cake and 1/4 cup softened mango sorbet each. Wrap each sandwich tightly with plastic wrap, and freeze for 2 hours.
2. Dissolve sweetener in lime juice and coconut milk; toss with blueberries, mango, strawberries, and peach slices.
3. To serve, unwrap the sandwiches and place each onto a dessert plate. Top with a mound of fruit and garnish with whipped cream and a mint sprig.

### 252. Mint-chip Coconut Milk Ice Cream Recipe

**Ingredients:**
- 24 fluid ounces canned coconut milk
- 1/3 cup agave syrup, or to taste

- 1 teaspoon peppermint extract, or to taste
- 3 ounces dark chocolate , chopped into small pieces

**Directions:**
1. Chill all the ingredients prior to preparing to quicken the freezing process
2. Blend coconut milk in a blender until smooth and evenly mixed; add agave syrup and peppermint extract and blend until smooth.
3. Transfer coconut milk mixture to an ice cream maker and follow manufacturer's instructions for ice cream, adding chocolate pieces when indicated. Freeze for 2 hours before serving.

### 253. No-churn Keto Ice Cream Recipe
**Ingredients:**
- 1 cup heavy whipping cream
- 2 tablespoons powdered zero-calorie sweetener (such as swerve)
- 1 tablespoon vodka
- 1 teaspoon vanilla extract
- 1/4 teaspoon xanthan gum
- 1 pinch salt

**Directions:**
1. Combine cream, sweetener, vodka, vanilla extract, xanthan gum, and salt in a wide-mouth pint-sized jar.
2. Blend cream mixture with an immersion blender in an up-and-down motion until cream has thickened and soft peaks have formed, 60 to 75 seconds. Cover jar and place in the freezer for three to four 4 hours, stirring every 30 to 40 minutes.

### 254. Snow Cream Recipe
**Ingredients:**
- 8 cups clean fresh snow
- 1 (14-ounce) can sweetened condensed milk
- 1 tablespoon vanilla extract

**Directions:**
1. Mix snow, sweetened condensed milk, and vanilla extract together in a bowl until well mixed.

### 255. Easy Snow Ice Cream Recipe
**Ingredients:**
- 1 (14-ounce) can sweetened condensed milk
- 3/4 cup white sugar
- 1 1/2 teaspoons vanilla extract
- 1 gallon clean fresh snow

**Directions:**
1. Stir sweetened condensed milk, sugar, and vanilla extract together in a huge bowl until smooth. Gradually stir snow into milk mixture until your desired consistency is reached.

### 256. Vanilla Ice Cream Viii Recipe
**Ingredients:**
- 8 cups milk
- 2 cups white sugar
- 1 tablespoon vanilla extract

**Directions:**
1. Combine milk, sugar and vanilla in freezer canister of ice cream maker.
2. Freeze according to manufacturer's instructions.

### 257. French-style Ice Cream
**Ingredients:**
- 6 eggs large egg yolks
- 3/4 cup sugar
- 1 <small>3/4</small> cups heavy cream heavy cream
- 1 <small>1/4</small> cups milk whole milk
- pinch salt of salt

**Directions:**
1. Set a medium bowl in a sizable bowl of ice water. In another medium bowl, whisk the egg yolks with 1/2 cup of the sugar until pale, about three minutes.
2. In a medium saucepan, combine the cream, milk, salt and remaining 1/4 cup of sugar and bring to a simmer, whisking before sugar is completely dissolved. Whisk the hot cream mixture in to the beaten egg yolks in a thin stream.
3. Transfer the mixture to the saucepan and cook over moderately low heat, stirring constantly with a wooden spoon, before custard is thick enough

to lightly coat the trunk of the spoon, about 4 minutes; don't let it boil. Pour the custard through a fine-mesh strainer in to the medium bowl in the ice water. Let cool completely, stirring frequently. Refrigerate the custard until cold, at least one hour.
4. Pour the custard into an ice cream maker with flavorings, if using, and freeze based on the manufacturer's instructions. Transfer the frozen custard to a plastic container, cover and freeze until firm, at least 3 hours

## 258. Peach-maple Ice Cream

**Ingredients:**
- 3/4 pound ripe peaches
- 1 tablespoon fresh lemon juice
- 1 cup heavy cream
- 1/2 cup milk
- 1/2 vanilla bean, split, seeds scraped
- 2 large eggs yolks
- 1/4 cup plus 2 tablespoons sugar
- pinch of salt
- 1/4 cup pure maple syrup
- 1 tablespoon bourbon, or more to taste

**Directions:**
1. Bring a little pot of water to a boil and fill a medium bowl with ice water. Cut a shallow X in the bottom of every peach and plunge it into the boiling water for 30 seconds. Transfer the peaches to the ice water to cool. Peel the peaches and cut them into 1/2-inch wedges; reserve the peach skins and pits. Transfer the peaches to a bowl and toss with the lemon juice. Cover the peaches and refrigerate.
2. In a medium saucepan, combine the cream and milk. Add the vanilla bean and seeds and peach skins and pits and bring to a simmer. Cover and remove from the heat. Let steep for 20 minutes. Strain the infused cream right into a bowl.
3. In a medium bowl, whisk the egg yolks with the sugar and salt. Whisk in half of the infused cream, then transfer the mixture to the saucepan, together with the remaining cream. Cook over moderate heat, stirring constantly with a wooden spoon, until slightly thickened and an instant-read thermometer inserted in the custard registers 165°, about five minutes. Immediately strain the custard into a clean bowl and stir in the maple syrup and bourbon. Refrigerate the custard until chilled, about 30 minutes.
4. In a blender, puree the peaches with 1 cup of the custard until smooth. Transfer the pureed peaches and the remaining custard to an ice cream maker and freeze according to the manufacturer's instructions. Transfer the ice cream to a plastic container. Press a sheet of plastic wrap directly onto the top and freeze until firm, about one hour.

## 259. Guinness Ice Cream Recipe

**Ingredients:**
- 2 cups heavy whipping cream
- 1 1/2 cups whole milk
- 1 cup white sugar
- 1 vanilla bean
- 6 large eggs yolks egg yolks, beaten
- 1 (12 fluid ounce) can or bottle irish stout beer (such as guinness)

**Directions:**
1. Combine cream, milk, and sugar in a saucepan over medium heat. Stir until sugar has dissolved, about five minutes.
2. Split the vanilla bean lengthwise with a sharp knife and scrape seeds into cream mixture. Place bean pod into mixture and bring to a boil. Remove from heat and discard vanilla bean pod.
3. Place egg yolks in a bowl. Gradually whisk in 1 cup hot cream mixture.
4. Whisk the egg yolk mixture back again to the saucepan and place over medium heat. Whisk constantly until slightly thickened, about 2-3 3 minutes. Mixture should coat the trunk of a spoon. Don't let the mixture boil.

5. Transfer cream mixture to a bowl and chill until cold, at least 2 hours to overnight.
6. Simmer Irish stout beer in a saucepan over low heat until reduced to 2/3 cup, in regards to a quarter-hour. Chill the stout beer syrup at least 2 hours to overnight.
7. Whisk together chilled cream mixture and beer syrup; pour into an ice cream maker and freeze according to manufacturer's directions.
8. When machine has finished, pack ice cream right into a airtight container and store in freezer.

### 260. Honey Vanilla Ice Cream Recipe
**Ingredients:**
- 2 cups milk
- 1 (7 inch) vanilla bean , split lengthwise
- 6 large eggs yolks egg yolks
- 1 cup packed brown sugar
- 3 tablespoons honey
- 1/4 teaspoon salt
- 2 cups heavy cream

**Directions:**
1. In a medium pan, heat the milk and vanilla bean to simmering. Do not boil. In a mixing bowl, whisk together the egg yolks, brown sugar, honey, and salt until light colored and frothy. While whisking constantly, slowly combine the hot milk with the egg mixture. Transfer the mixture back to the sauce pan. Cook over medium heat until mixture reaches 180 degrees Fahrenheit (82 degrees Celsius) when tested with a candy thermometer, or becomes thick enough to coat the trunk of a metal spoon. Remove from heat.
2. Remove the vanilla bean from the mixture and reserve. Strain custard into a huge bowl. Scrape seeds from the vanilla bean into the custard. (Vanilla bean pod may be used again.) Stir the heavy cream into the custard. Cover the top of custard with plastic wrap and refrigerate for 4 hours.
3. When cold, freeze within an ice cream maker based on the manufacturer's directions.

### 261. Vanilla Ice Cream Ix Recipe
**Ingredients:**
- 4 large eggs
- 2 1/2 cups white sugar
- 2 cups heavy cream
- 2 cups evaporated milk
- 5 cups whole milk
- 2 1/4 teaspoons vanilla extract
- 2 1/4 teaspoons lemon extract
- 1/2 teaspoon salt

**Directions:**
1. In a mixing bowl, beat eggs and sugar until stiff. Stir in cream, evaporated milk, dairy, vanilla, lemon extract and salt until well combined.
2. Pour into the freezer canister of an ice cream maker and freeze according to manufacturer's instructions.

### 262. Snow Ice Cream
**Ingredients:**
- 1 cup (8 oz.) sweetened condensed milk
- 1/3 cup sugar
- 1 teaspoon pure vanilla extract
- 4 cups snow
- sprinkles, for garnish if desired

**Directions:**
1. In a medium bowl, combine sweetened condensed milk, sugar and vanilla. Whisk until smooth. In a large bowl, pour condensed milk mixture over snow.
2. Stir to combine. Freeze 30 minutes to 1 hour or until almost solid. Scoop into bowls and serve. Garnish with sprinkles if desired.

### 263. Vegan Snickers Ice Cream Recipe
**Ingredients:**
- 2 cups ice cubes
- 1/2 cup soy milk
- 2 tablespoons crunchy peanut butter , or to taste
- 1 teaspoon carob powder, or more to taste

- 1 teaspoon agave nectar, or more to taste

**Directions:**
1. Place ice in a blender; add soy milk, peanut butter, carob powder, and agave nectar.
2. Blend mixture until smooth and thicken.

## 264. Salted Pecan-maple Ice Cream Recipe
**Ingredients:**
- 1/2 cup coarsely chopped pecans
- 2 tablespoons white sugar
- 1/2 teaspoon sea salt, or to taste
- 3/4 cup white sugar
- 1/4 cup real maple syrup
- 2 large eggs
- 1 teaspoon vanilla extract
- 1 drop maple-flavored extract, or to taste
- 3 cups half-and-half
- 1 pinch coarse sea salt, or to taste

**Directions:**
1. Place pecans right into a heavy saucepan over medium heat and toast the nuts, stirring constantly, until fragrant, one to two 2 minutes.
2. Sprinkle 2 tablespoons sugar over pecans and stir constantly before sugar melts to a light brown syrup and coats the pecans. Immediately pull the pan off the heat; sprinkle with 1/2 teaspoon sea salt.
3. Turn hot pecans out onto a bit of parchment paper and cool thoroughly; break apart any large clumps. Set candied pecans aside.
4. Whisk 3/4 cup sugar, maple syrup, eggs, vanilla extract, and maple flavoring in a sizable bowl until smooth. Slowly whisk in half-and-half.
5. Pour mixture into an ice cream maker and freeze according to manufacturer's instructions. Mix the candied pecans in to the softly-frozen ice cream. Sprinkle servings with a pinch of coarsely ground sea salt.

## 265. Divine Cherry Chocolate Ice Cream Recipe
**Ingredients:**
- 3 cups heavy cream
- 3 cups whole milk
- 1 cup white sugar
- 1 (10-ounce) jar maraschino cherries, with juice
- 8 large eggs yolks egg yolks
- 2 teaspoons almond extract
- 12 ounces bittersweet chocolate, chopped

**Directions:**
1. Stir together cream, milk, sugar, and the juice from the jar of cherries in a large saucepan over medium heat. Bring to a simmer, then remove from heat. Place the egg yolks into a sizable bowl, then whisk in hot cream, about 2 tablespoons at a time, until you have added 2 cups.
2. Whisk the hot yolks into the saucepan of hot cream, then cook on low, stirring constantly, before mixture reaches 170 degrees F (75 degrees C). It has thickened enough to coat the trunk of a metal spoon. Pour the mixture right into a container, cover, and refrigerate until cold, about 6 hours.
3. Chop the reserved maraschino cherries, then stir into the cold custard along with almond extract, and chopped chocolate. Pour into ice cream maker, and freeze according to manufacturer's directions.

## 266. Tropical Ice Cream Recipe
**Ingredients:**
- 2 cups heavy cream
- 1 1/3 cups 2% low-fat milk
- 2/3 cup pineapple and orange juice blend
- 3/4 cup sugar
- 1/3 cup flaked sweetened coconut
- 1/3 cup walnut pieces
- 1 large banana, sliced

**Directions:**
1. Whisk together cream, milk, pineapple-orange juice, and sugar until the sugar has dissolved. Pour into an ice cream maker and freeze according to manufacturer's instructions.

2. Five minutes prior to the ice cream is performed, add the coconut and walnut pieces. Two minutes prior to the ice cream is performed, add the sliced banana.

### 267. Peach-buttermilk Ice Cream

**Ingredients:**
- 1 1/2 pounds peaches (about 6 small), plus sliced peaches for serving
- 1 cup farm-fresh buttermilk
- 1 teaspoon grated lemons zest plus 2 tablespoons fresh lemon juice
- 6 large eggs yolks
- 2 cups heavy cream
- 1 cup sugar
- 1/8 teaspoon kosher salt
- 1 vanilla bean , split lengthwise, seeds scraped

**Directions:**
1. Bring a medium saucepan of water to a boil. Fill a huge bowl with ice water. Using a sharp paring knife, mark an X on the bottom of every peach. Add the peaches to the saucepan and blanch before skins start to peel away, 1 to 2 2 minutes. Transfer the peaches to the ice bath and let cool completely. Get rid of the saucepan.
2. Peel and chop the peaches. Transfer to a food processor and puree until smooth. Scrape into a huge bowl and whisk in the buttermilk, lemon zest and lemon juice. Cover and refrigerate until cold.
3. In a heatproof medium bowl, whisk the egg yolks. In the medium saucepan, simmer the cream with the sugar, salt and the vanilla bean and seeds over moderate heat, whisking occasionally, before sugar has dissolved, about five minutes. While whisking constantly, slowly stream half of the hot cream mixture in to the egg yolks. Pour the mixture back to the saucepan and cook over moderately low heat, whisking constantly, before custard is thick enough to coat the trunk of a spoon, 8 to ten minutes. Strain the custard through an excellent sieve set over a heatproof bowl and let cool to room temperature. Whisk in the chilled buttermilk-peach mixture. Press a sheet of plastic wrap directly onto the top of custard and refrigerate until cold, at least 3 hours.
4. Employed in 2 batches, freeze the ice cream base in an ice cream machine based on the manufacturer's instructions. Pack the ice cream into plastic containers and freeze until firm, at least 4 hours or overnight. Serve the ice cream topped with sliced peaches.

### 268. Espresso Chip Ice Cream Recipe

**Ingredients:**
- 3 large eggs yolks egg yolks
- 2 cups milk
- 2 1/2 cups whipping cream
- 2 teaspoons vanilla extract
- 1/2 cup brewed espresso , at room temperature
- 1/4 teaspoon salt
- 1 cup chocolate covered espresso beans , chopped
- 3/4 cup caramel topping

**Directions:**
1. Stir the egg yolks, milk, and cream together in a large pan over medium heat. Continue stirring, and cook the mixture until small bubbles form around the edges of the top, but do not boil. Remove from the heat, and stir in the vanilla extract, espresso, and salt. Cover, and refrigerate at least 6 hours.
2. Pour the cream mixture into an ice cream maker, and freeze for 20 minutes according to manufacturer's instructions. Stir in the espresso beans. Gently fold in the caramel sauce, and continue freezing until hard.

### 269. Strawberry Freeze Recipe

**Ingredients:**
- 1 cup buttermilk
- 3 cups fresh strawberries
- 1 cup white sugar, or to taste
- 3 cups buttermilk

**Directions:**
1. Place 1 cup buttermilk, strawberries, and sugar right into a blender.
2. Cover, and puree until smooth. Pour in the remaining 3 cups buttermilk and blend until combined. Pour into ice pop molds and freeze or if using an ice cream maker, freeze according to manufacturer's directions.

## 270. Cinnamon Ice Cream Ii Recipe

**Ingredients:**
- 3/4 cup heavy cream
- 2 tablespoons sour cream
- 6 large eggs
- 2/3 cup sugar
- 2 cups milk
- 1 tablespoon ground cinnamon
- 1 teaspoon vanilla extract

**Directions:**
1. In a medium bowl, stir together the heavy cream and sour cream. Reserve in a warm place for approximately an hour to thicken.
2. In another bowl, beat eggs with sugar using an electric mixer until pale. Stir in the milk and cinnamon, and transfer to a saucepan. Bring to a simmer over medium-low heat. Cook, stirring constantly, until thick enough to coat the trunk of a metal spoon. Stir in the vanilla, and remove from the heat. Reserve to cool.
3. When the custard has cooled, stir in the sour cream mixture. Freeze in an ice cream maker based on the manufacturer's instructions.

## 271. Dairy-free Coconut Candy Bar Ice Cream Recipe

**Ingredients:**
- 1 (15-ounce) can cream of coconut
- 1 (13.5 ounce) can coconut milk
- 1 cup unsweetened flaked coconut
- 2 (2-ounce) bars dark chocolate, chopped

**Directions:**
1. Whisk cream of coconut, coconut milk, and flaked coconut in a bowl. Cover and refrigerate for 8 hours or more.
2. Pour the chilled mixture into an ice cream maker and freeze according to manufacturer's directions until it reaches "soft-serve" consistency.
3. Melt the chocolate in a microwave-safe glass or ceramic bowl in 30-second intervals, stirring after each melting, for 1 to 3 minutes (depending on your microwave). Slowly drizzle chocolate into ice cream what machine is churning.
4. Transfer ice cream to a one- or two-quart lidded plastic container; cover surface with plastic wrap and seal. For best results, ice cream should ripen in the freezer for at least 2 hours or overnight.

## 272. Condensed-milk Ice Cream With Black Sesame Polvoron?

**Ingredients:**
- 2 cups heavy cream
- 1 (14-ounce) can sweetened condensed milk
- 1/4 cup brown rice flour
- 1/2 cup black sesame seeds
- 1/2 cup powdered milk
- 1/4 cup granulated sugar
- 1/4 cup unsalted butter, melted

**Directions:**
1. Place cream in a huge chilled bowl; beat with a power mixer until stiff peaks form, 2 to 3 three minutes. Gently fold in condensed milk until fully incorporated (do not overmix). Cover bowl with plastic wrap to ensure that plastic rests on surface of mixture. Freeze until firm, 8 to 10 hours.
2. Preheat oven to 325°F. Line a rimmed baking sheet with parchment paper. Spread rice flour in a thin layer on prepared baking sheet. Toast in preheated oven until flour smells nutty and is sandy in color, 12 to 14 minutes. Reserve. On a second parchment-lined rimmed baking sheet, spread sesame seeds in a thin, even layer, and toast until fragrant, six to eight 8 minutes. Let stand until cool.?

3. Place 1/3 cup toasted sesame seeds in the bowl of a food processor. Pulse until seeds are coarsely ground, about 8 times.?
4. Sift powdered milk, sugar, and toasted rice flour into a big bowl. Add ground sesame seeds and remaining toasted sesame seeds to bowl. Gently stir in melted butter. Let cool; transfer to an airtight container.?
5. To serve, spoon 3 small scoops of ice cream into a bowl, and sprinkle liberally with sesame mixture.

### 273. Pumpkin Pie Ice Cream Recipe

**Ingredients:**
- 1 cup pumpkins puree
- 2/3 cup white sugar
- 1 1/2 teaspoons pumpkins pie spice
- 1 cup whole milk
- 2 cups heavy whipping cream
- 1 teaspoon vanilla extract

**Directions:**
1. Mix pumpkin puree, sugar, and pumpkin pie spice together in a large bowl. Slowly whisk in milk, then whipping cream, then vanilla extract. Refrigerate to permit flavors to blend, 2 hours to overnight.
2. Transfer pumpkin mixture into an ice cream maker; churn for 15 to 20 minutes. Freeze according to manufacturer's directions until it reaches 'soft-serve' consistency.
3. Transfer ice cream to a lidded plastic container; cover surface with plastic wrap and seal. For best results, ice cream should 'bloom' in the freezer for at least 2 hours or overnight.

### 274. Easy Banana Ice Cream With Milk Chocolate Chunks

**Ingredients:**
- 3 ripe bananas
- 1 1/4 cups whole milk
- 1/3 cup sugar
- 1 teaspoon pure vanilla extract
- 1/8 teaspoon salt
- 1/2 cup heavy cream
- 3 ounces milk chocolate (preferably with nibs), chopped into 1/4-inch chunks

**Directions:**
1. In a blender, puree the bananas with the milk, sugar, vanilla, and salt until smooth. Transfer to a bowl and stir in a heavy cream and milk chocolate.
2. Pour the banana custard into an ice cream maker and freeze based on the manufacturer's instructions. Transfer the ice cream to an airtight container and freeze until firm, at least 4 hours. Let stand at room temperature for ten minutes before serving.

### 275. The Captain's Mango Ice Cream Recipe

**Ingredients:**
- 4 eaches mangoes, peeled and cubed
- 2 cups heavy whipping cream
- 3/4 cup packed dark brown sugar
- 1/4 cup light corn syrup
- 4 tablespoons spiced rum
- 1/2 teaspoon kosher salt

**Directions:**
1. Combine mangoes, cream, brown sugar, and corn syrup in a blender or food processor. Blend on high for 30 seconds.
2. Transfer to an airtight container. Stir in spiced rum and salt. Refrigerate, 8 hours to overnight.
3. Pour mixture into an ice cream maker and freeze according to manufacturer's instructions, about 20 minutes. Transfer to an airtight container and freeze until firm, about 4 hours.

### 276. Mudslide No-churn Ice Cream

**Ingredients:**
- 2 cups heavy cream
- 1 ounce 14.5- can sweetened condensed milk
- 1 cup chopped chocolate
- 1/4 cup hot fudge sauce, plus more for serving
- 2 tablespoons kahlua
- 2 tablespoons baileys irish cream

**Directions:**

1. In a stand mixer fitted with a whisk attachment, beat heavy cream until stiff peaks form, 5 minutes. Fold in sweetened condensed milk until fully combined, then fold in chocolate, fudge sauce, Kahlua, and Baileys.
2. Transfer mixture to a 9-x-5" loaf pan and add one more chocolate swirl on top. Freeze 5 hours. When ready to serve, let soften 10 minutes. Serve with warm hot fudge.

## 277. Coffee And Donuts Ice Cream Recipe
**Ingredients:**
- 4 eaches marble crullers (fried twisted stick doughnuts)
- 1 cup milk
- 2 tablespoons instant coffee granules
- 2 large eggs
- 3/4 cup white sugar
- 2 cups heavy cream

**Directions:**
1. Crumble or chop the crullers into small pieces. Do not over chop into crumbs, but make a variety of piece sizes. Set the doughnut pieces aside.
2. Gently heat the milk in a saucepan over low heat until hot but not boiling, and stir in the instant coffee granules until dissolved. Remove the milk mixture from the heat, and allow to cool.
3. Place the eggs in a mixing bowl, and beat for 3 minutes with an electric mixer until light, adding sugar about 2 tablespoons at a time until the sugar has been incorporated. Beat for 1 more minute, then beat the milk mixture and heavy cream into the eggs on low speed, until the mixture is smooth and creamy.
4. Place the mixture into an ice cream maker, and freeze according to manufacturer's instructions. When the ice cream is firm but not hard, lightly mix in the doughnut pieces. Pack the ice cream into a covered airtight container, and freeze for 6 to 8 hours, to ripen the flavor and firm the ice cream. Let the ice cream stand at room temperature for about 10 minutes before scooping into servings.

## 278. Vanilla-almond Ice Cream With Cherries And Pistachios
**Ingredients:**
- 6 large eggs yolks
- 1 1/2 cups heavy cream
- 1 1/2 cups whole milk
- 3/4 cup sugar
- 3/4 teaspoon kosher salt
- 1 vanilla bean , split lengthwise and seeds scraped
- 1/2 teaspoon pure almond extract
- 3/4 cup fresh cherries, pitted and halved
- 1/4 cup shelled pistachios, coarsely chopped

**Directions:**
1. Set a medium bowl in a large plate of ice water. In another medium bowl, beat the egg yolks until pale, one to two 2 minutes.
2. In a medium saucepan, whisk the cream with the milk, sugar, salt and the vanilla bean and seeds. Bring to a simmer, whisking, before sugar is completely dissolved. Very steadily whisk half of the hot cream mixture into the beaten egg yolks in a thin stream, then whisk this mixture into the saucepan. Cook over moderately low heat, stirring constantly with a wooden spoon, before custard is thick enough to lightly coat the back of the spoon, about 12 minutes; don't let it boil.
3. Strain the custard through a medium-mesh strainer into the bowl set in the ice water; discard the vanilla bean. Allow custard cool completely, stirring occasionally. Stir in the almond extract. Pour into a sizable resealable freezer bag and seal, pressing out the air. Lay the bag flat in the freezer and freeze until firm, at least 8 hours or overnight.
4. Working quickly, in batches if necessary, transfer the frozen custard to the plate of a food processor. Pulse at 5-second intervals until smooth.

Transfer the custard to a chilled 9-by-4-inch metal loaf pan and fold in the cherries and pistachios. Cover with plastic wrap and freeze until firm, about 6 hours or overnight.

## 279. Vanilla Ice Cream X Recipe

**Ingredients:**
- 1 frozen whipped topping (8 ounce) container frozen whipped topping thawed
- 1 can evaporated milk (12 fluid ounce) evaporated milk
- 1/2 can sweetened condensed milk (14 ounce) sweetened condensed milk
- 1 <small>1/2</small> teaspoons vanilla extract vanilla extract

**Directions:**
1. Beat whipped topping with evaporated and condensed milks and vanilla in a big bowl until smooth.
2. Pour into a round or rectangular container, seal tightly, and place in freezer every day and night.

## 280. Hazelnut Gelato Recipe

**Ingredients:**
- 2 cups whole milk
- 1 cup heavy whipping cream
- 1/3 cup white sugar
- 4 large eggs yolks egg yolks
- 1/3 cup white sugar
- 1/2 cup chocolate hazelnut spread
- 2 tablespoons instant espresso powder
- 1/2 teaspoon vanilla extract

**Directions:**
1. Combine milk, cream, and 1/3 cup sugar in a saucepan over medium heat; cook and stir until sugar dissolves, 3 to 5 minutes.
2. Beat egg yolks and 1/3 cup sugar together in a bowl until mixture is light yellow, about 4 minutes. Stir 1/2 cup milk mixture into egg mixture until smooth; pour into the remaining milk mixture in the saucepan, stirring continuously.
3. Cook, stirring continuously, until mixture thickens enough to coat the back of a metal spoon, 8 to 10 minutes; remove from heat.
4. Stir chocolate hazelnut spread, espresso powder, and vanilla extract into milk mixture until well combined; pour through a mesh strainer into a bowl. Refrigerate mixture until cold, about 3 hours.
5. Pour milk mixture into an ice cream maker and freeze according to manufacturer's instructions.

## 281. Instant Strawberry Ice Cream Recipe

**Ingredients:**
- 24 ounces frozen sweetened strawberries, cut into large chunks
- 1/2 cup sugar, plus
- 1 tablespoon sugar
- 1 1/2 cups heavy cream

**Directions:**
1. Place berries in blender. Whisk sugar into cream. With blender going, slowly add cream through opening in lid, stopping to stir the mixture three or four 4 times therefore the ice cream is smooth, with small items of berries.
2. Transfer to shallow pan and freeze to a scoopable texture, about 2 hours. Garnish with fresh strawberries, if you want.

## 282. How To Make Vanilla Ice Cream

**Ingredients:**
- 3/4 cup white sugar
- 1 cup heavy whipping cream
- 2 1/4 cups milk
- 2 teaspoons vanilla extract

**Directions:**
1. Stir sugar, cream, and milk into a saucepan over low heat until sugar has dissolved. Heat just until mix is hot and a little ring of foam appears around the edge.
2. Transfer cream mixture to a pourable container such as for example a big measuring cup. Stir in vanilla extract and chill mix thoroughly, at least 2 hours. (Overnight is most beneficial.)
3. Pour cold ice cream mix into an ice cream maker, start the device, and

churn according to manufacturer's directions, 20 to 25 minutes.
4. When ice cream is softly frozen, serve immediately or place a piece of plastic wrap on the ice cream and place in freezer to ripen, 2-3 3 hours.

### 283. Vanilla Bean Ice Cream
**Ingredients:**
- 2 cups whole milk
- 1 tablespoon plus 1 teaspoon cornstarch
- 1 1/2 ounces cream cheese, softened (3 tablespoons)
- 1 1/4 cups heavy cream
- 2/3 cup sugar
- 1 1/2 tablespoons light corn syrup
- 1 vanilla bean, split and seeds scraped
- 1/8 teaspoon kosher salt

**Directions:**
1. Fill a big bowl with ice water. In a little bowl, mix 2 tablespoons of the milk with the cornstarch. In another large bowl, whisk the cream cheese until smooth.
2. In a huge saucepan, combine the remaining milk with the heavy cream, sugar, corn syrup and vanilla bean and seeds. Bring the milk mixture to a boil and cook over moderate heat before sugar dissolves and the vanilla flavors the milk, about 4 minutes. Off heat, gradually whisk in the cornstarch mixture. Go back to a boil and cook over moderately high heat until the mixture is slightly thickened, about 1 minute.
3. Gradually whisk the hot milk mixture in to the cream cheese until smooth. Whisk in the salt. Set the bowl in the ice water bath and let stand, stirring occasionally, until cold, about 20 minutes.
4. Strain the ice cream base into an ice cream maker and freeze according to the manufacturer's instructions. Pack the ice cream into a plastic container.
5. Press a sheet of plastic wrap directly onto the top of ice cream and close with an airtight lid. Freeze the vanilla ice cream until firm, about 4 hours.

### 284. Roasted Peaches With Mascarpone Ice Cream
**Ingredients:**
- 4 large eggs yolks
- 3/4 cup plus 2 tablespoons sugar
- 2 cups whole milk
- 1 cup mascarpone (7 ounces)
- 1/2 teaspoon fresh lemon juice
- pinch of salt

**Directions:**
1. In a sizable bowl, using a handheld mixer, beat the egg yolks with 3/4 cup of the sugar at medium-high speed until fluffy, three minutes. In a saucepan, combine the milk with the remaining 2 tablespoons of the sugar and bring to a simmer. Slowly beat the warm milk in to the egg yolks at low speed. Scrape the custard in to the saucepan. Cook over moderate heat, stirring constantly with a wooden spoon, until thick enough to coat the back of the spoon, about 5 minutes; don't allow the custard boil.
2. Pour the custard right into a bowl set in a larger plate of ice water and whisk in the mascarpone, lemon juice and salt. Let stand until chilled, stirring occasionally, thirty minutes.
3. Pour the custard into an ice cream maker and freeze based on the manufacturer's instructions. Transfer the mascarpone ice cream to an airtight container and freeze until firm, at least 2 hours.
4. In a huge saucepan, combine the white wine, honey, water and sugar and bring to a boil. Boil until reduced by half, about thirty minutes. Add the rosemary sprig and let are a symbol of ten minutes; discard the rosemary.
5. Preheat the oven to 350°. Arrange the peaches within an 8-by-11-inch baking dish. Pour the rosemary syrup at the top and roast the peaches until tender, 40 minutes, basting and turning the peaches occasionally.

6. Scoop the mascarpone ice cream into bowls and top with the peach halves. Spoon the warm poaching liquid over the fruit and serve immediately.

### 285. Vanilla Cherry Ice Cream Recipe
**Ingredients:**
- 2 cups heavy cream
- 1 cup milk
- 3/4 cup white sugar
- 1 tablespoon vanilla extract
- 1 teaspoon almond extract
- 2 cups fresh cherries, pits removed and cut in half

**Directions:**
1. Combine the cream, milk, and sugar in a bowl. Stir until the sugar is completely dissolved. Stir in the vanilla and almond extract. Add the cherries.
2. Pour the mixture into an ice cream maker and churn based on the manufacturer's instructions. Transfer to a freezer-safe container and freeze for at least 2 hours before serving.

### 286. Graham Cracker Ice Cream Recipe
**Ingredients:**
- 2 cups fat free half-and-half
- 1/2 cup sugar
- 1/2 vanilla bean
- 3 eaches fat-free graham crackers, crushed

**Directions:**
1. Combine half-and-half and sugar in a huge bowl. Split vanilla bean lengthwise, scrape seeds into the bowl, and whisk to mix.
2. Pour cream mixture into ice cream maker, and process according to manufacturer's directions. When semi-frozen, sprinkle in the crushed graham crackers. Continue steadily to process until desired consistency is reached.

### 287. Vegan Pumpkin Ice Cream Recipe
**Ingredients:**
- 1/4 cup soy creamer
- 2 tablespoons arrowroot powder
- 1 3/4 cups soy creamer
- 1 cup soy milk
- 3/4 cup brown sugar
- 1 cup pumpkins puree
- 1 teaspoon vanilla extract
- 1 1/2 teaspoons pumpkins pie spice

**Directions:**
1. Mix 1/4 cup soy creamer with arrowroot and reserve. Whisk together 1 3/4 cup soy creamer, soy milk, brown sugar, pumpkin puree, vanilla extract, and pumpkin pie spice in a saucepan over medium heat, stirring frequently, until just boiling.
2. Remove the pan from heat; stir in the arrowroot mixture to thicken. Reserve to cool for thirty minutes.
3. Fill cylinder of ice cream freezer; freeze according to manufacturer's directions.

### 288. Orange-pineapple Ice Recipe
**Ingredients:**
- 1 (14-ounce) can sweetened condensed milk
- 1 (8-ounce) can crushed pineapple
- 1 gallon orange soda

**Directions:**
1. Combine condensed milk, pineapple and orange soda in freezer canister of ice cream maker. Freeze according to manufacturer's directions.

### 289. Fresh Fruit Ice Cream In A Baggie Recipe
**Ingredients:**
- 1 cup half-and-half cream
- 2 tablespoons white sugar
- 1 teaspoon vanilla extract
- 1/4 cup chopped fresh strawberries
- 4 cups ice cubes
- 1/4 cup kosher salt

**Directions:**
1. Combine the half and half, sugar, vanilla, and strawberries in a quart size resealable plastic bag. Press the air from the bag, seal, and shake bag to mix contents. Place the bag right into a gallon sized zip top bag. Add the ice to the gallon bag, press the air out, and seal bag.

2. Wrap bags in a soft towel. Shake continuously, until the contents of the tiny bag thickens into soft-serve ice cream, 5 to ten minutes.
3. Rinse the small bag quickly under cold water to clean off salt. Lay the ice cream filled baggie on a set surface. Use a wooden spoon handle to push the ice cream right down to underneath corner of the baggie. Snip off the corner, and squeeze ice cream right into a bowl.

## 290. Chocolate Hazelnut Tartufo Recipe
**Ingredients:**
- 2 cups milk whole milk
- 1 cup heavy cream heavy cream
- 1/3 cup sugar white sugar
- 4 eggs large egg yolks egg yolks
- 1/3 cup sugar white sugar
- 1/2 cup spread chocolate-hazelnut spread (such as Nutella)
- 2 tablespoons espresso instant espresso powder
- 1/2 teaspoon vanilla extract vanilla extract
- 3 ounces bittersweet chocolate fine quality bittersweet chocolate finely chopped
- 8 maraschino cherries cherries maraschino cherries
- 1/2 cup frozen whipped topping frozen whipped topping thawed

**Directions:**
1. Combine milk, cream, and 1/3 cup sugar in a medium saucepan over medium heat; stir before sugar dissolves, about three to five 5 minutes.
2. In another bowl, beat egg yolks and 1/3 cup sugar before egg yolks are light in color, about 4 minutes. Stir 1/2 cup of the milk mixture in to the egg yolks, then pour all the egg mixture in to the saucepan, stirring continuously. Cook, stirring continuously, until mixture thickens enough to coat the back of a metal spoon, 8 to ten minutes. Remove from heat.
3. Add the chocolate hazelnut spread, espresso powder, and vanilla, stirring until well combined. Pour through a mesh strainer right into a bowl. Refrigerate a long time until cold.
4. Pour into an ice cream maker and freeze according to manufacturer's directions. Transfer gelato into an airtight container and place in freezer until solid.
5. To help make the tartufo: Scoop 4-ounce portions of gelato and form into balls using your hands. Poke a hole in each ball and place 1 cherry in each, cover with gelato, and place on a baking sheet.
6. Roll gelato balls in the grated chocolate until coated and go back to the freezer until prepared to serve. Serve with whipped topping, if desired.

## 291. Truly Key Lime Pie Ice Cream Recipe
**Ingredients:**
- 1 (12 fluid ounce) can evaporated milk
- 1 (14-ounce) can sweetened condensed milk
- 2 cups milk
- 2/3 cup heavy cream
- 2 large eggs yolks egg yolks, beaten
- 1 cup white sugar
- 1 cup lime juice
- 2 teaspoons lemon extract
- 1 (3-ounce) package lime flavored jell-o mixes
- 6 large rectangular piece or 2 squares or 4 small rectangular pieces whole graham crackers

**Directions:**
1. In a saucepan over low heat, combine the evaporated milk, sweetened condensed milk, milk, and heavy cream. Cook until warm, whisking frequently. Once the mixture is hot to touch, whisk in the gelatin mix and sugar, stirring constantly until sugar and gelatin are completely dissolved. Whisk in the egg yolks, and remove from the heat. Stir in the lime juice and lemon extract.

2. Pour the mixture into an ice cream maker, and freeze based on the manufacturer's instructions. This recipe takes a little longer to create than the usual ice cream.
3. After the ice cream is thick, open the canister, and place large bits of graham cracker evenly on each side. They will break right into smaller pieces as the device churns. Mix for about 5 more minutes. Transfer to a freezer container, seal, and freeze until solid. I like to use 1 gallon resealable freezer bags.

## 292. Key Lime Ice Cream Recipe

**Ingredients:**
- 2 eggs large egg
- 1 <small>1/4</small> cups sugar white sugar
- 4 eggs large egg yolks egg yolks
- 1 tablespoon lemon zest lemon zest
- 2 <small>1/4</small> cups cream half-and-half cream
- 3/4 cup lime juice lime juice

**Directions:**
1. hisk together the eggs, egg yolks, sugar, lime juice, and lemon zest in a saucepan over medium heat until well-blended. Continuously stir the egg mixture with a wooden spoon until thickened, 7 to 8 minutes. The mixture ought to be thick enough to coat the trunk of the spoon. Remove from heat, and stir in the half and half until smooth. Strain the mixture through a fine sieve set over a clean bowl. Cover and chill the mixture in the refrigerator, stirring occasionally, until cool, about 1 hour.
2. Pour the chilled mixture into an ice cream maker and freeze according to manufacturer's directions until it reaches "soft-serve" consistency. Transfer ice cream to a one- or two-quart lidded plastic container; cover surface with plastic wrap and seal. For best results, ice cream should ripen in the freezer for at least 2 hours or overnight.

## 293. Maple Walnut Ice Cream Recipe

**Ingredients:**
- 1 1/2 cups heavy whipping cream
- 5 large eggs yolks egg yolks
- 1 1/2 cups milk
- 2 tablespoons white sugar
- 1 tablespoon corn syrup
- 3/4 cup maple syrup
- 1 teaspooncoarse salt
- 1/4 teaspoon vanilla extract
- 1 1/2 cups walnut halves
- 1/2 cup maple syrup
- 1 tablespoon maple syrup
- 1 pinch salt

**Directions:**
1. Pour cream into a large bowl and set a mesh strainer over the bowl. Whisk egg yolks together in a separate bowl.
2. Heat milk, sugar, and corn syrup together in a saucepan over medium-low heat until milk begins to steam, about 5 minutes. Slowly pour about 1/2 cup heated milk into the egg yolks, whisking constantly. Scrape egg yolk mixture into the saucepan with a heatproof spatula.
3. Cook and stir milk mixture constantly with the spatula, scraping the bottom of the saucepan often, until mixture thickens and coats the spatula, about 10 minutes. Remove saucepan from heat; pour mixture through the mesh strainer into the cream.
4. Stir 3/4 cup maple syrup, coarse salt, and vanilla into cream mixture, then place the bowl over a larger bowl of ice water; stir to cool to room temperature. Chill mixture in the refrigerator, about 2 hours.
5. Preheat oven to 275 degrees F (135 degrees C). Spread walnuts onto a baking sheet.
6. Toast walnuts in the preheated oven until they turn golden brown and become fragrant, about 15 minutes. Set nuts aside to cool to room temperature. Chop nuts coarsely.
7. Heat the 1/2 cup plus 1 tablespoon maple syrup in a saucepan until it comes to a boil. Stir in walnuts, and return to a boil. Stir nuts for 10

seconds, remove from heat; set aside to cool completely. The nuts will be wet and sticky when cooled.
8. Remove cream mixture from the refrigerator, pour into your ice cream maker, and freeze according to manufacturer's instructions. During the last few minutes of churning, stir in wet walnuts.

## 294. Ricotta Ice Cream With Honey And Almonds

**Ingredients:**
- 3/4 cup sliced almonds
- 1 pint vanilla ice cream
- 1 1/2 cups ricotta cheese
- 1/2 cup honey

**Directions:**
1. In a small frying pan, toast the almonds over moderately low heat, stirring frequently, until golden brown, about 5 minutes. Or toast them in a 350° oven for 5 to ten minutes. Let cool completely.
2. Put a big metal bowl in the freezer. Allow ice cream stand at room temperature until just starting to soften but nonetheless frozen. In a food processor, puree the ricotta and honey until smooth.
3. Take away the bowl from the freezer and put the ice cream in it. Stir until smooth. Stir in the ricotta mixture. Transfer the ice-cream mixture to a shallow stainless-steel pan and return it to the freezer, covered, until firm enough to scoop, about 60 minutes. Serve the ice cream topped with the toasted almonds.

## 295. Chai Tea Ice Cream Recipe

**Ingredients:**
- 3 cups whole milk, or more to taste
- 3 cups heavy whipping cream
- 3 cups white sugar
- 4 cinnamon sticks cinnamon sticks
- 4 tablespoons indian-style plain black tea
- 3 tablespoons garam masala (indian spice blend)
- 10 eaches black peppercorns
- 6 eaches cardamom pods
- 2 eaches whole star anise pods
- 1 teaspoon ground nutmeg
- 1 tablespoon vanilla extract
- 1 cup chopped semisweet chocolate

**Directions:**
1. Mix dairy, whipping cream, sugar, cinnamon sticks, tea, garam masala, peppercorns, cardamom pods, anise pods, and nutmeg together in a saucepan; bring to a simmer and cook for 20 minutes.
2. Strain mixture through a colander into a sizable bowl. Soon add up to 1 cup more milk to cut spice level and sweetness to your liking.
3. Pour milk mixture into an ice cream maker and churn according to the manufacturer's instructions.
4. Stir chocolate into the churned milk mixture and freeze, stirring occasionally, until soft and creamy, 4 to 5 hours.

## 296. Peanut Butter-banana V'ice Cream

**Ingredients:**
- 4 very ripe bananas
- 1/4 cup peanut butter (smooth or chunky)
- 1 tablespoon coconut oils
- 1/2 teaspoon ground cinnamon
- 1/4 teaspoon grated nutmeg
- pinch of kosher salt

**Directions:**
1. Slice bananas into 1/4"-thick rounds and devote a ziptop plastic bag. Lay the slices flat in a single layer in the freezer therefore the rounds freeze individually rather than in a large clump.
2. Freeze the bananas for at least 2 hours and up to overnight. Place the frozen bananas, peanut butter, coconut oil, cinnamon, nutmeg, and salt in a food processor or blender and let sit for 2 or 3 three minutes. Then puree until creamy and smooth. If you like a frozen yogurt consistency, then serve it up.
3. If you like a firmer ice cream experience, spoon it right into a

container and freeze for approximately an hour.

### 297. Pumpkin Ice Cream Recipe

**Ingredients:**
- 1 (15-ounce) can pumpkins
- 1 cup white sugar
- 1 teaspoon salt
- 1 teaspoon ground ginger
- 1 teaspoon ground cinnamon
- 1/2 teaspoon ground nutmeg
- 1 cup chopped pecans
- 1/2 gallon vanilla ice cream, softened
- 36 wafers vanilla wafers

**Directions:**
1. In a large bowl, combine pumpkin, sugar, salt, ginger, cinnamon and nutmeg and mix until well blended. Stir in pecans. Fold in ice cream.
2. Line a 9x13 inch dish or sealable plastic container with 18 cookies. Spread half the ice cream mixture over the cookies. Repeat layers. Freeze until firm.

### 298. Granny's Ice Cream Recipe

**Ingredients:**
- 4 large eggs whites egg whites
- 2/3 cup sour cream
- 1/2 cup white sugar
- vanilla

**Directions:**
1. In a big glass or metal mixing bowl, beat egg whites until foamy. Gradually add white sugar and vanilla, continuing to beat until soft peaks form. Carefully fold in sour cream until well blended. Fold in any additional flavorings or goodies now.
2. Place the mixture into the freezer and stir every 30 minutes or so until frozen. This could be made without stirring, however the texture will be icy instead of creamy. When you have an ice cream maker, you can put the ice cream mixture in the maker, and follow the manufacturer's instructions.

### 299. Cinnamon Ice Cream Recipe

**Ingredients:**
- 1 cup white sugar
- 1 1/2 cups half-and-half cream
- 2 large eggs, beaten
- 1 cup heavy cream
- 1 teaspoon vanilla extract
- 2 teaspoons ground cinnamon

**Directions:**
1. In a saucepan over medium-low heat, stir together the sugar and half-and-half. When the mixture to simmer, remove from heat, and whisk half of the mixture eggs.
2. Whisk quickly the eggs scramble. Pour the egg mixture the saucepan, and stir in the heavy cream.
3. Continue cooking over medium-low heat, stirring constantly, mixture is thick enough to coat of a metal spoon. Remove from heat, and whisk in vanilla and cinnamon. to cool.
4. Pour cooled mixture into an ice cream maker, and freeze manufacturer's instructions.

### 300. Strawberry Rosewater Ice Cream Recipe

**Ingredients:**
- 1 1/2 cups fresh strawberries, hulled
- 1/3 cup white sugar
- 3 eaches eggs yolks, beaten
- 1/2 pint milk
- 1/4 teaspoon salt
- 1/3 cup white sugar
- 1 pint heavy cream
- 1/4 cup rosewater

**Directions:**
1. Combine the strawberries and 1/3 cup sugar in a bowl; mash as well as a potato masher. Store the mixture in the refrigerator while preparing all of those other recipe.
2. Stir together the egg yolks, milk, salt and 1/3 cup sugar in a saucepan over medium heat. Heat to 175 degrees F (80 degrees C), making sure the mixture will not boil; transfer to a chilled bowl and move to the refrigerator to cool, stirring occasionally. Once cooled, stir in the cream, rosewater, and strawberry mixture.

3. Fill an ice cream maker with the mixture, and freeze based on the manufacturer's instructions.

## 301. Fig Ice Cream Recipe

**Ingredients:**
- 2 cups dried figs
- 2 tablespoons white sugar
- 1 teaspoon lemon juice
- 2 1/2 cups half-and-half
- 1/2 cup white sugar
- 3 large eggs yolks egg yolks
- 1 teaspoon salt
- 1 cup reduced-fat sour cream
- 1 teaspoon vanilla extract

**Directions:**
1. Soak figs in a plate of water until softened, three to four 4 hours. Drain figs and chop.
2. Combine chopped figs, 2 tablespoons sugar, and lemon juice in a saucepan over medium heat; cook and stir until until sugar is dissolved and figs begin to break down, 4 to 5 minutes. Remove saucepan from heat and cool to room temperature, 15 to 20 minutes. Cover saucepan with a lid and refrigerate.
3. Heat half-and-half in a heavy saucepan over medium-high heat until hot however, not boiling, 5 to 6 minutes. Remove saucepan from heat.
4. Whisk 1/2 cup sugar, egg yolks, and salt together in a bowl until smooth. Temper egg mixture by drizzling 1 to 2 2 tablespoons half-and-half into egg mixture, while consistently whisking egg mixture until slightly warmed. Pour egg mixture into half-and-half and return saucepan to medium-low heat; cook, whisking constantly, until custard is smooth and thickened, about five minutes.
5. Place saucepan with custard in the refrigerator, stirring occasionally, until chilled, about thirty minutes. Stir sour cream and vanilla extract into chilled custard. Cover saucepan and chill custard completely, at least 3 hours.
6. Process custard within an ice cream maker according to manufacturer's instructions. Stir fig mixture into ice cream within the last 5 minutes of processing. Transfer fig ice cream to a container and freeze until solid.

## 302. Coffee And Doughnuts Ice Cream Recipe

**Ingredients:**
- 3 doughnut (3-3/4" dia)s day-old glazed doughnuts, cut into 8 pieces
- 1 cup cold, strong, brewed coffee
- 1/2 cup sugar
- 2 cups heavy cream
- 1 (14-ounce) can sweetened condensed milk
- 1/2 cup milk
- 1 teaspoon vanilla extract

**Directions:**
1. Place the doughnut pieces within a layer in the bottom of a shallow dish. Pour just enough of the coffee over the doughnuts so the liquid is totally absorbed by the doughnuts. Put the dish in the freezer.
2. Mix the remaining coffee with the sugar, cream, sweetened condensed milk, milk, and vanilla in a bowl; stir.
3. Pour the mixture into an ice cream maker and freeze according to manufacturer's directions before ice cream cycle is completed. Fold the frozen doughnuts in to the mixture; transfer ice cream to a one- or two-quart lidded plastic container; cover surface with plastic wrap and seal. Ripen in the freezer for at least 12 hours.

## 303. Keto No-churn Strawberry Ice Cream Recipe

**Ingredients:**
- 1 cup heavy whipping cream
- 1/3 cup chopped strawberries
- 2 tablespoons low-calorie natural sweetener (such as swerve)
- 1 tablespoon vodka
- 1 teaspoon vanilla extract
- 1/4 teaspoon xanthan gum
- 1 pinch salt

**Directions:**
1. Combine heavy cream, strawberries, sweetener, vodka, vanilla extract, xanthan gum, and salt in a wide-mouth pint-size jar.
2. Using an immersion blender and an along motion, blend cream mixture for 60 to 75 seconds, or until thickened and soft peaks have formed.
3. Cover jar and freeze, stirring every 30 to 40 minutes, until ice cream reaches your ideal consistency, 3 to4 hours.

### 304. Frozen Vanilla Custard
**Ingredients:**
- 5 large eggs yolks
- 2/3 cup white sugar
- 1 pinch salt
- 1 cup whole milk
- 2 cups heavy cream
- 2 1/2 teaspoons pure vanilla extract

**Directions:**
1. Whisk egg yolks, sugar, and salt together until mixture changes from dark golden to pale yellow becomes fluffy.
2. Heat milk and cream in much saucepan over medium heat. Stir occasionally to avoid sticking to underneath. Cook just until mixture starts to simmer when little bubbles begin to appear on the top, 5 to 8 minutes. Remove from heat.
3. Whisk a ladleful of milk-cream mixture into the egg yolk mixture. Add another ladleful and whisk thoroughly before adding the next (this could keep the eggs from cooking). Gradually add the rest of the milk-cream mixture and whisk thoroughly. Whisk in vanilla. Cool completely (you can place the bowl in a more substantial bowl with ice water to cool it faster).
4. Pour cooled mixture right into a pitcher; cover. Refrigerate until ice cold or overnight.
5. Pour custard mixture into ice cream maker and process (according to manufacturer's instructions) until custard reaches the consistency of soft ice cream, about 20 minutes. Quickly transfer to a plastic container.
6. Place a bit of plastic wrap over the top of custard. Cover container and freeze until custard is firm enough to scoop, at least 3 hours.

### 305. Ice Cream In A Bag
**Ingredients:**
- 1 cup half-and-half
- 2 tablespoons granulated sugar
- 1/2 teaspoon pure vanilla extract
- 3 cups ice
- 1/3 cup kosher salt
- toppings of your choice

**Directions:**
1. In a little resealable plastic bag, combine half-and-half, sugar, and vanilla. Push out excess air and seal. Into a big resealable plastic bag, combine ice and salt.
2. Place small bag in the bigger bag and shake vigorously, 7 to ten minutes, until ice cream has hardened. Remove from bag and revel in with your preferred ice cream toppings.

### 306. Vanilla Ice Cream Vii Recipe
**Ingredients:**
- 1 quart heavy cream
- 1 1/4 cups milk
- 1 vanilla bean , split and scraped
- 1 1/4 cups white sugar, divided
- 10 large eggs yolks egg yolks
- 1 tablespoon vanilla extract

**Directions:**
1. In a heavy saucepan over medium heat, combine cream and milk. Place vanilla bean and scrapings in pot, and sprinkle with half the white sugar. Allow to just come to a boil.
2. Meanwhile, whisk the egg yolks alongside the rest of the sugar and the vanilla extract in a bowl. When the cream is ready, pour a third of it into the egg mixture, and whisk. Pour egg mixture into remaining hot cream and go back to heat until mixture coats the trunk of a metal spoon. Will not boil.

3. Strain custard and chill until cold. Then pour into the canister of an ice cream maker and freeze according to manufacturer's instructions.

### 307. Ice Cream Base Recipe

**Ingredients:**
- 1 cup heavy cream
- 3 cups half-and-half cream
- 8 large eggs yolks egg yolks
- 1 cup white sugar
- 1 teaspoon salt

**Directions:**
1. Pour the heavy cream and half-and-half cream heavy saucepan, place over medium-low heat, and heat until barely simmering, stirring frequently. Turn down to low.
2. Whisk together the egg yolks, sugar, and salt in bowl until thoroughly combined.
3. Slowly pour about 1/2 cup of hot cream mixture egg yolk mixture|is better, whisking constantly. Repeat more, whisking thoroughly before adding each additional 1/2 cup of hot cream to the egg yolk mixture. Pour the egg yolk mixture the saucepan with hot cream, and whisk constantly over medium-low heat mixture thickens coat of a spoon, 5 to 8 minutes. mixture boil.
4. Pour the ice cream base bowl to cool 20 minutes; place in refrigerator and chill overnight. , pour into an ice cream maker, and freeze manufacturer's directions. ice cream, pack covered container, and freeze for 2 hours or overnight before serving.

### 308. Unicorn Ice Cream

**Ingredients:**
- 3 cups heavy cream
- 1 11 cans -oz. sweetened condensed milk
- 1 teaspoon pure vanilla extract
- 2 drops each assorted food coloring (pink, purple, green, blue, yellow)
- sprinkles, for topping (optional)

**Directions:**
1. In a huge bowl using a hand mixer or in the bowl of a stand mixer using the whisk attachment, whisk heavy cream until medium peaks form.
2. Fold in sweetened condensed milk and vanilla until totally combined, then divide mixture among 5 bowls. Put in a different color food coloring to each bowl (we used pink, purple, green, blue and yellow) and stir until combined. Layer dollops of the colors in a 9"-x-5" loaf pan until you go out of the mixture.
3. Smooth the very best and run a knife through the mixture to swirl the colors (don't overmix if not the colors can be muddy; 4 to 5 swirls ought to be plenty). Top with sprinkles (if using) and freeze until firm, 5 hours. Remove from freezer and let soften, 5 to ten minutes, then scoop and serve.

### 309. Keto Strawberry Ice Cream Recipe

**Ingredients:**
- 5 eaches strawberries , hulled
- 2 1/2 cups heavy whipping cream
- 2/3 cup low-calorie natural sweetener (such as swerve)
- 1/2 cup water
- 2 teaspoons vanilla extract
- 1 teaspoon lemon juice
- 1/2 teaspoon vodka
- 1 pinch salt

**Directions:**
1. Place strawberries in a food processor or blender; puree until smooth.
2. Whisk strawberry puree, cream, sweetener, water, vanilla extract, lemon juice, vodka, and salt together in a bowl; pour into an ice cream maker.
3. Process ice cream according to manufacturer's instructions. Transfer to a freezer-safe container and freeze until firm.

### 310. Easy Pistachio Ice Cream Recipe

**Ingredients:**
- 1 (14-ounce) can sweetened condensed milk

- 1 1/2 cups milk
- 1 (3.4-ounce) package instant pistachio pudding mixes

**Directions:**
1. Mix sweetened condensed milk, milk, and pudding mix together in a bowl; transfer to an ice cream maker and process according to manufacturers' instructions.

## 311. Roman's Dairy-free Chocolate-coconut Ice Cream

**Ingredients:**
- 3 cups unsweetened coconut milk
- 3 tablespoons agave syrup
- 1 1/4 cups sugar
- 2/3 cup unsweetened cocoa powder
- 3 large eggs yolks
- 1 tablespoon pure vanilla extract
- 1/2 cup unsweetened coconut flakes

**Directions:**
1. Set a fine-mesh sieve in a big bowl set over a bowl of ice water.
2. In a huge saucepan, whisk the coconut milk and agave syrup over moderately low heat until warm. In a medium heatproof bowl, whisk the sugar and cocoa powder. Gradually whisk in 1 cup of the warm coconut milk until smooth, then whisk in the egg yolks. Scrape the cocoa paste into the saucepan and whisk until blended. Cook the custard over moderate heat, whisking constantly, for about 6 minutes, until scorching and slightly thickened; don't let it boil. Immediately strain the custard into the prepared bowl and stir in the vanilla. Stir the custard until chilled.
3. Freeze the custard within an ice cream maker based on the manufacturers' directions. Transfer the ice cream to a big plastic container and freeze until firm, at least 4 hours.
4. In a little skillet, toast the coconut flakes over low heat until lightly browned, 4 minutes. Transfer to a plate and let cool. Serve the ice cream topped with toasted coconut.

## 312. Keto Ice Cream

**Ingredients:**
- 2 15 cans 2 (15-oz.) coconut milk
- 2 cups heavy cream
- 1/4 cup swerve confectioner's sweetener
- 1 teaspoon pure vanilla extract
- pinch kosher salt

**Directions:**
1. Chill coconut milk in the fridge at least 3 hours, ideally overnight.
2. Make whipped coconut: Spoon coconut cream into a big bowl, leaving liquid in can, and use a hand mixer to beat coconut cream until very creamy.
3. Reserve. Make whipped cream: In another large bowl utilizing a hand mixer (or in a plate of a stand mixer), beat heavy cream until soft peaks form.
4. Beat in sweetener and vanilla. Fold whipped coconut into whipped cream, then transfer mixture into a loaf pan. Freeze until solid, about 5 hours.

## 313. Strawberry Shortcake No-churn Ice Cream

**Ingredients:**
- 2 cups heavy cream
- 1 14 cans -oz. sweetened condensed milk
- 2 cups chopped strawberries, plus more for topping
- 1 cup chopped poundcake, plus more for topping

**Directions:**
1. In a stand mixer fitted with the whisk attachment, beat heavy cream until stiff peaks form. Fold in sweetened condensed milk, strawberries, and pound cake.
2. Transfer mixture to a 9"-x-5" loaf pan and smooth top with a spatula. Top with additional strawberries and pound cake and freeze until firm, 5 hours. When prepared to serve, remove from freezer to let soften, 10 minutes.

### 314. Homemade Pumpkin Frozen Yogurt Recipe

**Ingredients:**
- 2 cups plain whole milk yogurt
- 1 cup whipping cream
- 1 cups raw sugar
- 1 cup pumpkins puree
- 3 tablespoons brandy
- 1 teaspoon vanilla extract
- 1 teaspoon pumpkins pie spice
- teaspoonsea salt

**Directions:**
1. Combine the yogurt, cream, sugar, pumpkin puree, brandy, vanilla extract, pumpkin pie spice, and salt in a mixing bowl. Whisk together until the sugar and salt have completely dissolved. Cover, and refrigerate overnight.
2. Pour the chilled mixture into an ice cream maker and freeze according to manufacturer's directions until it reaches "soft-serve" consistency, about 20 minutes. Transfer ice cream to a one- or two-quart lidded container.
3. For best results, ice cream should ripen in the freezer for at least 2 hours or overnight.

### 315. Homemade Peanut Butter Ice Cream Recipe

**Ingredients:**
- 1 (14-ounce) can sweetened condensed milk
- 1 (12-ounce) can evaporated milk
- 1 1/4 cups whole milk
- 1/2 cup peanut butter (no sweetener added)
- 1/4 cup white sugar
- 2 teaspoons vanilla extract
- 6 eaches peanut butter cups, chopped

**Directions:**
1. Combine sweetened condensed milk, evaporated milk, whole milk, peanut butter, sugar, and vanilla extract in an ice cream maker. Stir until sugar dissolves. Freeze according to manufacturer's directions until it reaches soft-serve consistency, adding peanut butter cups halfway through freezing cycle.
2. Transfer ice cream to a one- or two-quart lidded plastic container; cover surface with plastic wrap and seal. For best results, ice cream should ripen in the freezer for at least 2 hours or overnight.

### 316. Vanilla Ice Cream Ii Recipe

**Ingredients:**
- 6 large eggs
- 6 (12 fluid ounce) cans evaporated milk
- 1 (14-ounce) can sweetened condensed milk
- 3 cups white sugar
- 1 1/2 teaspoons vanilla extract
- 2 cups milk , or as needed

**Directions:**
1. Combine eggs, evaporated milk, condensed milk, sugar, and vanilla and mix well.
2. Pour mixture into an ice cream maker. Add milk, if necessary, for mixture to attain the fill line. Freeze according to manufacturer's directions.

### 317. Vanilla Ice Cream V Recipe

**Ingredients:**
- 2 quarts half-and-half cream
- 1/2 pint heavy cream
- 1 1/2 cups white sugar
- 4 teaspoons vanilla extract
- 1 pinch salt

**Directions:**
1. Combine half-and-half, cream, sugar, vanilla and salt in freezer container of ice cream maker.
2. Freeze according to manufacturer's instructions.

### 318. Chocolate Syrup Ice Cream Recipe

**Ingredients:**
- 2 pints heavy cream , chilled
- 1/3 cup unsweetened cocoa powder
- 3/4 cup chocolate syrup
- 2 (14-ounce) cans sweetened condensed milk
- 1/4 teaspoon ground cinnamon

**Directions:**

1. In a large bowl, beat cream with cocoa until stiff peaks form. Stir in chocolate syrup, sweetened condensed milk and cinnamon. Pour into a shallow dish or plastic container, cover and freeze 8 hours or until firm.

### 319. Sparkling Ice Cream

**Ingredients:**
- 2 cups heavy cream
- 1 145 cans 1 (14.5-oz.) sweetened condensed milk
- 2 tablespoons honey
- 2 tablespoons prosecco
- gold and silver sprinkles, for garnish

**Directions:**
1. In a stand mixer fitted with a whisk attachment, or utilizing a hand mixer, beat heavy cream until stiff peaks form, five minutes.
2. Fold in sweetened condensed milk and honey until fully combined, then fold in prosecco. Transfer mixture to a 9-x-5" loaf pan and top with sprinkles. Freeze for 5 hours. When prepared to serve, let soften ten minutes.
3. Serve in flutes with an increase of Prosecco if desired.

### 320. Ice Cream Salad Recipe

**Ingredients:**
- 1/2 (8-ounce) package reduced-fat cream cheese, softened
- 3 ounces marshmallow creme
- 1/2 cup reduced-fat vanilla yogurt
- 1 large apple, cut into chunks
- 1 cup sliced strawberries
- 1/2 cup jicama, cut into matchsticks
- 1/2 cup mandarin orange segments
- 1/2 cup blueberries
- 1/2 cup chopped walnuts, toasted
- 8 cones flat bottomed ice cream cones

**Directions:**
1. Beat cream cheese, marshmallow creme, and vanilla yogurt together in a bowl until smooth.
2. Mix apple, strawberries, jicama, mandarin orange segments, blueberries, and walnuts in a sizable bowl.
3. Pour cream cheese mixture over fruit and toss to mix. Cover and refrigerate until well chilled.
4. Scoop fruit and cream cheese mixture into ice cream cones to serve.

### 321. Nesquik Frostee No-churn Ice Cream

**Ingredients:**
- 3 cups heavy cream
- 1 145 cans 1 14.5-oz. sweetened condensed milk
- 1/3 cup Nesquik chocolate flavor powder

**Directions:**
1. In a big mixing bowl, beat heavy cream using an electric mixer until stiff peaks form, 5 to 6 minutes.
2. Mix in the sweetened condensed milk and Nesquik. Pour mixture right into a loaf pan and freeze for at least 4 hours, or until firm. (The texture is a lot like soft serve.) Optional: Dust ice cream with a light sprinkling of Nesquik powder before serving.

### 322. Chunky Banana Nut Chip Ice Cream Recipe

**Ingredients:**
- 4 medium (7" to 7-7/8" long)s bananas, broken into chunks
- 1 tablespoon lemon juice
- 1 teaspoon vanilla extract
- 1 cup white sugar
- 1 1/3 cups heavy cream, chilled
- 2/3 cup cold milk
- 1/2 cup chopped toasted walnuts
- 1/2 cup miniature semisweet chocolate chips

**Directions:**
1. In a blender or food processor, combine bananas, lemon juice, vanilla, sugar, cream and milk. Puree until smooth. Transfer mixture to the freezer canister of an ice cream maker and freeze according to manufacturer's instructions.
2. When ice cream starts to stiffen, add walnuts and chocolate chips.

## 323. Easy Ice Cream In A Bag Recipe

**Ingredients:**
- 1/4 cup milk
- 1/4 cup half-and-half
- 1 tablespoon white sugar
- 1/4 teaspoon vanilla extract
- 1 cup ice cubes, or as needed
- 3 tablespoons ice cream rock salt

**Directions:**
1. Combine milk, half-and-half, sugar, and vanilla extract in a pint-size resealable plastic bag; seal tightly.
2. Put a scoop of ice, 3 tablespoons ice cream rock salt, and the bag containing the milk-cream mixture right into a gallon-size resealable plastic bag; seal tightly.
3. Rock the bag backwards and forwards (usually do not shake) until contents thicken into ice cream, about 10 minutes. Wipe salt from the very best of the pint-size bag before opening to prevent salt from getting into the ice cream.

## 324. Chocolate Frosty Recipe

**Ingredients:**
- 1 quart chocolate milk
- 1 (14-ounce) can sweetened condensed milk
- 1 (8-ounce) container frozen whipped topping (such as cool whip®), thawed

**Directions:**
1. Mix chocolate milk, sweetened condensed milk, and whipped topping in a large bowl.
2. Pour mixture into an ice cream maker and freeze according to manufacturer's instructions.

## 325. Pecan Caramel Ice Cream Recipe

**Ingredients:**
- 1 cup caramel ice cream topping
- 3 1/2 cups milk
- 1 (14-ounce) can sweetened condensed milk (such as eagle brand®)
- 1 (3.5 ounce) package instant vanilla pudding mix
- 1 teaspoon vanilla extract
- 1/2 teaspoon salt
- 1 1/2 cups coarsely chopped pecans, or more to taste

**Directions:**
1. Place caramel ice cream topping right into a microwave-safe container and heat in microwave until slightly warmed and softened, 10 to 30 seconds.
2. Whisk caramel topping, milk, sweetened condensed milk, instant vanilla pudding mix, vanilla extract and salt in a huge mixing bowl until pudding mix has dissolved and batter is smooth.
3. Cover bowl and chill batter thoroughly, at least 6 hours to overnight.
4. Pour chilled batter into an ice cream maker and freeze according to manufacturer's instructions; stir pecans into soft ice cream at end of freezing time.
5. Serve soft if desired. If a harder ice cream is recommended, pack pecan ice cream right into a lidded container and freeze to desired consistency

## 326. Smooth Raspberry Ice Cream Recipe

**Ingredients:**
- 4 cups fresh raspberries
- 2 large eggs
- 1 1/3 cups white sugar
- 1 1/2 cups half-and-half
- 1 cup heavy whipping cream
- 1/4 cup light corn syrup
- 1 tablespoon lemon juice

**Directions:**
1. Puree raspberries in a blender or food processor; pour mixture through a strainer to eliminate seeds.
2. Beat eggs and sugar together in a bowl until smooth. Stir raspberry puree, half-and-half, cream, corn syrup, and lemon juice into the egg-sugar mixture.
3. Transfer raspberry cream mixture to the ice cream maker. Freeze according to the manufacturer's instructions.

## 327. Chef John's Strawberry Ice Cream Recipe

**Ingredients:**
- 12 ounces fresh strawberries, hulled
- 3/4 cup white sugar
- 2 cups heavy whipping cream
- 1 cup milk
- 1 teaspoon vanilla extract
- 1 tiny pinch salt
- 2 drops red food coloring

**Directions:**
1. Place strawberries and sugar in a blender and pulse until pureed; steep for ten minutes.
2. Pour cream, milk, vanilla extract, and salt into strawberry mixture; blend until smooth and slightly thickened, 10 to 15 seconds. Whisk red food color into cream mixture.
3. Pour strawberry mixture into the container of an ice cream maker and freeze according to the manufacturer's instructions. Transfer ice cream to a sealable container, cover the ice cream with plastic wrap, seal the container, and freeze, 2 hours to overnight.
4. Process within an ice cream maker until thick. Immediately transfer to a sealable container, cover with plastic wrap, cover the bowl with a lid and freeze for 2 hours to overnight.

## 328. Ice Cream Cones

**Ingredients:**
- 1 large sheet heavy-duty aluminum foil (20x12 inch)
- 2 large eggs whites large egg whites, room temperature
- 1/2 cup white sugar
- 1/2 cup packed all-purpose flour, plus more if needed
- 2 tablespoons whole milk
- 2 tablespoons melted butter
- 1 tablespoon cold water, or as needed
- 1/4 teaspoon vanilla extract
- 1 teaspoon kosher salt

**Directions:**
1. Preheat oven to 400 degrees F (200 degrees C). Line a rimmed baking sheet with a silicone baking mat.
2. Fold aluminum foil in half and bunch it up to create a solid cone form with a pointy end and a wider end about how big is an ice cream cone. This will be utilized to shape the cones if they come out of the oven.
3. Whisk egg whites and sugar together in a mixing bowl until mixture is smooth and shiny, about 2 minutes. Add flour, milk, melted butter, water, vanilla, and salt. Whisk together until thoroughly combined.
4. Ladle about one to two 2 tablespoons batter on 1 side of silicone mat on prepared baking sheet. Gently swirl the batter with the trunk of the ladle outwards to make a fairly thin flat circle 5 or 6 inches in diameter. If necessary, you may use a pastry brush to even the thickness. If batter seems too thin, add a bit more flour. If too thick, more water. Bake in batches, 2 per batch.
5. Bake in preheated oven until edges are browned around the outside few inches, about 8 minutes.
6. Gently loosen among the circles. While still hot, place the aluminum foil cone mold using one end and roll the circle right into a cone shape, pressing together the pointed bottom to seal it. Put on a cooking rack seam side down. You may need to put the pan back the oven for one minute to heat the next circle; they must be hot to wrap around the mold. Repeat for the rest of the cones.

## 329. Easy Chocolate Ice Cream Recipe

**Ingredients:**
- 1 (14-ounce) can sweetened condensed milk
- 2/3 cup chocolate syrup
- 2 cups heavy cream

**Directions:**
1. Line a 9x5 inch loaf pan with aluminum foil. In a sizable bowl, stir together condensed milk and chocolate syrup until color is even. In another bowl, whip cream until stiff peaks form.

2. Fold cream into chocolate mixture and pour all into prepared pan. Cover and freeze 6 hours, until firm.

## 330. Pumpkin Ice Cream

**Ingredients:**
- 1 15 cans 1 (15-oz.) pumpkins puree
- 2 cups whole milk
- 2 cups heavy cream
- 1 cup packed brown sugar
- 6 large eggs yolks
- 1 teaspoon pure vanilla extract
- 1 teaspoon cinnamon
- 1/2 teaspoon ginger
- 1/2 teaspoon nutmeg
- 1/4 teaspoon kosher salt

**Directions:**
1. The day before you intend to churn, freeze the plate of your ice cream maker. As your ice cream base will have to chill as well, we suggest which makes it the night time before, too.
2. In a medium saucepan over medium heat, whisk together pumpkin puree, milk, and cream. When mixture starts to boil, remove from heat and set aside. In a sizable bowl, whisk brown sugar and egg yolks until pale and thick ribbons form, three to four 4 minutes. (You might use a hand mixer.) Whisking constantly, gradually add about 50 % of hot pumpkin mixture to eggs, one ladle at a time, to warm mixture through.
3. Pour mixture back to saucepan with remaining pumpkin mixture. Return pan over low heat and cook, stirring frequently with a wooden spoon, until mixture thickens, making sure the mixture never comes up to a simmer, about 4 to five minutes. To check on if the mixture is done, coat the trunk of your wooden spoon with the mixture and swipe your finger through the mixture.
4. If your finger leaves a clean line, your mixture is good to go-this will be at around 170°, if you are using a candy thermometer.
5. When the custard is adequately thickened, stir in vanilla and spices. Strain into a sizable bowl and place over an ice bath. Let cool to room temperature, then cover and chill at least 3 hours, up to overnight. Whenever your custard is chilled as well as your ice cream maker bowl is frozen, churn ice cream according to manufacturer's instructions, about a quarter-hour, scraping sides occasionally.
6. When ice cream is soft-serve consistency, transfer to another container and freeze until hardened, 2-3 3 hours, up to overnight.

## 331. Richer Than Rich German Chocolate Ice Cream Recipe

**Ingredients:**
- 3 cups milk
- 6 ounces german sweet chocolate
- 1 1/2 cups white sugar
- 2 1/2 tablespoons all-purpose flour
- 1/4 teaspoon salt
- 2 large eggs, beaten
- 1 1/2 cups heavy cream
- 1 teaspoon vanilla extract
- 1/2 cup shredded sweetened coconut
- 1 cup chopped pecans, toasted

**Directions:**
1. Heat milk, chocolate, sugar, flour, and salt in a saucepan over low heat. Cook before chocolate melts, stirring occasionally. Stir about 1/2 cup of the hot chocolate mixture in to the eggs, then stir the egg mixture in to the saucepan. Increase heat to medium and continue cooking and stirring before mixture is thickened, about five minutes. Pour chocolate egg mixture into a bowl. Cover and refrigerate until chilled, at least 2 hours. Stir in the heavy cream and vanilla extract.
2. Pour the chilled mixture into an ice cream maker and freeze according to manufacturer's directions until it reaches "soft-serve" consistency. Stir in the coconut and pecans. Transfer ice cream to a one- or two-quart

lidded plastic container; cover surface with plastic wrap and seal. For best results, ice cream should ripen in the freezer for at least 2 hours or overnight.

### 332. Cherry Cheesecake Frozen Yogurt Recipe

**Ingredients:**
- 1 (8-ounce) package cream cheese, softened
- 1 cup white sugar
- 1 tablespoon lemon juice
- 3 cups plain greek yogurt
- 2 cups pitted, chopped fresh cherries

**Directions:**
1. In a huge bowl, mash the cream cheese with sugar until thoroughly combined; stir in the lemon juice, and mix in the yogurt, in regards to a cup at a time, before mixture is smooth and creamy. Mix in the cherries. Cover the bowl with plastic wrap, and chill until very cold, at least 4 hours.
2. Pour the mixture into an ice cream freezer, and freeze according to manufacturer's instructions. For firmer texture, pack the frozen yogurt right into a covered container, and freeze for many hours.

### 333. Peanut Butter Ice Cream Recipe

**Ingredients:**
- 4 cups half-and-half cream
- 3 cups non-fat dry milk
- 3 cups milk
- 1 1/2 cups sugar
- 1 1/2 cups peanut butter
- 4 teaspoons vanilla extract

**Directions:**
1. Pour the half-and-half, dry milk, and milk into a big saucepan over low heat. Cook until heated, stirring to dissolve the dry milk. Stir in the peanut butter and sugar until smooth and sugar has dissolved. Remove from heat, and stir in the vanilla. Cool mixture, and refrigerate.
2. Stir the mixture, or merge a blender before pouring into an ice cream maker. Freeze based on the manufacturer's instructions.

### 334. Quick Ice Cream Recipe

**Ingredients:**
- 3/4 cup prepared fat free vanilla pudding
- 1 (8-ounce) container fat free frozen whipped topping, thawed

**Directions:**
1. Fold the pudding alongside the whipped topping.
2. Go back to whipped topping container and freeze 8 hours or overnight with lid slightly open.

### 335. Irish Cream Ice Cream Recipe

**Ingredients:**
- 2 cups half-and-half
- 1/2 cup white sugar
- 1/2 cup brown sugar
- 2 cups heavy whipping cream
- 1 tablespoon vanilla extract
- 1/2 cup irish cream liqueur

**Directions:**
1. Beat together half-and-half, white sugar, and brown sugar in a sizable bowl with an electric mixer on medium speed before sugars have dissolved.
2. Stir heavy cream and vanilla extract in to the mixture until smooth.
3. Pour the mixture into an ice cream maker and freeze according to manufacturer's instructions.
4. About 2 minutes prior to the end of freezing time, pour Irish cream liqueur in to the ice cream maker; permit the machine to complete freezing the ice cream.
5. Transfer ice cream right into a freezer-proof container with a tight lid and place in freezer until ice cream is hardened, at least 4 hours.

### 336. Peanut Butter Banana Ice Cream Recipe

**Ingredients:**
- 4 eaches ripe bananas, cut into 1-inch slices
- 1/4 cup peanut butter

**Directions:**

1. Arrange banana slices on a baking sheet and freeze, 8 hours to overnight.
2. Process frozen bananas in a food processor until evenly chopped; add peanut butter and process until thick and creamy.

### 337. Reese's N'ice Cream
**Ingredients:**
- 8 large ripe bananas. sliced into coins
- 1/2 cup smooth peanut butter smooth peanut butter, plus 1/4 c melted peanut butter
- 1 teaspoon pure vanilla extract
- 1 cup chopped reese's, plus more for topping
- 1/4 cup melted chocolate

**Directions:**
1. Freeze bananas until frozen, about 2 hours. In a food processor, blend together bananas, 1/2 cup peanut butter, and vanilla.
2. Pour mixture into a loaf pan and fold in Reese's. Drizzle top with melted chocolate and melted peanut butter then scatter more Reese's at the top. Freeze until solid, about 3 hour

### 338. No-cook Eggnog Ice Cream Recipe
**Ingredients:**
- 2 cups eggnog
- 2 cups heavy cream
- 1 (10-ounce) can sweetened condensed milk
- 1 teaspoon vanilla extract , or to taste

**Directions:**
1. Mix eggnog, heavy cream, condensed milk, and vanilla in a sizable bowl. Pour the mixture into an ice cream maker and freeze according to manufacturer's directions until it reaches "soft-serve" consistency.
2. Transfer ice cream to a one- or two-quart lidded plastic container; cover surface with plastic wrap and seal. For best results, ice cream should ripen in the freezer for at least 2 hours or overnight.

### 339. Lavender Ice Cream Recipe
**Ingredients:**
- 3 cups milk
- 2 sprigs (blank)s stems of fresh lavender flowers
- 8 large eggs yolks egg yolks
- 1 1/2 cups white sugar
- 3 cups heavy cream

**Directions:**
1. Heat the milk and lavender in a 3-quart saucepan over low heat until warmed through. Remove from heat, and invite lavender to infuse for approximately 20 minutes. Remove flowers.
2. Beat the egg yolks and sugar together in large bowl. Whisk the lavender-infused milk into the egg mixture, then pour it back to the saucepan. Heat the mixture over low heat, whisking constantly, before mixture thickens and will coat the trunk of a spoon, 7 to ten minutes. Remove from heat, and cool slightly, about five minutes. Stir in the heavy cream. Transfer the mixture to a bowl, and chill in refrigerator at least 4 hours.
3. Pour the chilled mixture into an ice cream maker and freeze according to manufacturer's directions until it reaches "soft-serve" consistency. Transfer ice cream to a lidded container; cover surface with plastic wrap and seal. For best results, ice cream should be place in the freezer at least 2 hours or overnight.

### 340. Coconut-avocado Ice Cream Recipe
**Ingredients:**
- 1 1/2 cups milk
- 1 cup coconut cream
- 1/2 cup white sugar
- 2 (1/2 pound) avocados , peeled and pitted
- 3/4 teaspoon lemon juice

**Directions:**
1. Puree milk, coconut cream, sugar, avocados, and lemon juice in a blender until smooth. Pour right into a bowl, cover, and refrigerate for many hours until cold. Freeze within an ice cream machine according to manufacturer's directions, then freeze overnight.

2. Allow ice cream to soften in refrigerator for ten minutes before serving.

## 341. Gelato Recipe

**Ingredients:**
- 2 cups milk
- 1 cup heavy cream
- 4 large eggs yolks egg yolks
- 1/2 cup sugar

**Directions:**
1. In a medium saucepan, mix milk and cream. Warm until foam forms around the edges. Remove from heat.
2. In a sizable bowl, beat the egg yolks and sugar until frothy. Gradually pour the warm milk in to the egg yolks, whisking constantly. Return mixture to saucepan; cook over medium heat, stirring with a wooden spoon until the mixture gels slightly and coats the back of the spoon. If small egg lumps begin to show, remove from heat immediately.
3. Pour the mixture through a sieve or fine strainer right into a bowl. Cover, and chill for several hours or overnight.
4. Pour the mixture into an ice cream maker, and freeze based on the manufacturer's instructions. Transfer to a sealed container, and freeze until firm. If the gelato is too firm, stick it in the refrigerator until it reaches the required consistency.

## 342. Frozen Strawberry Yogurt Recipe

**Ingredients:**
- 1 pound fresh strawberries
- 3/4 cup white sugar
- 1 tablespoon vanilla extract
- 1/4 cup half-and-half
- 1 (32-ounce) container plain yogurt

**Directions:**
1. Place strawberries, sugar, vanilla extract, and half-and-half in a blender; puree until smooth. Add yogurt and pulse until combined.
2. Pour the mixture into an ice cream maker and freeze according to manufacturer's instructions. Transfer frozen yogurt to a lidded plastic container. Cover surface with plastic wrap and seal. For best results, let it ripen in the freezer for at least 2 hours or overnight before serving.

## 343. Olive Oil Ice Cream

**Ingredients:**
- 1/2 cup granulated sugar
- 2 tablespoons nonfat powdered milk
- 1/4 teaspoon xanthan gum
- 1 1/3 cups whole milk
- 2 tablespoons light corn syrup
- 1 1/3 cups heavy cream
- 1/4 cup grassy extra-virgin olive oils (such as red ridge farm durant arbequina), plus more for garnish
- 1/2 teaspoon kosher salt
- flaky sea salt (such as maldon)

**Directions:**
1. Stir together sugar, powdered milk, and xanthan gum in a little bowl. Whisk together milk and corn syrup in a medium saucepan. Add sugar mixture, and whisk until smooth. Heat mixture over medium, whisking often, until sugar has fully dissolved, three to four 4 minutes. (Usually do not simmer.) Remove from heat, and whisk in cream. Cover and chill at least 6 hours. For better still texture and flavor, chill mixture up to 24 hours. Base can be stored within an airtight container in freezer for three months; thaw completely before using.
2. Whisk together chilled base, olive oil, and kosher salt until well combined. (There it's still little droplets of oil on the surface.) Pour mixture into freezer bowl of a 1 1/2-quart electric ice cream maker and proceed according to manufacturer's directions until ice cream has the texture of soft-serve, about 35 minutes. (Instructions and times may vary.)
3. Quickly transfer ice cream to a freezer-safe container; press parchment paper directly onto surface. Cover container, and freeze

until firm, at least 6 hours. Ice cream can be kept in freezer up to three months. To serve, garnish with olive oil and flaky sea salt.

### 344. Spiced Ginger-peach Ice Cream Recipe
**Ingredients:**
- 1 cup milk
- 3/4 cup white sugar
- 1/4 teaspoon salt
- 3 ounces peach puree
- 3/4 teaspoon ground ginger
- 1/2 teaspoon ground cinnamon, or more to taste
- 1/4 teaspoon vanilla extract
- 3 large eggs yolks egg yolks, lightly beaten
- 2 cups heavy whipping cream
- 4 small slice (blank)s fresh peach slices, diced, or more to taste

**Directions:**
1. Whisk milk, sugar, and salt together in a saucepan over medium heat; bring to a simmer. Stir peach puree, ginger, cinnamon, and vanilla extract; simmer until flavors blend, 5 to 10 minutes.
2. Place egg yolks in a little bowl. Slowly pour 1/2 cup hot milk mixture into eggs, whisking constantly. Pour warmed egg mixture into the milk mixture in the saucepan over medium heat. Cook, stirring occasionally, until thick, 5 to ten minutes. Strain egg mixture right into a chilled bowl and refrigerate, stirring occasionally, until chilled, about 2 hours.
3. Whisk cream into chilled egg mixture; add peaches and stir.
4. Pour peach mixture in to the container of an ice cream maker and freeze according to the manufacturer's instructions.

### 345. Strawberry, Lemon And Vanilla Ice Cream Parfait
**Ingredients:**
- 1 pound strawberries, hulled and quartered
- 1/4 cup granulated sugar
- 1 tablespoon fresh orange juice
- 1/2 teaspoon pure vanilla extract
- 3/4 cup heavy cream
- 1 pint vanilla ice cream
- 4 graham crackers, coarsely crushed
- 1 pint lemon sorbet

**Directions:**
1. In a food processor, combine the strawberries with the sugar, orange juice and vanilla and pulse before strawberries are coarsely chopped. Let stand before strawberries release some of their juice, about ten minutes. Process the strawberries until smooth.
2. In a medium bowl, utilizing a hand-held mixer, beat the cream at medium speed until soft peaks form.
3. Spoon 2 tablespoons of the strawberry sauce into 4 parfait glasses. Top with a scoop of vanilla ice cream, a sprinkling of the crushed graham crackers, a scoop of the lemon sorbet and another 2 tablespoons of the strawberry sauce. Top the parfaits with a dollop of the whipped cream and finish with a sprinkling of the graham crackers. Serve immediately.

### 346. Pineapple Whip Recipe
**Ingredients:**
- 1 cup heavy whipping cream
- 6 fluid ounces pineapple juice (such as dole®)
- 1/3 cup white sugar
- 1 teaspoon fresh lemon juice

**Directions:**
1. Whisk cream, pineapple juice, and sugar in a bowl until sugar is dissolved; stir in lemon juice. Refrigerate until well chilled, at least 6 hours.
2. Transfer pineapple mixture to an ice cream maker and process according to manufacturer's instructions.

### 347. Mint Mojito Coffee Ice Cream Recipe
**Ingredients:**
- 2 cups whole milk
- 1/3 cup coarsely ground coffee beans
- 3/4 cup brown sugar, divided

- 1 bunch fresh mint leaves, crushed
- 6 large eggs yolks large egg yolks
- 1 cup heavy whipping cream
- 1/3 cup white rum
- 1/3 cup chopped chocolate

**Directions:**
1. Heat milk, ground coffee, 1/4 cup brown sugar, and mint in a saucepan over low heat until warmed through, 7 to ten minutes.
2. Whisk egg yolks and remaining 1/2 cup brown sugar in a bowl; slowly whisk in about 1 cup hot milk mixture. Pour egg yolk mixture into saucepan and continue steadily to heat until custard is thickened, about five minutes.
3. Line a sieve with cheesecloth and strain custard into a large bowl; discard solids. Whisk heavy cream into custard. Cover and refrigerate until chilled, 4 to 5 hours.
4. Stir rum and chocolate into chilled custard and pour into an ice cream maker. Freeze according to manufacturer's directions.

## 348. Vegan Banana Ice Cream Recipe

**Ingredients:**
- 2 large frozen bananas, cut into small chunks
- 1 cup unsweetened almond milk
- 1 tablespoon chopped pecans
- 1 pinch ground cinnamon , or to taste

**Directions:**
1. Blend bananas, almond milk, pecans, and cinnamon together in a blender or food processor until smooth and creamy.

## 349. Cinnamon Black Walnut Ice Cream Recipe

**Ingredients:**
- 4 cups heavy cream
- 4 cups half-and-half
- 2 cups white sugar
- 2 1/2 cups chopped black walnuts
- 1 tablespoon vanilla extract
- 1 teaspoon ground cinnamon
- 1/2 teaspoon salt

**Directions:**
1. In a huge bowl, stir together the heavy cream, half-and-half, sugar, walnuts, vanilla, cinnamon, and salt. Cover and refrigerate for thirty minutes.
2. Pour the mixture into the plate of an ice cream maker and freeze as directed by the product manufacturer

## 350. Snow Ice Cream Recipe

**Ingredients:**
- 1 gallon clean fresh snow
- 1 (14-ounce) can sweetened condensed milk

**Directions:**
1. Mix snow and sweetened condensed milk together in a bowl until perfectly mixed.

## 351. Mermaid Ice Cream

**Ingredients:**
- 3 cups heavy cream
- 1 14 cans -oz. sweetened condensed milk
- 1 teaspoon pure vanilla extract
- green, blue, and purple food coloring
- sprinkles, for topping (optional)

**Directions:**
1. In a big bowl utilizing a hand mixer or in the plate of a stand mixer using the whisk attachment, beat heavy cream until medium peaks form.
2. Fold in sweetened condensed milk and vanilla until totally combined, then divide mixture among five bowls. Put in a different color food coloring to each bowl (we used different amounts of green, blue, and purple) and stir until combined. Layer dollops of the colors in a 9"-x-5" loaf pan until you go out of the mixture.
3. Run a knife through the mixture to swirl the colors three or four 4 times and smooth top.
4. Top with sprinkles (if using) and freeze until firm, 5 hours. Remove from freezer and let soften, 5 to 10 minutes, then scoop and serve.

## 352. No-churn Cake Batter Ice Cream Recipe

**Ingredients:**

- 2 cups heavy whipping cream
- 1 (14-ounce) can sweetened condensed milk
- 1 1/4 cups cake mix with candy bits (such as pillsbury funfetti), or more to taste

**Directions:**

1. Beat cream with an electric mixer in a sizable bowl until stiff peaks form.
2. Stir condensed milk and cake mix together in another bowl. Fold cake mix mixture into whipped cream. Pour mixture into a freezer-safe container, cover the container, and freeze until ice cream is defined, 6 hours to overnight.

# OTHER FAVORITE RECIPES

## 353. Strawberry Ice Cream Milk Shake
Servings: 8
Cooking Time: 30 Minutes
**Ingredients:**
- 1 cup cold whole milk
- ¾ cup granulated sugar
- 2 cups cold heavy cream
- 1 teaspoon vanilla extract
- 1 cup strawberries hulled
- ½ cup ice

**Directions:**
1. Put ice water in a large mixing bowl. Place a small bowl on top of the large bowl with ice. Pour cold milk and sugar into the small bowl and whisk until the sugar is dissolved. Stir in the cream and vanilla. Stir to combine.
2. Place the cold freezer bowl in the Cuisinart Ice Cream Maker. Turn on the machine and pour in the mixture. Add one package of crushed Oreos five minutes before the time ends.
3. Stop in 25 minutes until the mixture becomes soft and creamy.
4. Transfer into an air-tight container and freeze overnight.
5. Place strawberries, ice, and 2 cups of milkshake in a blender. Pulse until smooth.
6. Serve immediately.

**Nutrition Info:** Calories per serving: 193 ; Protein: 1.9g; Carbs: 17.4g; Fat: 13.1g Sugar: 7g

## 354. Basil Soft Serve Ice Cream
Servings: 6
Cooking Time: 35 Minutes
**Ingredients:**
- 2 cups heavy cream
- 1 cup milk
- 3/4 cup sugar
- 1 Tbs. vanilla extract
- 1 ½ cups packed basil

**Directions:**
1. Refer to note at the beginning of the chapter about freezing bowl.
2. Place the milk and cream in a bowl, and mix them together until well combined. Use a whisk to mix in the sugar. Continue to whisk for about 4 minutes until the sugar dissolves. Mix in the vanilla extract.
3. Place all the ingredients in a food processor or blender, and puree.
4. Pour the ingredients into your ice cream maker, and let it churn for 25 minutes.
5. Serve immediately.

## 355. Strawberry English Muffin With Honey Ice Cream Sandwich
Servings: 2
Cooking Time: 15 Min
**Ingredients:**
- 1 pack of English muffins
- organic honey to pour atop
- small pack of strawberries

**Directions:**
1. Toast your English muffins in a toaster just like you would for breakfast.
2. Spread about 4-5 strawberries on top of your warm muffin.
3. Squeeze out and drizzle honey over both inside pieces of the English muffin.
4. Add a scoop of Ice Cream (that you made from this book) between the two pieces of English muffins. Enjoy!

## 356. Vegan Chocolate Made Mint Milkshake
Servings: 9
Cooking Time: 40 Minutes
**Ingredients:**
- 3/4 cup water
- 1 1/4 cups full fat coconut milk or coconut cream (as thick as possible)
- 2/3 cup organic cane sugar
- 2/3 cup unsweetened cocoa powder
- 1/4 tsp sea salt
- 6 ounces vegan dark chocolate, finely chopped
- 11/2 tsp mint extract
- ½ cup sliced frozen bananas

**Directions:**
1. Refer to note at the beginning of the chapter about freezing bowl.

2. Put the first 5 ingredients in a large saucepan, and heat it on medium-high heat. Mix the ingredients together using a whisk. Allow the mixture to come to a low boil. Continue to whisk often, and remain cooking on a low boil for 1 minute.
3. Take the pan off the heat, and mix in the chocolate and mint extract using the whisk. Continue to mix until the chocolate is melted.
4. Place the mixture in a blender with the bananas, and blend on high speed for about 30 seconds.
5. Allow the mixture to cool
6. Pour the ingredients into your ice cream maker, and let it churn for 10-15 minutes, until desired consistency is reached.
7. Serve immediately.

### 357. Berries Sorbet

Servings: 8
Cooking Time: 15 Minutes
**Ingredients:**
- 1/3 cup water
- ¼ cup sugar
- 1 12-ounce package frozen blackberries
- 4 cups mixed berries

**Directions:**
1. Place water and sugar in a saucepan. Bring to a boil until sugar dissolves. Remove from heat and allow to chill in the fridge for at least 2 hours.
2. Place all ingredients in a blender. Pulse until smooth.
3. Turn on the Cuisinart and pour in the mixture.
4. Churn for 10 minutes.
5. Transfer in an airtight container and freeze overnight.

**Nutrition Info:** Calories per serving: 299 ; Protein: 4.3g; Carbs: 56.5g; Fat: 7.2g Sugar: 20.1g

### 358. Big Banana Nutella Soft Serve Ice Cream

Servings: 6
Cooking Time: 35 Minutes
**Ingredients:**
- 2 cups heavy cream
- 1 cup milk
- 3/4 cup sugar
- 1 Tbs. vanilla extract
- 1 cup sliced Bananas
- 6 tbs. Nutella

**Directions:**
1. Refer to note at the beginning of the chapter about freezing bowl.
2. Place the milk and cream in a bowl, and mix them together until well combined. Use a whisk to mix in the sugar. Continue to whisk for about 4 minutes until the sugar dissolves. Then mix in the vanilla extract.
3. Place all the ingredients in a food processor or blender, and puree.
4. Pour the ingredients into your ice cream maker, and let it churn for 25 minutes.
5. Serve immediately.

### 359. Vegan Ridiculous Raspberry Coconut Frozen Yogurt

Servings: 1 Quart
Cooking Time: 2 Hours 35 Minutes
**Ingredients:**
- 2 cups coconut yogurt
- 1/4 cup sugar or maple syrup
- 1/2 teaspoon vanilla extract
- 1/4 cup shredded coconut
- ½ cup raspberries

**Directions:**
1. Refer to note at the beginning of the chapter about freezing bowl.
2. Puree the raspberries in a food processor or blender.
3. Place the yogurt in a bowl. Use a whisk to mix in the sugar. Continue to whisk for about 4 minutes until the sugar dissolves. Then mix in the vanilla extract, and raspberry puree.
4. Pour the ingredients into your ice cream maker, and let it churn for 25 minutes. About 5 minutes before the ice cream is done churning add the shredded coconut to your ice cream maker.
5. Put the frozen yogurt in an airtight container and place in the freezer for at least 2 hours, until desired consistency is reached.

## 360. White Chocolate Chip Cookie Dough Frozen Yogurt

Servings: 1 Quart
Cooking Time: 2 Hours 35 Minutes
**Ingredients:**
- 1 quart container full-fat plain yogurt
- ¼ teaspoon salt
- 1 cup sugar
- 1 tablespoon vanilla extract
- ½ cup prepackaged cookie dough cut into small chunks
- ½ cup finely chopped white chocolate chips

**Directions:**
1. NOTE: Freeze your ice cream bowl for at least 24hrs prior to starting!
2. Place the yogurt in a bowl. Use a whisk to mix in the sugar and salt. Continue to whisk for about 4 minutes until the sugar dissolves. Then mix in the vanilla extract.
3. Pour the ingredients into your ice cream maker, and let it churn for 25 minutes. About 5 minutes before the ice cream is done churning add the cookie dough and white chocolate to your ice cream maker.
4. Put the frozen yogurt in an airtight container and place in the freezer for at least 2 hours, until desired consistency is reached.

## 361. Pistachio Berry Frozen Yogurt

Servings: 7
Cooking Time: 10 Minutes
**Ingredients:**
- 1 cup heavy cream
- 1 cup Greek yogurt
- 1 cup milk
- ½ cup honey
- 2 tablespoons lemon juice
- ½ cup strawberries, hulled
- ¼ cup toasted pistachio nuts, chopped

**Directions:**
1. Place all ingredients except the pistachio nuts in a food processor. Pulse until smooth.
2. Turn on the Cuisinart and pour in the mixture.
3. Churn for 10 minutes.
4. Transfer in an airtight container and freeze overnight.
5. Garnish with pistachio nuts before serving.

**Nutrition Info:** Calories per serving: 204; Protein: 3.7g; Carbs: 26g; Fat: 10.7g Sugar: 24.7g

## 362. Mouth Watering Maple Bacon Milkshake

Servings: 6
Cooking Time: 25 Minutes
**Ingredients:**
- 2 cups heavy cream
- 1 cup milk
- 3/4 cup sugar
- 1 teaspoons vanilla extract
- 6 slices finely chopped cooked thick cut bacon
- ½ cup maple syrup

**Directions:**
1. Refer to note at the beginning of the chapter about freezing bowl.
2. Place the milk and cream in a bowl, and mix them together until well combined. Use a whisk to mix in the sugar. Continue to whisk for about 4 minutes until the sugar dissolves. Then mix in the vanilla extract, and maple syrup.
3. Pour the ingredients into your ice cream maker, and let it churn for 10-15 minutes, until desired consistency is reached. About 5 minutes before the ice cream is done churning add the bacon to your ice cream maker.
4. Serve immediately.

## 363. Amazing Key Lime Sorbet

Servings: 4
Cooking Time: 3 Hours
**Ingredients:**
- 3 cups cold water
- 2 ¼ cup fresh key lime juice
- 2 3/4 cup sugar
- 1 tablespoon lime zest

**Directions:**
1. NOTE: Freeze your ice cream bowl for at least 24hrs prior to starting!
2. Mix together the water and sugar in a large sauce pan on medium heat.

Allow the mixture to come to a boil. Then lower to low heat, and let the mixture simmer until the sugar dissolve. Allow the mixture to cool completely.
3. Mix the lime juice and zest with the cooled mixture.
4. Pour the ingredients into your ice cream maker, and let it churn for 25-30 minutes.
5. Place in an airtight container for up to 2 hours, until desired consistency is reached.

### 364. Cherry Fig Mint Milkshake

Servings: 6
Cooking Time: 25 Minutes
**Ingredients:**
- 2 cups heavy cream
- 1 cup milk
- 3/4 cup sugar
- 2 teaspoons vanilla extract
- ¼ cup lemon juice
- ¼ cup cherries
- 2 cups peeled, diced figs
- 2 teaspoons chopped fresh mint

**Directions:**
1. NOTE: Freeze your ice cream bowl for at least 24hrs prior to starting!
2. Place the milk and cream in a bowl, and mix them together until well combined. Use a whisk to mix in the sugar. Continue to whisk for about 4 minutes until the sugar dissolves. Then mix in the vanilla extract, lemon juice, cherries and mint.
3. Pour the ingredients into your ice cream maker, and let it churn for 10-15 minutes, until desired consistency is reached. About 5 minutes before the ice cream is done churning add the figs to your ice cream maker.
4. Serve immediately.

### 365. Cinnamon Clove Coffee Frozen Yogurt

Servings: 1.5 Quarts
Cooking Time: 2 Hours 35 Minutes
**Ingredients:**
- 1 quart container full-fat plain yogurt
- ¼ teaspoon salt
- 1 cup sugar
- 2 teaspoons cinnamon
- 1 tablespoon cloves pulverized
- 1 teaspoon vanilla extract
- 1 cup strong brewed coffee or espresso
- 1 tablespoon coffee grounds

**Directions:**
1. NOTE: Freeze your ice cream bowl for at least 24hrs prior to starting!
2. Place the yogurt in a bowl. Use a whisk to mix in the sugar and salt. Continue to whisk for about 4 minutes until the sugar dissolves. Then mix in the vanilla extract, coffee, and coffee grounds, cloves and cinnamon.
3. Pour the ingredients into your ice cream maker, and let it churn for 25 minutes.
4. Put the frozen yogurt in an airtight container and place in the freezer for at least 2 hours, until desired consistency is reached.

### 366. Vegan "oh So" Soy Vanilla Soft Serve Ice Cream

Servings: Makes 1 Quart
Cooking Time: 35 Minutes
**Ingredients:**
- 1 pound silken tofu
- ½ cup plus 2 tablespoons organic or granulated sugar
- ½ teaspoon kosher salt
- 1 vanilla bean, split lengthwise
- ¾ cup refined coconut oil, melted, cooled slightly

**Directions:**
1. Refer to note at the beginning of the chapter about freezing bowl.
2. Put the first 3 ingredients in a blender. Then add in the vanilla bean seeds. Puree the mixture until its smooth, around 15 seconds. Turn the blender to medium speed, and slowly drizzle in the coconut oil. Blend the mixture until its thick, but don't over blend it.
3. Pour the ingredients into your ice cream maker, and let it churn for 25 minutes.
4. Serve immediately.

### 367. Mulberry Ginger Sorbet

Servings: 8
Cooking Time: 20 Minutes
**Ingredients:**
- ¾ cup sugar
- ¾ cup water
- Juice from 1 tablespoon grated ginger
- 4 cups mulberries
- 2 tablespoon raspberry liqueur

**Directions:**
1. Place water and sugar in a saucepan. Bring to a boil until sugar dissolves. Remove from heat and allow to chill in the fridge for at least 2 hours.
2. Place all ingredients in a blender and pulse until smooth.
3. Turn on the Cuisinart and pour in the mixture.
4. Churn for 15 minutes.
5. Transfer in an airtight container and freeze overnight.

**Nutrition Info:** Calories per serving: 71; Protein: 1.1g; Carbs: 17.4g; Fat: 0.3g Sugar: 8g

### 368. Ice Cream Pizza

Servings: 8
Cooking Time: 30 Minutes
**Ingredients:**
- 1 cup cold whole milk
- ¾ cup granulated sugar
- 2 cups cold heavy cream
- 1 teaspoon vanilla extract
- 1 commercial pizza dough, cooked according to package instructions
- 5 pieces Oreo cookies, crushed
- ½ cups M&Ms, chopped
- ½ cup hot fudge sauce

**Directions:**
1. Put ice water in a large mixing bowl. Place a small bowl on top of the large bowl with ice. Pour cold milk and sugar into the small bowl and whisk until the sugar is dissolved. Stir in the cream and vanilla. Stir to combine.
2. Place the cold freezer bowl in the Cuisinart Ice Cream Maker. Turn on the machine and pour in the mixture. Add one package of crushed Oreos five minutes before the time ends.
3. Stop in 25 minutes until the mixture becomes soft and creamy.
4. Transfer into an air-tight container and freeze overnight.
5. Spread ice cream in a dough and top with Oreo cookies and M&Ms. Drizzle with hot fudge sauce.
6. Slice and serve.

**Nutrition Info:** Calories per serving: 387; Protein: 11g; Carbs: 35.9g; Fat: 22.7g Sugar: 19.8g

### 369. Maple Frozen Yogurt

Servings: 4
Cooking Time: 10 Minutes
**Ingredients:**
- 1 cup chopped pecans
- ½ cup + 1 tablespoon maple syrup
- 2 cups non-fat Greek yogurt
- ½ cup heavy cream
- teaspoon vanilla extract
- 1 tablespoon rum

**Directions:**
1. Place the pecans and 1 tablespoon maple syrup in a non-stick pan and stir until the syrup becomes dry. Set aside to cool.
2. In a cold bowl, combine the yogurt, cream, maple syrup, vanilla extract, and rum.
3. Turn on the Cuisinart and pour in the mixture.
4. Churn for 10 minutes.
5. Five minutes before the churning stops, add maple pecans.
6. Transfer in an airtight container and freeze overnight.

**Nutrition Info:** Calories per serving: 425; Protein: 13.9g; Carbs: 40.5g; Fat: 23.7g Sugar: 34.9g

### 370. Deep Dark Chocolate Sorbet

Servings: 3
Cooking Time: 5 Hours
**Ingredients:**
- 2 cups water
- 1 cup unsweetened cocoa powder
- 3/4 cup agave
- 1 tablespoon lime zest

**Directions:**

1. Refer to note at the beginning of the chapter about freezing bowl.
2. Mix together the water and agave in a medium saucepan on medium heat. Stir frequently until the agave dissolve. Mix in the cocoa powder and let the mixture come to a simmer. Let the mixture cook for 3 minutes. Allow the mixture to cool completely. Then refrigerate covered for 2 hours.
3. Pour the ingredients into your ice cream maker, and let it churn for 25-30 minutes.
4. Place in an airtight container for up to 2 hours, until desired consistency is reached.

### 371. "crispy" Kit Kat Ice Cream

Servings: 6
Cooking Time: 2 Hours 50 Minutes
**Ingredients:**
- 2 cups heavy cream
- 1 cup milk
- 3/4 cup sugar
- 1 tablespoon vanilla extract
- 1 ½ cups chopped mini kit kats

**Directions:**
1. Refer to note at the beginning of the chapter about freezing bowl.
2. Place the milk and cream in a bowl, and mix them together until well combined. Use a whisk to mix in the sugar. Continue to whisk for about 4 minutes until the sugar dissolves. Then mix in the vanilla extract.
3. Pour the ingredients into your ice cream maker, and let it churn for 25 minutes. About 5 minutes before the ice cream is done churning add the kit kats to your ice cream maker.
4. Put the ice cream in an airtight container and place in the freezer for around 2 hours. Allow the ice cream to thaw for 15 minutes before serving.

### 372. Chocolate Frozen Yogurt

Servings: 5
Cooking Time: 10 Minutes
**Ingredients:**
- 4 cups plain and unsweetened yogurt
- ½ cup cane sugar
- ¼ cup cocoa powder
- 1 teaspoon vanilla extract

**Directions:**
1. Place all ingredients in a food processor and pulse until smooth.
2. Turn on the Cuisinart and pour in the mixture.
3. Churn for 10 minutes.
4. Transfer in an airtight container and freeze overnight.

**Nutrition Info:** Calories per serving: 150 ; Protein: 7.6g; Carbs: 16.7g; Fat: 6.9g Sugar: 14g

### 373. Chocolate Peanut Butter Soft Serve Ice Cream

Servings: 6
Cooking Time: 40 Minutes
**Ingredients:**
- 2 cups heavy cream
- 1 cup milk
- 3/4 cup sugar
- 1 Tbs. vanilla extract
- 1/2 cup peanut butter slightly melted
- 2 ounces semi-sweet chocolate

**Directions:**
1. Refer to note at the beginning of the chapter about freezing bowl.
2. Melt the chocolate in a medium sauce pan on low heat. Allow the chocolate to cool a bit.
3. While the chocolate is cooling, place the milk and cream in a bowl, and mix them together until well combined. Use a whisk to mix in the sugar. Continue to whisk for about 4 minutes until the sugar dissolves. Mix in the vanilla extract. Then whisk in the peanut butter, and then the chocolate.
4. Pour the ingredients into your ice cream maker, and let it churn for 25 minutes.
5. Serve immediately.

### 374. Easy Coconut Sorbet

Servings: 6
Cooking Time: 15 Minutes
**Ingredients:**
- 1 cup coconut water
- ¾ cup sugar
- 2 cans coconut milk

**Directions:**
1. Place coconut water and sugar in a saucepan. Bring to a boil until the sugar dissolves.
2. Remove from the heat and place in the fridge to chill for at least 3 hours.
3. Turn on the Cuisinart and pour in the water-sugar mixture and coconut milk.
4. Churn for 10 minutes.
5. Transfer in an airtight container and freeze overnight.

**Nutrition Info:** Calories per serving: 69; Protein: 0.8g; Carbs: 16.5g; Fat: 0.2g Sugar: 15.1g

### 375. Double Fudge Chocolate Gelato

Servings: 4-6
Cooking Time: 2 Hours 35 Minutes
**Ingredients:**
- 1/2 cup heavy cream
- 2 cups milk
- 3/4 cup sugar
- 1/4 teaspoon salt
- 7 ounces high quality dark chocolate fudge
- 1 teaspoon vanilla extract

**Directions:**
1. NOTE: Freeze your ice cream bowl for at least 24hrs prior to starting!
2. Melt the chocolate, and allow it to cool a little bit.
3. Place the milk and cream in a bowl, and mix them together until well combined. Use a whisk to mix in the sugar and salt. Continue to whisk for about 4 minutes until the sugar and salt dissolve. Then mix in the vanilla extract. Finally mix in the fudge until well combined.
4. Pour the ingredients into your ice cream maker, and let it churn for 25 minutes.
5. Put the gelato in an airtight container and place in the freezer for up to 2 hours, until desired consistency is reached.

### 376. Buttermilk Frozen Yogurt

Servings: 7
Cooking Time: 10 Minutes
**Ingredients:**
- 1 cup sugar
- ½ cup light corn syrup
- ¼ cup water
- 1/8 teaspoon salt
- 2 cups whole plain Greek yogurt
- 1 cup buttermilk, shaken
- 5 teaspoons fresh lemon juice

**Directions:**
1. Place the sugar, corn syrup, and water in a saucepan. Bring to a boil over low heat while stirring constantly. Add the salt. Continue stirring until the sugar dissolves. Remove from heat and set aside.
2. In a cold bowl, mix together the sugar mixture, Greek yogurt, buttermilk, and lemon juice.
3. Turn on the Cuisinart and pour in the mixture.
4. Churn for 10 minutes.
5. Transfer in an airtight container and freeze overnight.
6. Garnish with chocolate chips and coconut flakes before serving.

**Nutrition Info:** Calories per serving:182 ; Protein: 4g; Carbs: 38.2g; Fat: 2.6g Sugar: 37.7g

### 377. Mango Tango Sorbet

Servings: 5
Cooking Time: 10 Minutes
**Ingredients:**
- 2 ripe mangoes, peeled and diced
- 1 cup white sugar
- 1 lime, juiced
- 2 cups tangerine juice

**Directions:**
1. Place all ingredients in a blender. Pulse until smooth.
2. Turn on the Cuisinart and pour in the mixture.
3. Churn for 10 minutes.
4. Transfer in an airtight container and freeze overnight.

**Nutrition Info:** Calories per serving: 256; Protein: 1.2g; Carbs: 66g; Fat: 0g Sugar:55 g

### 378. Watermelon Sorbet

Servings: 7
Cooking Time: 15 Minutes

**Ingredients:**
- 1 cup sugar
- 1 cup water
- ¼ cup lemon juice
- 3 cups watermelon, peeled and seeded

**Directions:**
1. Place the water and sugar in a saucepan and bring to a boil over medium heat until the sugar dissolves. Remove from the heat and place in the fridge to chill for at least 3 hours.
2. Once cooled, place the water-sugar mixture into a blender and add the rest of the ingredients. Pulse until smooth.
3. Turn on the Cuisinart and pour in the mixture.
4. Churn for 10 minutes.
5. Transfer in an airtight container and freeze overnight.

**Nutrition Info:** Calories per serving: 77; Protein: 0.4g; Carbs: 19.8g; Fat: 0.1g Sugar: 12.3g

## 379. Kiwi Sorbet

Servings: 6
Cooking Time: 15 Minutes
**Ingredients:**
- ¾ cup granulated sugar
- ¾ cup water
- 2 pounds ripe kiwi fruit, peeled and sliced

**Directions:**
1. Place the water and sugar in a saucepan. Bring to a boil until the sugar dissolves.
2. Remove from the heat and place in the fridge to chill for at least 3 hours.
3. Place the kiwi slices in a blender and add the chilled sugar mixture. Pulse until smooth. Allow to chill for another two hours.
4. Turn on the Cuisinart and pour in the mixture.
5. Churn for 10 minutes.
6. Transfer in an airtight container and freeze overnight.

**Nutrition Info:** Calories per serving: 159; Protein: 0.6g; Carbs: 41.1g; Fat: 0.1g Sugar: 39.3g

## 380. Cinnamon Coconut Lemon Blackberry Gelato

Servings: 4-6
Cooking Time: 2 Hours 35 Minutes
**Ingredients:**
- 1/2 cup heavy cream
- 2 cups milk
- 3/4 cup sugar
- 1/2 cup sliced Coconut
- 1/2 cup finely chopped Blackberries
- 1 tablespoon vanilla extract
- 1 teaspoon lemon
- 1 teaspoon cinnamon

**Directions:**
1. NOTE: Freeze your ice cream bowl for at least 24hrs prior to starting!
2. Puree the strawberries in a food processor or blender.
3. Place the milk and cream in a bowl, and mix them together until well combined. Use a whisk to mix in the sugar. Continue to whisk for about 4 minutes until the sugar dissolves. Then mix in the vanilla extract, cinnamon, lemon, blackberry puree along with the finely chopped coconut.
4. Pour the ingredients into your ice cream maker, and let it churn for 25 minutes.
5. Put the gelato in an airtight container and place in the freezer for up to 2 hours, until desired consistency is reached.

## 381. Blueberry Frozen Yogurt

Servings: 6
Cooking Time: 10 Minutes
**Ingredients:**
- 2 ½ cups blueberries, fresh or frozen
- 2/3 cup honey
- 1 small lemon, zested and juiced
- ¼ teaspoon salt
- 2 cups full fat yogurt, chilled

**Directions:**
1. Place all ingredients in a food processor. Pulse until smooth.
2. Turn on the Cuisinart and pour in the mixture.
3. Churn for 10 minutes.

4. Transfer in an airtight container and freeze overnight.

**Nutrition Info:** Calories per serving: 262; Protein: 5.12 g; Carbs: 61g; Fat: 1.6g Sugar: 58.9g

## 382. Vegan Radical Raspberry Chocolate Soft Serve Ice Cream

Servings: 9
Cooking Time: 50 Minutes
**Ingredients:**
- 3/4 cup water
- 1 1/4 cups full fat coconut milk or coconut cream (as thick as possible)
- 2/3 cup organic cane sugar
- 2/3 cup unsweetened cocoa powder
- 1/4 tsp sea salt
- 6 ounces vegan dark chocolate, finely chopped
- 1/2 tsp pure vanilla extract
- 1/2 cup raspberries

**Directions:**
1. Refer to note at the beginning of the chapter about freezing bowl.
2. Put the first 5 ingredients in a large saucepan, and heat it on medium-high heat. Mix the ingredients together using a whisk. Allow the mixture to come to a low boil. Continue to whisk often, and remain cooking on a low boil for 1 minute.
3. Take the pan off the heat, and mix in the chocolate and vanilla extract using the whisk. Continue to mix until the chocolate is melted.
4. Place the mixture in a blender with the raspberries, and blend on high speed for about 30 seconds or until the raspberries are pureed.
5. Allow the mixture to cool
6. Pour the ingredients into your ice cream maker, and let it churn for 25 minutes.
7. Serve immediately.

## 383. Oreo Ice Cream Bar Dessert

Servings: 8
Cooking Time: 25 Minutes
**Ingredients:**
- 1 cup cold whole milk
- ¾ cup granulated sugar
- 2 cups cold heavy cream
- 1 teaspoon vanilla extract
- 36 pieces Oreo cookies, crushed
- 6 tablespoons melted butter
- 1 cup commercial chocolate syrup
- 1 cup whipping cream

**Directions:**
1. Put ice water in a large mixing bowl. Place a small bowl on top of the large bowl with ice. Pour cold milk and sugar into the small bowl and whisk until the sugar is dissolved. Stir in the cream and vanilla. Stir to combine.
2. Place the cold freezer bowl in the Cuisinart Ice Cream Maker. Turn on the machine and pour in the mixture. Add one package of crushed Oreos five minutes before the time ends.
3. Stop in 25 minutes until the mixture becomes soft and creamy.
4. Transfer into an air-tight container and freeze overnight.
5. Prepare the cookie dough by mixing together crushed Oreo cookies, melted butter, and chocolate syrup. Mix until a dough is formed.
6. Use half of the dough mixture and press firmly into a baking pan. Spread ice cream evenly on top. Place in the fridge and allow cream to freeze.
7. Once frozen, press the remaining dough on top.
8. Serve with whipped cream.

**Nutrition Info:** Calories per serving: 512; Protein: 8g; Carbs: 56g; Fat: 30 g Sugar: 43 g

## 384. Vanilla Ice Cream Sponge Cake

Servings: 12
Cooking Time: 25 Minutes
**Ingredients:**
- 1 cup cold whole milk
- ¾ cup granulated sugar
- 2 cups cold heavy cream
- 1 teaspoon vanilla extract
- 1-pound sponge cake, sliced to 1-inch thick
- 1 cup strawberry slices
- Whipped cream

**Directions:**

1. Put ice water in a large mixing bowl. Place a small bowl on top of the large bowl with ice. Pour cold milk and sugar into the small bowl and whisk until the sugar is dissolved. Stir in the cream and vanilla. Stir to combine.
2. Place the cold freezer bowl in the Cuisinart Ice Cream Maker. Turn on the machine and pour in the mixture. Add one package of crushed Oreos five minutes before the time ends.
3. Stop in 25 minutes until the mixture becomes soft and creamy.
4. Transfer into an air-tight container and freeze overnight.
5. In a springform pan, place slices of sponge cake.
6. Spread ice cream on top and top with strawberry slices.
7. Repeat the process until you make three layers of sponge cake, ice cream, and strawberry.
8. Top with whipped cream.
9. Place in the fridge to set for two hours.

**Nutrition Info:** Calories per serving:281 ; Protein: 3.9g; Carbs: 38.3g; Fat: 12.7g Sugar: 20.3g

### 385. Rhubarb Ice Cream Cake

Servings: 16
Cooking Time: 35 Minutes
**Ingredients:**
- 4 stalks fresh rhubarb, chopped
- 1 medium gala apple, chopped
- ½ cup water
- 1 cup raspberries
- ½ cup white sugar
- 1 cup cold whole milk
- ¾ cup granulated sugar
- 2 cups cold heavy cream
- 1 teaspoon vanilla extract

**Directions:**
1. Place in a bowl the rhubarb, apple, water, raspberries, and sugar. Boil over medium flame and simmer for 10 minutes. Drain and set aside in the fridge. Reserve the juices.
2. In a bowl, mix together the graham crackers and butter to form a dough. Press dough in spring form pan and place in the fridge to chill.
3. Put ice water in a large mixing bowl. Place a small bowl on top of the large bowl with ice. Pour cold milk and sugar into the small bowl and whisk until the sugar is dissolved. Stir in the cream and vanilla. Stir to combine.
4. Place the cold freezer bowl in the Cuisinart Ice Cream Maker. Turn on the machine and pour in the mixture. Add one package of crushed Oreos five minutes before the time ends.
5. Stop in 25 minutes until the mixture becomes soft and creamy.
6. Place in a spring form pan and top with the chilled fruit sauce.

**Nutrition Info:** Calories per serving: 121; Protein:1.22 g; Carbs: 13.8g; Fat: 7.3g Sugar: 12.2g

### 386. White Chocolate Citrus Rose Frozen Yogurt

Servings: 1 Quart
Cooking Time: 2 Hours 35 Minutes
**Ingredients:**
- 1 quart container full-fat plain yogurt
- ¼ teaspoon salt
- 1 cup sugar
- 1 teaspoon vanilla extract
- 6 ounces chopped white chocolate
- ½ teaspoon citrus extract
- ½ teaspoon rose water

**Directions:**
1. NOTE: Freeze your ice cream bowl for at least 24hrs prior to starting!
2. Melt the white chocolate and let it cool a bit
3. Place the yogurt in a bowl. Use a whisk to mix in the sugar and salt. Continue to whisk for about 4 minutes until the sugar dissolves. Then mix in the vanilla extract, rose water, citrus extract and white chocolate.
4. Pour the ingredients into your ice cream maker, and let it churn for 25 minutes.
5. Put the frozen yogurt in an airtight container and place in the freezer for

### 387. Walnut Mint Pomegranate Frozen Yogurt

Servings: 1 Quart
Cooking Time: 2 Hours 35 Minutes
**Ingredients:**
- 1 quart container full-fat plain yogurt
- ¼ teaspoon salt
- 1 cup sugar
- 1 tablespoon mint extract
- 1 cup 100% pomegranate juice
- 1/2 cup walnuts

**Directions:**
1. NOTE: Freeze your ice cream bowl for at least 24hrs prior to starting!
2. Place the yogurt in a bowl. Use a whisk to mix in the sugar and salt. Continue to whisk for about 4 minutes until the sugar dissolves. Then mix in the mint extract, and pomegranate juice.
3. Pour the ingredients into your ice cream maker, and let it churn for 25 minutes. About 5 minutes before the ice cream is done churning add the chocolate chips to your ice cream maker.
4. Put the frozen yogurt in an airtight container and place in the freezer for at least 2 hours, until desired consistency is reached.

### 388. Ice Cream Sliders

Servings: 6
Cooking Time: 25 Minutes
**Ingredients:**
- 1 cup cold whole milk
- ¾ cup granulated sugar
- 2 cups cold heavy cream
- 1 teaspoon vanilla extract
- 10 pieces vanilla wafers
- Toppings of your choice (nuts, graham crackers, marshmallows)
- Commercial caramel sauce

**Directions:**
1. Put ice water in a large mixing bowl. Place a small bowl on top of the large bowl with ice. Pour cold milk and sugar into the small bowl and whisk until the sugar is dissolved. Stir in the cream and vanilla. Stir to combine.
2. Place the cold freezer bowl in the Cuisinart Ice Cream Maker. Turn on the machine and pour in the mixture. Add one package of crushed Oreos five minutes before the time ends.
3. Stop in 25 minutes until the mixture becomes soft and creamy.
4. Transfer into an air-tight container and freeze overnight.
5. Place the ice cream on a bowl and top with wafers and toppings of your choice. Drizzle with caramel sauce.
6. Serve immediately.

**Nutrition Info:** Calories per serving: 352; Protein: 3.1g; Carbs: 44.1g; Fat: 18.5g Sugar: 31.6g

### 389. Watermelon Strawberry Frozen Yogurt

Servings: 12
Cooking Time: 10 Minutes
**Ingredients:**
- 1 cup watermelon, cubed and seeds removed
- 2 cups frozen strawberries, hulled
- 1 banana, peeled
- ¼ cup honey
- A pinch of salt
- 4 cups Greek yogurt

**Directions:**
1. Place all ingredients in a food processor. Pulse until smooth.
2. Turn on the Cuisinart and pour in the mixture.
3. Churn for 10 minutes.
4. Transfer in an airtight container and freeze overnight.

**Nutrition Info:** Calories per serving: 97; Protein: 3.2g; Carbs: 16.2g; Fat: 2.8g Sugar: 13.3g

### 390. Fun Fig Mint Milkshake

Servings: 6
Cooking Time: 25 Minutes
**Ingredients:**
- 2 cups heavy cream
- 1 cup milk
- 3/4 cup sugar
- 2 teaspoons vanilla extract

- 1/4 cup lemon juice
- 2 cups peeled, diced figs
- 2 teaspoons chopped fresh mint

**Directions:**
1. Refer to note at the beginning of the chapter about freezing bowl.
2. Place the milk and cream in a bowl, and mix them together until well combined. Use a whisk to mix in the sugar. Continue to whisk for about 4 minutes until the sugar dissolves. Then mix in the vanilla extract, lemon juice, and mint.
3. Pour the ingredients into your ice cream maker, and let it churn for 10-15 minutes, until desired consistency is reached. About 5 minutes before the ice cream is done churning add the figs to your ice cream maker.
4. Serve immediately.

### 391. Frozen Cantaloupe Yogurt

Servings: 6
Cooking Time: 10 Minutes
**Ingredients:**
- 3 cups non-fat Greek yogurt
- 2/3 cup white sugar
- 1 teaspoon vanilla extract
- 1 cup cantaloupe flesh

**Directions:**
1. Place all ingredients in a food processor. Pulse until smooth.
2. Turn on the Cuisinart and pour in the mixture.
3. Churn for 10 minutes.
4. Transfer in an airtight container and freeze overnight.

**Nutrition Info:** Calories per serving: 126; Protein: 9.3g; Carbs: 21.7g; Fat: 0.3g Sugar: 20g

### 392. Chocolate Matcha Gelato

Servings: 4-6
Cooking Time: 2 Hours 35 Minutes
**Ingredients:**
- 1/2 cup heavy cream
- 2 cups milk
- 3/4 cup sugar
- 1 teaspoon vanilla extract
- 1 tablespoon matcha
- 2 ounces chopped dark chocolate

**Directions:**
1. Refer to note at the beginning of the chapter about freezing bowl.
2. Place the milk and cream in a bowl, and mix them together until well combined. Use a whisk to mix in the sugar. Continue to whisk for about 4 minutes until the sugar dissolves. Then mix in the vanilla extract. Finally whisk in the matcha until well mixed.
3. Pour the ingredients into your ice cream maker, and let it churn for 25 minutes. About 5 minutes before the ice cream is done churning add the chocolate to your ice cream maker.
4. Put the gelato in an airtight container and place in the freezer for up to 2 hours, until desired consistency is reached.

### 393. Grape Sorbet

Servings: 6
Cooking Time: 10 Minutes
**Ingredients:**
- 4 cups seedless grapes
- 1/3 cup granulated sugar
- 2 tablespoon lemon juice

**Directions:**
1. Place the grapes and sugar in a blender and pulse until smooth.
2. Pass the mixture through a sieve to remove the skin.
3. Add the lemon juice to the grape puree.
4. Turn on the Cuisinart and pour in the mixture.
5. Churn for 10 minutes.
6. Transfer in an airtight container and freeze overnight.

**Nutrition Info:** Calories per serving: 100; Protein: 1g; Carbs: 26g; Fat: 0g Sugar: 18g

### 394. Snicker Doodle Ice Cream Sandwiches

Servings: 24
Cooking Time: 1 Hours, 15min
**Ingredients:**
- 1 1/2 cups all-purpose flour
- 1 teaspoon baking soda
- 1 teaspoon cream of tartar
- 1 cup sugar, divided
- 1/2 cup unsalted butter

- 1/4 teaspoon kosher salt
- 1 large egg, room temperature
- 2 1/4 teaspoons ground cinnamon

**Directions:**
1. Whisk flour, baking soda, and cream of tartar in a medium bowl. For best results, use an electric mixer on medium
2. Beat butter in a large bowl, about 2 to 2 1/2 minutes, beating the mix until light and fluffy
3. Take the dough, put it into a ball, wrap ball in plastic wrap then chill it for about a 30min.
4. Preheat oven to 400°F. Put parchment paper on 2 baking sheets.
5. Take the remaining 1/4 cup sugar and cinnamon, in a small bowl and mix it.
6. Roll balls in cinnamon sugar using your hands to do so into a tablespoonful of dough balls.
7. Transfer dough balls to baking sheet about 1" - 2" apart from each other.
8. Bake until golden brown on the edges. About 10 minutes
9. Transfer to a wire rack to cook

### 395. Agave Lemon Chocolate Sorbet

Servings: 3
Cooking Time: 5 Hours
**Ingredients:**
- 2 cups water
- 1 cup unsweetened cocoa powder
- 3/4 cup agave
- 2 tablespoons lemon juice

**Directions:**
1. NOTE: Freeze your ice cream bowl for at least 24hrs prior to starting!
2. Mix together the water and agave in a medium saucepan on medium heat. Stir frequently until the agave dissolve. Mix in the cocoa powder and lemon juice and let the mixture come to a simmer. Let the mixture cook for 3 minutes. Allow the mixture to cool completely. Then refrigerate covered for 2 hours.
3. Pour the ingredients into your ice cream maker, and let it churn for 25-30 minutes.
4. Place in an airtight container for up to 2 hours, until desired consistency is reached.

### 396. Berry Ice Cream Cake

Servings: 8
Cooking Time: 25 Minutes
**Ingredients:**
- 1 cup graham crackers, crushed
- ¼ cup butter
- 1 cup cold whole milk
- ¾ cup granulated sugar
- 2 cups cold heavy cream
- 1 teaspoon vanilla extract
- 2 cups of frozen berries, assorted

**Directions:**
1. In a bowl, mix together the graham crackers and butter to form a dough. Press dough in spring form pan and place in the fridge to chill.
2. Put ice water in a large mixing bowl. Place a small bowl on top of the large bowl with ice. Pour cold milk and sugar into the small bowl and whisk until the sugar is dissolved. Stir in the cream and vanilla. Stir to combine.
3. Place the cold freezer bowl in the Cuisinart Ice Cream Maker. Turn on the machine and pour in the mixture. Add one package of crushed Oreos five minutes before the time ends.
4. Stop in 25 minutes until the mixture becomes soft and creamy.
5. Transfer into a prepared spring form pan and top with berries of your choice.
6. Freeze for 4 hours.
7. Cut into wedges before serving.

**Nutrition Info:** Calories per serving: 277; Protein: 2.9g; Carbs: 23.8g; Fat: 19.5g Sugar: 23g

### 397. Dark Chocolate Coconut Frozen Yogurt

Servings: 8
Cooking Time: 20 Minutes
**Ingredients:**
- 1 14-ounce coconut milk
- ¼ cup honey
- 2 teaspoons cocoa powder
- 1 tablespoon arrowroot powder

- A pinch of salt
- 1 ½ cup plain yogurt
- ½ cup semi-sweet chocolate chips
- ½ cup dried coconut flakes

**Directions:**
1. In a saucepan, add the coconut milk, honey, cocoa, and arrowroot. Bring to a boil over low heat until the mixture slightly thickens. Make sure to mix constantly. Remove from the heat and set aside to cool.
2. In a cold bowl, mix together salt and yogurt. Add the coconut milk mixture. Whisk until smooth.
3. Turn on the Cuisinart and pour in the mixture.
4. Churn for 10 minutes.
5. Transfer in an airtight container and freeze overnight.
6. Garnish with chocolate chips and coconut flakes before serving.

**Nutrition Info:** Calories per serving: 242; Protein: 4g; Carbs: 35g; Fat: 9g Sugar: 18g

## 398. Succulent Waffle Cookie Ice Cream Sandwich

Servings: 6
Cooking Time: 5 Minutes
**Ingredients:**
- 1 cup flour
- 1 tbsp. sugar
- 2 tsp. baking powder
- ½ tsp. cinnamon
- ¼ tsp. salt
- 1 egg
- 1 cup milk
- 1 ½ tbs. melted butter

**Directions:**
1. Crack eggs and mix in a bowl with salt and pepper.
2. Pour 2 tbsps. Milk to the eggs and whisk. Mix in the other ingredients until the batter is smooth.
3. Spray your waffle maker with oil. Pour 2 tbsp. batter into the waffle maker and cook until crispy. Repeat until all the batter is used.
4. Put a scoop of ice cream (that you made from this book) in the middle of two waffles.

5. Drizzle honey over the top for a sweeter experience.

## 399. Apple Chocolate Gelato

Servings: 4-6
Cooking Time: 2 Hours 35 Minutes
**Ingredients:**
- 1/2 cup heavy cream
- 2 cups milk
- 3/4 cup sugar
- 1 teaspoon vanilla extract
- 1 cup apples
- ½ cup finely chopped semi-sweet chocolate

**Directions:**
1. NOTE: Freeze your ice cream bowl for at least 24hrs prior to starting!
2. Puree the apples in a food processor or blender.
3. Place the milk and cream in a bowl, and mix them together until well combined. Use a whisk to mix in the sugar. Continue to whisk for about 4 minutes until the sugar dissolves. Then mix in the vanilla extract and apple puree.
4. Pour the ingredients into your ice cream maker, and let it churn for 25 minutes. About 5 minutes before the ice cream is done churning add the chocolate to your ice cream maker.
5. Put the gelato in an airtight container and place in the freezer for up to 2 hours, until desired consistency is reached.

## 400. Lemon Strawberry Sorbet

Servings: 6
Cooking Time: 15 Minutes
**Ingredients:**
- 1 cup water
- 1 cup sugar
- 2 teaspoons lemon zest
- 1 cup lemon juice, freshly squeezed
- 1 cup fresh strawberries, hulled

**Directions:**
1. Place the water and sugar in a saucepan and bring to a boil over medium heat until the sugar dissolves. Remove from the heat and place in the fridge to chill for at least 3 hours.

2. Once cooled, place the water-sugar mixture into a blender and add the rest of the ingredients. Pulse until smooth.
3. Turn on the Cuisinart and pour in the mixture.
4. Churn for 10 minutes.
5. Transfer in an airtight container and freeze overnight.

**Nutrition Info:** Calories per serving: 82; Protein: 0.3g; Carbs: 21.4g; Fat: 0.2g Sugar: 18.5g

## 401. Cinnamon Maple Bacon Milkshake

Servings: 6
Cooking Time: 25 Minutes
**Ingredients:**
- 2 cups heavy cream
- 1 cup milk
- 3/4 cup sugar
- 1 teaspoon cinnamon
- 1 teaspoons vanilla extract
- 6 slices finely chopped cooked thick cut bacon
- ½ cup maple syrup

**Directions:**
1. NOTE: Freeze your ice cream bowl for at least 24hrs prior to starting!
2. Place the milk and cream in a bowl, and mix them together until well combined. Use a whisk to mix in the sugar. Continue to whisk for about 4 minutes until the sugar dissolves. Then mix in the vanilla extract, cinnamon and maple syrup.
3. Pour the ingredients into your ice cream maker, and let it churn for 10-15 minutes, until desired consistency is reached. About 5 minutes before the ice cream is done churning add the bacon to your ice cream maker.
4. Serve immediately.

## 402. Orange Dream Soda Ice Cream

Servings: 6
Cooking Time: 2 Hours 50 Minutes
**Ingredients:**
- 2 cups heavy cream
- 1 cup milk
- 3/4 cup sugar
- 1 teaspoon vanilla extract
- 20 ounces of your favorite orange soda

**Directions:**
1. Refer to note at the beginning of the chapter about freezing bowl.
2. Place the milk and cream in a bowl, and mix them together until well combined. Use a whisk to mix in the sugar. Continue to whisk for about 4 minutes until the sugar dissolves. Then mix in the vanilla extract and orange soda.
3. Pour the ingredients into your ice cream maker, and let it churn for 25 minutes.
4. Put the ice cream in an airtight container and place in the freezer for around 2 hours. Allow the ice cream to thaw for 15 minutes before serving.

## 403. Chocolaty Chocolate Pretzel Gelato

Servings: 4-6
Cooking Time: 2 Hours 35 Minutes
**Ingredients:**
- 1/2 cup heavy cream
- 2 cups milk
- 3/4 cup sugar
- 1 teaspoon vanilla extract
- 7 ounces semi-sweet chocolate
- 4 ounce pretzels

**Directions:**
1. Refer to note at the beginning of the chapter about freezing bowl.
2. Melt the chocolate, and allow it to cool a little bit.
3. Place the milk and cream in a bowl, and mix them together until well combined. Use a whisk to mix in the sugar. Continue to whisk for about 4 minutes until the sugar dissolves. Then mix in the vanilla extract. Finally mix in the chocolate
4. Place the pretzels in a food processor, and process until the cookies are no bigger than chocolate chips. If you don't have a food processor place the pretzels in a large resealable plastic bag, and seal it shut. Use your hands, a mallet, or a rolling pin to crush the pretzels.

5. Pour the ingredients into your ice cream maker, and let it churn for 25 minutes. About 5 minutes before the ice cream is done churning add the pretzels to your ice cream maker.
6. Put the gelato in an airtight container and place in the freezer for up to 2 hours, until desired consistency is reached.

## 404. Blackberry Sugar-free Keto Frozen Yogurt

Servings: 10
Cooking Time: 10 Minutes
**Ingredients:**
- 4 cups blackberries
- 1 cup Greek yogurt
- 1 tablespoon lemon juice
- 1 teaspoon vanilla extract

**Directions:**
1. Place all ingredients in a food processor. Pulse until smooth. Place in the fridge to chill.
2. Turn on the Cuisinart and pour in the mixture.
3. Churn for 10 minutes.
4. Transfer in an airtight container and freeze overnight.

**Nutrition Info:** Calories per serving: 63; Protein: 4g; Carbs: 10g; Fat: 0g Sugar: 3g

## 405. Strawberry Basil Frozen Yogurt

Servings: 6
Cooking Time: 10 Minutes
**Ingredients:**
- 1-pound strawberries, hulled
- 1 lemon, zested and juiced
- ½ cup sugar
- ¼ cup fresh basil leaves
- 1 ½ cups whole Greek yogurt
- 1 tablespoon honey

**Directions:**
1. Place the strawberries, lemon zest, juice, sugar, and basil leaves in a food processor. Pulse until smooth.
2. Place the mixture in a bowl and add the yogurt and honey. Whisk until combined. Chill in the fridge.
3. Turn on the Cuisinart and pour in the mixture.
4. Churn for 10 minutes.
5. Transfer in an airtight container and freeze overnight.

**Nutrition Info:** Calories per serving: 106 ; Protein: 2.7g; Carbs: 20.4g; Fat: 2.2g Sugar: 17.8g

## 406. Vanilla Peanut Butter Layer

Servings: 5
Cooking Time: 25 Minutes
**Ingredients:**
- 1 cup cold whole milk
- ¾ cup granulated sugar
- 2 cups cold heavy cream
- 1 teaspoon vanilla extract
- 2 packs graham cracker, crushed
- ½ cup smooth peanut butter
- ¼ cup toasted peanuts, crushed

**Directions:**
1. Put ice water in a large mixing bowl. Place a small bowl on top of the large bowl with ice. Pour cold milk and sugar into the small bowl and whisk until the sugar is dissolved. Stir in the cream and vanilla. Stir to combine.
2. Place the cold freezer bowl in the Cuisinart Ice Cream Maker. Turn on the machine and pour in the mixture. Add one package of crushed Oreos five minutes before the time ends.
3. Stop in 25 minutes until the mixture becomes soft and creamy.
4. Transfer into an air-tight container and freeze overnight.
5. Assemble the dessert by putting crushed graham cracker in the bottom of a parfait glass then layer with vanilla ice cream and peanut butter.
6. Repeat until three layers are formed.
7. Garnish with toasted peanuts.
8. Serve immediately.

**Nutrition Info:** Calories per serving: 521; Protein: 14.1g; Carbs: 42.8g; Fat: 34.5g Sugar: 24.9 g

## 407. Mint Greek Frozen Yogurt

Servings: 10
Cooking Time: 10 Minutes
**Ingredients:**
- 3 cups plain Greek yogurt
- 1 cup sugar

- ¼ cup lemon juice
- 2 teaspoons vanilla
- 1/8 teaspoon salt
- 2 tablespoons mint, chopped finely

**Directions:**
1. Place the yogurt, sugar, lemon juice, vanilla, and salt in a cold bowl. Whisk until smooth. Add the chopped mint.
2. Turn on the Cuisinart and pour in the mixture.
3. Churn for 10 minutes.
4. Transfer in an airtight container and freeze overnight.

**Nutrition Info:** Calories per serving: 84; Protein: 2g; Carbs: 15g; Fat: 1g Sugar: 5g

## 408. Aromatic Rose Gelato

Servings: 4-6
Cooking Time: 2 Hours 35 Minutes
**Ingredients:**
- 1/2 cup heavy cream
- 2 cups milk
- 3/4 cup sugar
- 1 teaspoon rose extract

**Directions:**
1. Refer to note at the beginning of the chapter about freezing bowl.
2. Place the milk and cream in a bowl, and mix them together until well combined. Use a whisk to mix in the sugar. Continue to whisk for about 4 minutes until the sugar dissolves. Then mix in the rose extract.
3. Pour the ingredients into your ice cream maker, and let it churn for 25 minutes.
4. Put the gelato in an airtight container and place in the freezer for up to 2 hours, until desired consistency is reached.

## 409. Vegan Chunky Chocolate Banana Milkshake

Servings: 9
Cooking Time: 40 Minutes
**Ingredients:**
- 3/4 cup water
- 1 1/4 cups full fat coconut milk or coconut cream (as thick as possible)
- 2/3 cup organic cane sugar
- 2/3 cup unsweetened cocoa powder
- 1/4 tsp sea salt
- 6 ounces vegan dark chocolate, finely chopped
- 1/2 tsp pure vanilla extract
- ½ cup sliced frozen bananas

**Directions:**
1. Refer to note at the beginning of the chapter about freezing bowl.
2. Put the first 5 ingredients in a large saucepan, and heat it on medium-high heat. Mix the ingredients together using a whisk. Allow the mixture to come to a low boil. Continue to whisk often, and remain cooking on a low boil for 1 minute.
3. Take the pan off the heat, and mix in the chocolate and vanilla extract using the whisk. Continue to mix until the chocolate is melted.
4. Place the mixture in a blender with the bananas, and blend on high speed for about 30 seconds.
5. Allow the mixture to cool
6. Pour the ingredients into your ice cream maker, and let it churn for 10-15 minutes, until desired consistency is reached.
7. Serve immediately.

## 410. Lingering Lemon Mint Sorbet

Servings: 4
Cooking Time: 3 Hours 10 Minutes
**Ingredients:**
- ½ cup lemon juice
- 1 cup boiling water
- 1 cup chopped mint
- Zest of 1 lemon
- 1 cup sugar

**Directions:**
1. Refer to note at the beginning of the chapter about freezing bowl.
2. Mix together the sugar, lemon zest, and mint in a heat safe bowl. Then pour in the water, and stir frequently until sugar dissolves. Let the mixture sit for 20 minutes. Then strain it into another bowl. Mix in the lemon juice and let the mixture cool totally.
3. Pour the ingredients into your ice cream maker, and let it churn for 25-30 minutes.

4. Place in an airtight container for up to 2 hours, until desired consistency is reached.

## 411. Aromatic Earl Grey Tea Ice Cream

Servings: 6
Cooking Time: 2 Hours 50 Minutes
**Ingredients:**
- 2 cups heavy cream
- 1 cup milk
- 3/4 cup sugar
- 1 teaspoon vanilla extract
- 4 tablespoons earl grey tea

**Directions:**
1. Refer to note at the beginning of the chapter about freezing bowl.
2. Put the milk in a pan and bring it to a simmer. Add in the tea, take the pot off the heat, and allow to seep for 5 minutes. Discard the tea, and allow milk to cool.
3. Place the milk and cream in a bowl, and mix them together until well combined. Use a whisk to mix in the sugar. Continue to whisk for about 4 minutes until the sugar dissolves. Then mix in the vanilla extract.
4. Pour the ingredients into your ice cream maker, and let it churn for 25 minutes.
5. Put the ice cream in an airtight container and place in the freezer for around 2 hours. Allow the ice cream to thaw for 15 minutes before serving.

## 412. Raspberry Lavender Sorbet

Servings: 6
Cooking Time: 5 Hours 35 Minutes
**Ingredients:**
- 3 cups, mashed raspberries
- ½ teaspoon lavender
- 3/4 cup sugar
- 1/2 teaspoon salt
- 2 tablespoons vanilla extract
- 2 ½ teaspoons lime juice

**Directions:**
1. NOTE: Freeze your ice cream bowl for at least 24hrs prior to starting!
2. Use a food processor or blender to puree the lavender, sugar, raspberries, and vanilla extract. Then blend in the salt and lime juice. Strain the mixture into a bowl, and refrigerate covered for 2-3 hours.
3. Pour the ingredients into your ice cream maker, and let it churn for 25-30 minutes.
4. Place in an airtight container for up to 2 hours, until desired consistency is reached.

## 413. Blueberry Pumpkin Spice Waffle Ice Cream Sandwich

Servings: 6
Cooking Time: 5 Minutes
**Ingredients:**
- 1 cup flour
- 1 tbsp. sugar
- 2 tsp. baking powder
- ½ tsp. cinnamon
- ½ tsp. pumpkin spice
- 1 cup blueberries (organic)
- ¼ tsp. salt
- 1 egg
- 1 cup milk
- 1 ½ tbs. melted butter

**Directions:**
1. Crack eggs and mix in a bowl with salt and pepper.
2. Pour 2 tbsps. Milk to the eggs and whisk. Mix in the other ingredients until the batter is smooth.
3. Spray your waffle maker with oil. Pour 2 tbsp. batter into the waffle maker and cook until crispy. Repeat until all the batter is used.
4. Put a scoop of ice cream (that you made from this book) in the middle of two waffles.
5. Drizzle honey over the top for a sweeter experience.

## 414. Cherry Mango Sorbet

Servings: 2
Cooking Time: 15 Minutes
**Ingredients:**
- 1 cup frozen mango chunks
- ½ cup frozen pineapple chunks
- 1 cup preserved cherries
- 1 tablespoon water

**Directions:**

1. Place all ingredients in a blender. Pulse until smooth.
2. Turn on the Cuisinart and pour in the mixture.
3. Churn for 15 minutes.
4. Transfer in an airtight container and freeze overnight.

**Nutrition Info:** Calories per serving: 202 ; Protein: 1.7g; Carbs: 51.7g; Fat: 0.3g Sugar: 32g

## 415. Lemon Frozen Yogurt

Servings: 4
Cooking Time: 10 Minutes
**Ingredients:**
- ¾ cup sugar
- 2 tablespoons lemon juice
- 1/3 tablespoon lemon zest
- ½ teaspoon vanilla
- 2 cups plain yogurt

**Directions:**
1. Place all ingredients in a food processor. Pulse until smooth. Place in the fridge to chill.
2. Turn on the Cuisinart and pour in the mixture.
3. Churn for 10 minutes.
4. Transfer in an airtight container and freeze overnight.

**Nutrition Info:** Calories per serving: 151 ; Protein: 4.2g; Carbs: 25.1g; Fat: 4g Sugar: 23.4g

## 416. Caribbean Pineapple Mint Sorbet

Servings: 9
Cooking Time: 2 Hours 40 Minutes
**Ingredients:**
- 1 diced, peeled, and cored small pineapple
- 2 tablespoons lemon juice
- ½ cup mint
- 1 cup plus 2 tablespoons sugar

**Directions:**
1. NOTE: Freeze your ice cream bowl for at least 24hrs prior to starting!
2. Puree the pineapple, mint and lemon juice in a food processor or blender. Then add in the sugar and puree until the sugar dissolves.
3. Pour the ingredients into your ice cream maker, and let it churn for 25-30 minutes.
4. Place in an airtight container for up to 2 hours, until desired consistency is reached.

## 417. Neapolitan Frozen Yogurt

Servings: 10
Cooking Time: 10 Minutes
**Ingredients:**
- 1 cup cherries, pitted
- ½ cup icing sugar
- 1 lemon, juiced
- 2 cups plain Greek yogurt
- ½ cup frozen mango chunks
- 2 tablespoons honey
- ¼ cup frozen blueberries
- Mint leaves for garnish

**Directions:**
1. Place the cherries, icing sugar, and lemon juice in a food processor. Pulse until smooth.
2. Place in a bowl and add the yogurt. Allow to chill in the fridge for 30 minutes.
3. Turn on the Cuisinart and pour in the mixture.
4. Churn for 10 minutes.
5. Five minutes before churning ends, add the mango, honey, and blueberries.
6. Transfer in an airtight container and freeze overnight.
7. Serve with mint.

**Nutrition Info:** Calories per serving: 66; Protein: 2.1g; Carbs: 10.9g; Fat: 2g Sugar: 9.4g

## 418. Healthy Greek Frozen Yogurt

Servings: 5
Cooking Time: 10 Minutes
**Ingredients:**
- 4 cups frozen fruit of your choice
- ½ cup plain Greek yogurt
- 2 teaspoons vanilla extract
- 3 tablespoons honey

**Directions:**
1. Place all ingredients in a food processor. Pulse until smooth.

2. Turn on the Cuisinart and pour in the mixture.
3. Churn for 10 minutes.
4. Transfer in an airtight container and freeze overnight.

**Nutrition Info:** Calories per serving: 200; Protein: 2.9g; Carbs: 48.8g; Fat: 0.2g Sugar: 47g

### 419. Plum Sorbet

Servings: Makes 1 Quart
Cooking Time: 4 Hours 35 Minutes
**Ingredients:**
- 2 pounds pitted, quartered plums
- 1 tablespoon light corn syrup
- 1 cup sugar
- ¼ teaspoon salt

**Directions:**
1. Refer to note at the beginning of the chapter about freezing bowl.
2. Use a food processor or blender to puree the plums. Put in the sugar and corn syrup, and process for about another 30 seconds. Then blend in the salt. Strain the mixture into a bowl, and refrigerate covered for 2-3 hours.
3. Pour the ingredients into your ice cream maker, and let it churn for 25-30 minutes.
4. Place in an airtight container for up to 2 hours, until desired consistency is reached.

### 420. Orange Sorbet

Servings: 7
Cooking Time: 15 Minutes
**Ingredients:**
- 1 orange, zest, and juice
- 2 cups water
- 1 1/3 cups sugar
- 3 cups fresh orange juice
- 4 tablespoons lemon juice

**Directions:**
1. Place all ingredients in a saucepan. Turn on the heat and allow to simmer for 5 minutes or until the sugar dissolves.
2. Remove from the heat and place in the fridge to cool for 2 hours.

3. Turn on the Cuisinart and pour in the mixture.
4. Churn for 10 minutes.
5. Transfer in an airtight container and freeze overnight.

**Nutrition Info:** Calories per serving: 146; Protein: 1g; Carbs: 35.9g; Fat: 0.2g Sugar: 30.6g

### 421. Berry Pumpkin Spice Frozen Yogurt

Servings: 1.5 Quarts
Cooking Time: 2 Hours 35 Minutes
**Ingredients:**
- 1 quart container full-fat plain yogurt
- ¼ teaspoon salt
- 1 cup sugar
- 1 tablespoon vanilla extract
- 1 cup raspberries
- 1 cup blueberries
- 2 tablespoons pumpkin spice

**Directions:**
1. NOTE: Freeze your ice cream bowl for at least 24hrs prior to starting!
2. Puree the raspberries, blueberries and pumpkin spice in a food processor or blender
3. Place the yogurt in a bowl. Use a whisk to mix in the sugar and salt. Continue to whisk for about 4 minutes until the sugar dissolves. Then mix in the vanilla extract, berry and pumpkin spice puree.
4. Pour the ingredients into your ice cream maker, and let it churn for 25 minutes.
5. Put the frozen yogurt in an airtight container and place in the freezer for at least 2 hours, until desired consistency is reached.

### 422. Vegan Chocolate Soft Serve Ice Cream

Servings: 9
Cooking Time: 50 Minutes
**Ingredients:**
- 3/4 cup water
- 1 1/4 cups full fat coconut milk or coconut cream (as thick as possible)
- 2/3 cup organic cane sugar
- 2/3 cup unsweetened cocoa powder
- 1/4 tsp sea salt

- 6 ounces vegan dark chocolate, finely chopped
- 1/2 tsp pure vanilla extract

**Directions:**
1. Refer to note at the beginning of the chapter about freezing bowl.
2. Put the first 5 ingredients in a large saucepan, and heat it on medium-high heat. Mix the ingredients together using a whisk. Allow the mixture to come to a low boil. Continue to whisk often, and remain cooking on a low boil for 1 minute.
3. Take the pan off the heat, and mix in the chocolate and vanilla extract using the whisk. Continue to mix until the chocolate is melted.
4. Place the mixture in a blender, and blend on high speed for about 30 seconds.
5. Allow the mixture to cool
6. Pour the ingredients into your ice cream maker, and let it churn for 25 minutes.
7. Serve immediately.

### 423. Creamy White Chocolate Rose Frozen Yogurt

Servings: 1 Quart
Cooking Time: 2 Hours 35 Minutes
**Ingredients:**
- 1 quart container full-fat plain yogurt
- ¼ teaspoon salt
- 1 cup sugar
- 1 teaspoon vanilla extract
- 6 ounces chopped white chocolate
- ½ teaspoon rose water

**Directions:**
1. Refer to note at the beginning of the chapter about freezing bowl.
2. Melt the white chocolate and let it cool a bit
3. Place the yogurt in a bowl. Use a whisk to mix in the sugar and salt. Continue to whisk for about 4 minutes until the sugar dissolves. Then mix in the vanilla extract, rose water and white chocolate.
4. Pour the ingredients into your ice cream maker, and let it churn for 25 minutes.

5. Put the frozen yogurt in an airtight container and place in the freezer for at least 2 hours, until desired consistency is reached.

### 424. Vegan Pistachio "punch" Chocolate Chunk Gelato

Servings: 4
Cooking Time: 2 Hours 35 Minutes
**Ingredients:**
- 2 cups shelled, roasted, salted pistachios
- 1 can coconut milk
- I/2 cup arrowroot
- ¾ cup sugar
- 1 teaspoon lime juice
- 4 ounces chopped vegan chocolate

**Directions:**
1. Refer to note at the beginning of the chapter about freezing bowl.
2. Pulse the pistachios in a food processor for about 3 minutes
3. Place all ingredients EXCEPT the chocolate in a blender. Blend on high speed until smooth.
4. Pour the mixture into your ice cream maker, and let it churn for 25 minutes. About 5 minutes before the ice cream is done churning add the chocolate to your ice cream maker.
5. Put the gelato in an airtight container and place in the freezer for up to 2 hours, until desired consistency is reached.

### 425. Lemon Scented Rose Gelato

Servings: 4-6
Cooking Time: 2 Hours 35 Minutes
**Ingredients:**
- 1/2 cup heavy cream
- 2 cups milk
- 3/4 cup sugar
- 1 teaspoon rose extract
- juice of ½ lemon

**Directions:**
1. NOTE: Freeze your ice cream bowl for at least 24hrs prior to starting!
2. Place the milk and cream in a bowl, and mix them together until well combined. Use a whisk to mix in the sugar. Continue to whisk for about 4

minutes until the sugar dissolves. Then mix in the rose extract.
3. Pour the ingredients into your ice cream maker, and let it churn for 25 minutes.
4. Put the gelato in an airtight container and place in the freezer for up to 2 hours, until desired consistency is reached.

### 426. Frozen Nanaimo Pie

Servings: 16
Cooking Time: 40 Minutes
**Ingredients:**
- ¾ cup graham cracker crumbs
- 1/3 cup shredded coconut
- 1/3 cup chopped walnut
- ¼ cup cocoa powder
- ¼ cup brown sugar
- 1/3 cup melted butter
- 1 cup cold whole milk
- ¾ cup granulated sugar
- 2 cups cold heavy cream
- 1 teaspoon vanilla extract
- 2 tablespoons semi-sweet chocolate, chopped
- ¼ cup whipping cream

**Directions:**
1. In a bowl, combine the graham crackers, coconut, walnut, cocoa powder, brown sugar, and butter to form a dough.
2. Press the dough in a spring form pan and set aside in the fridge to set.
3. In a bowl, mix together the graham crackers and butter to form a dough. Press dough in spring form pan and place in the fridge to chill.
4. Put ice water in a large mixing bowl. Place a small bowl on top of the large bowl with ice. Pour cold milk and sugar into the small bowl and whisk until the sugar is dissolved. Stir in the cream and vanilla. Stir to combine.
5. Place the cold freezer bowl in the Cuisinart Ice Cream Maker. Turn on the machine and pour in the mixture. Add one package of crushed Oreos five minutes before the time ends.
6. Stop in 25 minutes until the mixture becomes soft and creamy.
7. Pour into the prepared pan and top with whipping cream and chocolate chips.

**Nutrition Info:** Calories per serving: 151; Protein: 1.4g; Carbs: 12.3g; Fat: 11.36g Sugar: 5.3g

### 427. Vegan Chunky Chocolate Almond Ice Cream

Servings: 9
Cooking Time: 3 Hours 15 Minutes
**Ingredients:**
- 3/4 cup water
- 1 1/4 cups full fat coconut milk or coconut cream (as thick as possible)
- 2/3 cup organic cane sugar
- 2/3 cup unsweetened cocoa powder
- 1/4 tsp sea salt
- 6 ounces vegan dark chocolate, finely chopped
- 1/2 tsp pure vanilla extract
- ½ cup chopped almonds

**Directions:**
1. Refer to note at the beginning of the chapter about freezing bowl.
2. Put the first 5 ingredients in a large saucepan, and heat it on medium-high heat. Mix the ingredients together using a whisk. Allow the mixture to come to a low boil. Continue to whisk often, and remain cooking on a low boil for 1 minute.
3. Take the pan off the heat, and mix in the chocolate and vanilla extract using the whisk. Continue to mix until the chocolate is melted.
4. Place the mixture in a blender, and blend on high speed for about 30 seconds.
5. Allow the mixture to cool
6. Pour the ingredients into your ice cream maker, and let it churn for 25 minutes. About 5 minutes before the ice cream is done churning add the snickers to your ice cream maker.
7. Put the ice cream in an airtight container and place in the freezer for around 2 hours. Allow the ice cream to thaw for 15 minutes before serving.

### 428. Strawberry Vanilla Frozen Yogurt

Servings: 6

Cooking Time: 10 Minutes
**Ingredients:**
- 3 cups non-fat Greek yogurt
- 2/3 cup white sugar
- 1 teaspoon vanilla extract
- 1 cup strawberries, hulled

**Directions:**
1. Place all ingredients in a food processor. Pulse until smooth.
2. Turn on the Cuisinart and pour in the mixture.
3. Churn for 10 minutes.
4. Transfer in an airtight container and freeze overnight.

**Nutrition Info:** Calories per serving: 124; Protein: 9.2g; Carbs: 21.2g; Fat: 0.3g Sugar: 19.8g

### 429. Sugar Cookie Sandwich With Ice Cream

Servings: 10
Cooking Time: 25 Minutes
**Ingredients:**
- 1 cup cold whole milk
- ¾ cup granulated sugar
- 2 cups cold heavy cream
- 1 teaspoon vanilla extract
- 20 cinnamon sugar cookies

**Directions:**
1. Put ice water in a large mixing bowl. Place a small bowl on top of the large bowl with ice. Pour cold milk and sugar into the small bowl and whisk until the sugar is dissolved. Stir in the cream and vanilla. Stir to combine.
2. Place the cold freezer bowl in the Cuisinart Ice Cream Maker. Turn on the machine and pour in the mixture. Add one package of crushed Oreos five minutes before the time ends.
3. Stop in 25 minutes until the mixture becomes soft and creamy.
4. Transfer into an air-tight container and freeze overnight.
5. Spread the ice cream in between two sugar cookies.
6. Serve immediately.

**Nutrition Info:** Calories per serving: 369; Protein: 6g; Carbs: 54g; Fat: 14.6g Sugar: 37.1g

### 430. Pumpkin Frozen Yogurt

Servings: 4
Cooking Time: 10 Minutes
**Ingredients:**
- 2 cups plain Greek yogurt
- 4 ounces low-fat cream cheese, softened
- ½ cup canned pumpkin, mashed
- ¼ cup brown sugar
- 1 tablespoon pumpkin pie spice
- 1 teaspoon vanilla extract

**Directions:**
1. Place all ingredients in a food processor. Pulse until smooth.
2. Turn on the Cuisinart and pour in the mixture.
3. Churn for 10 minutes.
4. Transfer in an airtight container and freeze overnight.

**Nutrition Info:** Calories per serving: 198; Protein:12 g; Carbs: 24g; Fat: 7g Sugar:20 g

### 431. Caramel & Pistachio Milkshake

Servings: 6
Cooking Time: 25 Minutes
**Ingredients:**
- 2 cups heavy cream
- 1 cup milk
- 1 cup brown sugar
- 1 teaspoon vanilla extract
- 2 ounces caramel
- 1/3 cup finely chopped pistachios
- 1 tablespoon butter

**Directions:**
1. NOTE: Freeze your ice cream bowl for at least 24hrs prior to starting!
2. Melt the butter in a small skillet on medium heat. Add the Pistachios, and cook for about 5 minutes, until they become lightly browned.
3. Place the milk and cream in a bowl, and mix them together until well combined. Use a whisk to mix in the sugar. Continue to whisk for about 4 minutes until the sugar dissolves. Then mix in the vanilla extract.
4. Pour the ingredients into your ice cream maker, and let it churn for 10-15 minutes, until desired consistency is reached. About 5 minutes before

the ice cream is done churning add the caramel to your ice cream maker.

## 432. Vegan Big Blackberry Soy Frozen Yogurt

Servings: 1 Quart
Cooking Time: 2 Hours 30 Minutes
**Ingredients:**
- 2 ¾ cups unsweetened plain soy yogurt
- 1¼ blackberry jam

**Directions:**
1. Refer to note at the beginning of the chapter about freezing bowl.
2. Place the yogurt in a bowl and mix in the jam. Use a hand mixer to beat the mixture for 5 minutes.
3. Pour the ingredients into your ice cream maker, and let it churn for 25 minutes.
4. Put the frozen yogurt in an airtight container and place in the freezer for at least 2 hours, until desired consistency is reached.

## 433. Luscious Lavender Sour Cherry Sorbet

Servings: 6
Cooking Time: 5 Hours 35 Minutes
**Ingredients:**
- 3 cups pitted, sliced sour cherries
- ½ teaspoon lavender
- 3/4 cup sugar
- 1/2 teaspoon salt
- 2 tablespoons vanilla extract
- 2 ½ teaspoons lime juice

**Directions:**
1. Refer to note at the beginning of the chapter about freezing bowl.
2. Use a food processor or blender to puree the lavender, sugar, cherries, and vanilla extract. Then blend in the salt and lime juice. Strain the mixture into a bowl, and refrigerate covered for 2-3 hours.
3. Pour the ingredients into your ice cream maker, and let it churn for 25-30 minutes.
4. Place in an airtight container for up to 2 hours, until desired consistency is reached.

## 434. Brown Sugar Honey Mango Frozen Yogurt

Servings: 1 Quart
Cooking Time: 2 Hours 35 Minutes
**Ingredients:**
- 1 quart container full-fat plain yogurt
- ¼ teaspoon salt
- 1 cup sugar
- 1 teaspoon vanilla extract
- 8 ounces mango
- 1/4 cup honey
- 2 tablespoons brown sugar

**Directions:**
1. NOTE: Freeze your ice cream bowl for at least 24hrs prior to starting!
2. Puree the strawberries in a food processor or blender.
3. Place the yogurt in a bowl. Use a whisk to mix in the sugar and salt. Continue to whisk for about 4 minutes until the sugar dissolves. Then mix in the vanilla extract, honey, brown sugar and mango puree.
4. Pour the ingredients into your ice cream maker, and let it churn for 25 minutes.
5. Put the frozen yogurt in an airtight container and place in the freezer for at least 2 hours, until desired consistency is reached.

## 435. Mint Cookies 'n Sea Salt "silkshake"

Servings: 6
Cooking Time: 25 Minutes
**Ingredients:**
- 2 cups heavy cream
- 1 cup milk
- 3/4 cup sugar
- 1 teaspoon sea salt
- 1 teaspoon vanilla extract
- 1 ½ teaspoons mint extract
- 10 chocolate sandwich cookies

**Directions:**
1. Freeze bowl (Refer to note on page XX about freezing bowl)
2. Place the milk and cream in a bowl, and mix them together until well combined. Use a whisk to mix in the sugar. Continue to whisk for about 4 minutes until the sugar dissolves.

Then mix in the vanilla, sea salt and mint extract.
3. Place the sandwich cookies in a food processor, and process until the cookies are finely processed. If you don't have a food processor place the cookies in a large resealable plastic bag, and seal it shut. Use your hands, a mallet, or a rolling pin to crush the cookies.
4. Pour the ingredients into your ice cream maker, and let it churn for 10-15 minutes, until desired consistency is reached. About 5 minutes before the ice cream is done churning add the cookies to your ice cream maker.

### 436. Strawberry Lime Sorbet

Servings: 4
Cooking Time: 3 Hours
**Ingredients:**
- 2 cups water
- 3 pounds chilled strawberries
- 2 ½ cup sugar
- 5 chilled limes

**Directions:**
1. NOTE: Freeze your ice cream bowl for at least 24hrs prior to starting!
2. Mix together the water and sugar in a large sauce pan on medium heat. Allow the mixture to come to a boil. Then lower to low heat, and let the mixture simmer until the sugar dissolve. Allow the mixture to cool completely.
3. Puree the strawberries in a food processor or blender until smooth. Then add the zest of 3 limes, juice of 5 limes, and the cooled syrup. Blend until all ingredients are mixed.
4. Mix the lime juice and zest with the cooled mixture.
5. Pour the ingredients into your ice cream maker, and let it churn for 25-30 minutes.
6. Place in an airtight container for up to 2 hours, until desired consistency is reached.

### 437. Cherry Pineapple Chocolate Milkshake

Servings: 6
Cooking Time: 25 Minutes
**Ingredients:**
- 2 cups heavy cream
- 1 cup milk
- 3/4 cup sugar
- 1 teaspoon vanilla extract
- ¼ cup pineapples
- 1 cup cherry juice
- ¼ cup semi-sweet chocolate chips

**Directions:**
1. NOTE: Freeze your ice cream bowl for at least 24hrs prior to starting!
2. Place the milk and cream in a bowl, and mix them together until well combined. Use a whisk to mix in the sugar. Continue to whisk for about 4 minutes until the sugar dissolves. Then mix in the vanilla extract, and cherry juice.
3. Pour the ingredients into your ice cream maker, and let it churn for 10-15 minutes, until desired consistency is reached. About 5 minutes before the ice cream is finished churning, add in the pineapples and chocolate chips.

### 438. Dulce De Leche Frozen Yogurt

Servings: 8
Cooking Time: 10 Minutes
**Ingredients:**
- 1 ½ cups plain whole milk yogurt
- 1 cup commercial Dulce de Leche
- 1 cup heavy cream
- 1/8 teaspoon salt
- ½ teaspoon vanilla extract

**Directions:**
1. Place all ingredients in a chilled bowl. Whisk until well-combined.
2. Turn on the Cuisinart and pour in the mixture.
3. Churn for 10 minutes.
4. Transfer in an airtight container and freeze overnight.

**Nutrition Info:** Calories per serving: 200; Protein: 4.5g; Carbs: 26.3g; Fat: 9.8g Sugar: 21.5g

### 439. Passion Fruit Sorbet

Servings: 8
Cooking Time: 15 Minutes

**Ingredients:**
- 1 cup boiling water
- ¾ cup sugar
- 8 passion fruit, flesh scooped
- Juice from 1 lemon

**Directions:**
1. Place water and sugar in a saucepan. Bring to a boil until sugar dissolves. Remove from heat and allow to chill in the fridge for at least 2 hours.
2. While the sugar syrup is chilling, place the passion fruit in a blender and pulse until smooth. Pass the mixture into a sieve to remove the seeds. Discard the seeds and save the juice.
3. Mix the passion fruit juice with the sugar syrup and add the lemon juice.
4. Turn on the Cuisinart and pour in the mixture.
5. Churn for 10 minutes.
6. Transfer in an airtight container and freeze overnight.

**Nutrition Info:** Calories per serving: 55; Protein: 0.4g; Carbs: 13.9g; Fat: 0.2g Sugar: 6g

### 440. Vegan Sweet Chocolate Strawberry Chunk Gelato

Servings: Makes 2 ½ Cups
Cooking Time: 2 Hours 35 Minutes
**Ingredients:**
- 1 cup refrigerated coconut cream
- 1 cup pitted dates
- 1 cup frozen banana pieces
- 3 tablespoons cocoa powder
- 1/2 teaspoon salt
- ½ cup strawberry cut into chunk

**Directions:**
1. Refer to note at the beginning of the chapter about freezing bowl.
2. Place all ingredients EXCEPT the strawberries in a blender. Blend on high speed until smooth.
3. Pour the mixture into your ice cream maker, and let it churn for 25 minutes. About 5 minutes before the ice cream is done churning add the strawberries to your ice cream maker.
4. Put the gelato in an airtight container and place in the freezer for up to 2 hours, until desired consistency is reached.

### 441. Pumpkin Cinnamon Raisin Gingerbread Frozen Yogurt

Servings: 1 Quart
Cooking Time: 2 Hours 35 Minutes
**Ingredients:**
- 1 quart container full-fat plain yogurt
- ¼ teaspoon salt
- 1 cup sugar
- 1 teaspoon vanilla extract
- 1/2 cup pumpkin
- ¼ cup raisins
- 2 tablespoons molasses
- 1 teaspoon cinnamon
- ¼ teaspoon ginger

**Directions:**
1. NOTE: Freeze your ice cream bowl for at least 24hrs prior to starting!
2. Place all the ingredients in a blender and blend on high until pureed and sugar dissolves.
3. Pour the ingredients into your ice cream maker, and let it churn for 25 minutes. About 5 minutes before the ice cream is done churning add the raisins to your ice cream maker.
4. Put the frozen yogurt in an airtight container and place in the freezer for at least 2 hours, until desired consistency is reached.

### 442. Mango Pineapple Sorbet

Servings: 6
Cooking Time: 10 Minutes
**Ingredients:**
- 1 cup fresh ripe mango, peeled and cubed (seed removed)
- 1 cup pineapple tidbits
- ¼ cup water
- 1 teaspoon lemon juice
- ½ cup sugar
- ½ teaspoon salt

**Directions:**
1. Place all ingredients in a blender. Pulse until smooth.
2. Place in the fridge to chill for 2 hours.
3. Turn on the Cuisinart and pour in the mixture.
4. Churn for 10 minutes.

5. Transfer in an airtight container and freeze overnight

**Nutrition Info:** Calories per serving: 74 ; Protein: 0.4g; Carbs: 19g; Fat: 0.1g Sugar: 10g

## 443. "stuffed" Snickers Soft Serve Ice Cream

Servings: 6
Cooking Time: 35 Minutes
**Ingredients:**
- 2 cups heavy cream
- 1 cup milk
- 3/4 cup sugar
- 1 Tbs. vanilla extract
- 1 ½ cups chopped mini snickers bars

**Directions:**
1. Refer to note at the beginning of the chapter about freezing bowl.
2. Place the milk and cream in a bowl, and mix them together until well combined. Use a whisk to mix in the sugar. Continue to whisk for about 4 minutes until the sugar dissolves. Mix in the vanilla extract.
3. Pour the ingredients into your ice cream maker, and let it churn for 25 minutes. About 5 minutes before the ice cream is done churning add the snickers to your ice cream maker.
4. Serve immediately.

## 444. Mulberry Frozen Yogurt

Servings: 12
Cooking Time: 10 Minutes
**Ingredients:**
- 2 cups heavy cream
- 1 ½ cups Greek yogurt
- 1 cup milk
- ½ cup honey
- 2 tablespoons lemon juice
- ½ cup mulberries

**Directions:**
1. Place all ingredients in a food processor. Pulse until smooth.
2. Turn on the Cuisinart and pour in the mixture.
3. Churn for 10 minutes.
4. Transfer in an airtight container and freeze overnight.

5. Garnish with pistachio nuts before serving.

**Nutrition Info:** Calories per serving: 157; Protein: 6.3g; Carbs: 15.7g; Fat: 8.3g Sugar: 15.3g

## 445. Mango Madness Chili Lime Sorbet

Servings: 6-8
Cooking Time: 2 Hours 40 Minutes
**Ingredients:**
- 3 peeled, pitted, and diced large mangos
- 1 tablespoon chili powder
- 2 cups simple syrup
- 1/4 cup fresh lime juice
- Pinch of salt

**Directions:**
1. Refer to note at the beginning of the chapter about freezing bowl.
2. Puree the mangos in a food processor or blender. Then add in the remaining ingredients and blend on low until combined.
3. Pour the ingredients into your ice cream maker, and let it churn for 25-30 minutes.
4. Place in an airtight container for up to 2 hours, until desired consistency is reached.

## 446. Meyer Lemon Sorbet

Servings: 3
Cooking Time: 15 Minutes
**Ingredients:**
- 1 cup water
- 1 cup sugar
- 2 teaspoons lemon zest
- 1 cup lemon juice, freshly squeezed

**Directions:**
1. Place all ingredients in a saucepan. Turn on the heat and allow to simmer for 5 minutes or until the sugar dissolves.
2. Remove from the heat and place in the fridge to cool for 2 hours.
3. Turn on the Cuisinart and pour in the mixture.
4. Churn for 10 minutes.
5. Transfer in an airtight container and freeze overnight.

**Nutrition Info:** Calories per serving:148 ; Protein: 0.3g; Carbs: 39.1g; Fat: 0.2g Sugar: 34.7g

## 447. Caramel Frozen Squares

Servings: 8
Cooking Time: 25 Minutes
**Ingredients:**
- 1 cup cold whole milk
- ¾ cup granulated sugar
- 2 cups cold heavy cream
- 1 teaspoon vanilla extract
- 1 ½ cups packed light brown sugar
- ½ cup evaporated milk
- 7 tablespoons butter, melted
- ½ teaspoon vanilla extract
- 1 13-ounce packaged pecan shortbread cookies, crushed

**Directions:**
1. Put ice water in a large mixing bowl. Place a small bowl on top of the large bowl with ice. Pour cold milk and sugar into the small bowl and whisk until the sugar is dissolved. Stir in the cream and vanilla. Stir to combine.
2. Place the cold freezer bowl in the Cuisinart Ice Cream Maker. Turn on the machine and pour in the mixture. Add one package of crushed Oreos five minutes before the time ends.
3. Stop in 25 minutes until the mixture becomes soft and creamy.
4. Transfer into an air-tight container and freeze overnight.
5. In a saucepan over medium flame, mix together the brown sugar and milk. Bring to a boil and allow to simmer for 3 minutes. Remove from heat add a tablespoon of butter and vanilla. Set aside. This will be the caramel sauce.
6. Coat a 9x13 inch pan with cooking spray and press the crumb into the dish.
7. Spread the ice cream carefully and evenly on top. Top with the remaining cookie crumbs and pour in sauce.

**Nutrition Info:** Calories per serving:539 ; Protein: 4.9g; Carbs: 44.7g; Fat: 38.4g Sugar: 16g

## 448. Banana Pineapple Coconut Gelato

Servings: 4-6
Cooking Time: 2 Hours 35 Minutes
**Ingredients:**
- 1/2 cup heavy cream
- 2 cups milk
- 3/4 cup sugar
- 1 tablespoon vanilla extract
- ½ cup sliced banana
- ½ cup chopped pineapple
- ½ cup chopped coconut

**Directions:**
1. NOTE: Freeze your ice cream bowl for at least 24hrs prior to starting!
2. Puree the bananas in a food processor or blender.
3. Place the milk and cream in a bowl, and mix them together until well combined. Use a whisk to mix in the sugar. Continue to whisk for about 4 minutes until the sugar dissolves. Then mix in the vanilla extract and banana puree.
4. Pour the ingredients into your ice cream maker, and let it churn for 25 minutes. About 5 minutes before the ice cream is done churning add the walnuts to your ice cream maker.
5. Put the gelato in an airtight container and place in the freezer for up to 2 hours, until desired consistency is reached.

## 449. Lime-mango Sorbet

Servings: 8
Cooking Time: 15 Minutes
**Ingredients:**
- ½ cup water
- ¼ cup sugar
- 5 cups ripe mango cubes
- 1 teaspoon lime zest
- ¼ lime juice

**Directions:**
1. Place sugar and water in a saucepan. Bring to a boil until the sugar dissolves.
2. Remove from the heat and place in the fridge to chill for at least 3 hours.
3. Place all ingredients in a blender and add the chilled sugar mixture. Pulse

until smooth. Allow to chill for another two hours.
4. Turn on the Cuisinart and pour in the mixture.
5. Churn for 10 minutes.
6. Transfer in an airtight container and freeze overnight.

**Nutrition Info:** Calories per serving: 88; Protein: 1g; Carbs: 22g; Fat: 1g Sugar: 19g

## 450. Candy Cane Ice Cream Sandwiches

Servings: 6
Cooking Time: 35 Minutes
**Ingredients:**
- 1 lb. Sugar cookie dough
- vanilla ice cream
- Crushed candy canes
- Sprinkle of cinnamon

**Directions:**
1. First, make sure you preheat oven to 345 degrees F. Take the sugar cookie dough and make them into 1 tablespoon balls and place them on the parchment baking sheet paper. Put them in the oven and bake till lightly golden brown
2. Approximately 10 minutes.
3. Let the cookies cool for about 5 minutes on baking sheets
4. You can then move them to wire rack to cool.
5. Once cool, place giant scoop of ice cream onto one cookie and sandwich with another cookie on top. Roll in lightly crushed candy canes and freeze for about 30min.

## 451. Black Cherry Kiwi Cotton Candy Gelato

Servings: 4-6
Cooking Time: 2 Hours 35 Minutes
**Ingredients:**
- 1/2 cup heavy cream
- 2 cups milk
- 3/4 cup sugar
- 1 teaspoon vanilla extract
- 1 teaspoon cotton candy extract
- 1 cup black cherries
- ½ cup finely chopped kiwi

**Directions:**
1. NOTE: Freeze your ice cream bowl for at least 24hrs prior to starting!
2. Puree the apples in a food processor or blender.
3. Place the milk and cream in a bowl, and mix them together until well combined. Use a whisk to mix in the sugar. Continue to whisk for about 4 minutes until the sugar dissolves. Then mix in the vanilla extract and black cherry puree.
4. Pour the ingredients into your ice cream maker, and let it churn for 25 minutes. About 5 minutes before the ice cream is done churning add the kiwi to your ice cream maker.
5. Put the gelato in an airtight container and place in the freezer for up to 2 hours, until desired consistency is reached.

## 452. Mango Texas Toast Ice Cream Sandwich

Servings: 2
Cooking Time: 15 Min
**Ingredients:**
- 1 loaf of Texas Toast bread (thick slices)
- organic honey to pour atop
- 1 mango (peeled & sliced)

**Directions:**
1. Toast your Texas Toast in a toaster. It should be nice and firm and golden brown.
2. Spread some of the mango slices on top of your Texas Toast.
3. Squeeze out and drizzle honey over both inside pieces of the Texas Toast.
4. Add a scoop of Ice Cream (that you made from this book) between the two pieces of Texas Toast and Enjoy!

## 453. Clementine Sorbet

Servings: Makes 1 Quart
Cooking Time: 4 Hours 35 Minutes
**Ingredients:**
- 20 chilled, peeled, and segmented clementines
- 1 cup sugar
- ¼ teaspoon salt

**Directions:**

1. Refer to note at the beginning of the chapter about freezing bowl.
2. Use a food processor or blender to puree the clementines. Strain the puree until you have 4 ½ cups of juice. Place the juice and sugar back in the blender or food processor. Process until sugar dissolves. Then pulse in the salt until combined.
3. Pour the ingredients into your ice cream maker, and let it churn for 25-30 minutes.
4. Place in an airtight container for up to 2 hours, until desired consistency is reached.

### 454. Peach Mango Frozen Yogurt

Servings: 5
Cooking Time: 4 Minutes
**Ingredients:**
- 1 ½ cups Greek yogurt
- 1 cup sliced peaches
- 1 cup diced mango
- ½ cup sugar
- 1 teaspoon vanilla extract

**Directions:**
1. Place all ingredients in a food processor. Pulse until smooth.
2. Turn on the Cuisinart and pour in the mixture.
3. Churn for 10 minutes.
4. Transfer in an airtight container and freeze overnight.

**Nutrition Info:** Calories per serving: 182; Protein: 14.8g; Carbs: 31g; Fat: 1g
Sugar: 29 g

### 455. Lemon Blueberry Frozen Yogurt

Servings: 5
Cooking Time: 20 Minutes
**Ingredients:**
- ½ cup fresh lemon juice
- 1 tablespoon grated lemon zest
- 2/3 cup sugar
- ¾ cup blueberries
- ¼ cup honey
- 2 cups plain whole milk yogurt
- ½ cup heavy cream

**Directions:**
1. In a saucepan, place the lemon juice, zest, sugar, and blueberries. Add a little water. Turn on the heat to medium low. Allow the mixture to simmer until the blueberries turn into a jam-like consistency. Set aside to cool.
2. In a cold bowl, whisk together the honey, yogurt, and heavy cream.
3. Turn on the Cuisinart and pour in the mixture.
4. Churn for 10 minutes.
5. Five minutes before the churning stops, add the blueberry mixture.
6. Transfer in an airtight container and freeze overnight.

**Nutrition Info:** Calories per serving: 245 ; Protein: 4.1g; Carbs: 42.6g; Fat: 7.8g
Sugar: 40.5g

### 456. Finger Lickin' Honey Lavender Milkshake

Servings: 6
Cooking Time: 25 Minutes
**Ingredients:**
- 2 cups heavy cream
- 1 cup milk
- 3/4 cup sugar
- 1 ½ teaspoon lavender extract
- 1/3 cup honey

**Directions:**
1. Refer to note at the beginning of the chapter about freezing bowl.
2. Place the milk and cream in a bowl, and mix them together until well combined. Use a whisk to mix in the sugar. Continue to whisk for about 4 minutes until the sugar dissolves. Then mix in the lavender extract, and honey.
3. Pour the ingredients into your ice cream maker, and let it churn for 10-15 minutes, until desired consistency is reached.
4. Serve immediately.

### 457. Vegan Sensuous Strawberries N Cream Ice Cream

Servings: Makes 1 Quart
Cooking Time: 35 Minutes
**Ingredients:**
- 1 pound silken tofu
- ½ cup plus 2 tablespoons organic or granulated sugar

- ½ teaspoon kosher salt
- 1 vanilla bean, split lengthwise
- ¾ cup refined coconut oil, melted, cooled slightly
- 1 cup sliced strawberries

**Directions:**
1. Refer to note at the beginning of the chapter about freezing bowl.
2. Put the first 3 ingredients in a blender. Then add in the vanilla bean seeds and strawberries. Puree the mixture until its smooth, around 15 seconds. Turn the blender to medium speed, and slowly drizzle in the coconut oil. Blend the mixture until its thick, but don't over blend it.
3. Pour the ingredients into your ice cream maker, and let it churn for 25 minutes.
4. Put the ice cream in an airtight container and place in the freezer for around 2 hours. Allow the ice cream to thaw for 15 minutes before serving.

### 458. Blueberry Honey English Muffin Ice Cream Sandwich

Servings: 2
Cooking Time: 15 Min
**Ingredients:**
- 1 pack of English muffins
- organic honey to pour atop
- small pack of blueberries

**Directions:**
1. Toast your English muffins in a toaster just like you would for breakfast.
2. Spread about 4-5 blueberries on top of your warm muffin.
3. Squeeze out and drizzle honey over both inside pieces of the English muffin.
4. Add a scoop of Ice Cream (that you made from this book) between the two pieces of English muffins.
5. Enjoy!

### 459. Wonderful Watermelon Sorbet

Servings: Makes 1 Quart
Cooking Time: 2 Hours 40 Minutes
**Ingredients:**
- 3 1/2 cups sliced seedless watermelon
- 6 ounce chilled pineapple juice
- 3/4 cup chilled ginger ale
- ½ cup fresh lime juice
- 1/3 cup grenadine

**Directions:**
1. Refer to note at the beginning of the chapter about freezing bowl.
2. Puree all ingredients in a food processor or blender.
3. Pour the ingredients into your ice cream maker, and let it churn for 25-30 minutes.
4. Place in an airtight container for up to 2 hours, until desired consistency is reached.

### 460. Lemon Mint Melon Sorbet

Servings: 4
Cooking Time: 3 Hours 10 Minutes
**Ingredients:**
- ½ cup lemon juice
- 1 cup boiling water
- 1 cup chopped mint
- ½ cup melon
- Zest of 1 lemon
- 1 cup sugar

**Directions:**
1. NOTE: Freeze your ice cream bowl for at least 24hrs prior to starting!
2. Mix together the sugar, lemon zest, mint and melon in a heat safe bowl. Then pour in the water, and stir frequently until sugar dissolves. Let the mixture sit for 20 minutes. Then strain it into another bowl. Mix in the lemon juice and let the mixture cool totally.
3. Pour the ingredients into your ice cream maker, and let it churn for 25-30 minutes.
4. Place in an airtight container for up to 2 hours, until desired consistency is reached.

### 461. Avocado Sorbet

Servings: 5
Cooking Time: 20 Minutes
**Ingredients:**
- 2/3 to ¾ cup avocado meat, cut into chunks
- ½ cup agave syrup

- ½ cup coconut milk
- ¼ cup fresh lime juice

**Directions:**
1. Place all ingredients in a blender and pulse until smooth.
2. Turn on the Cuisinart and pour in the mixture.
3. Churn for 10 minutes.
4. Transfer in an airtight container and freeze overnight.

**Nutrition Info:** Calories per serving: 159; Protein: 1.1g; Carbs: 21g; Fat: 8.8g Sugar: 11g

### 462. Honey Peach Gelato

Servings: 4-6
Cooking Time: 2 Hours 35 Minutes
**Ingredients:**
- 1/2 cup heavy cream
- 2 cups milk
- 3/4 cup sugar
- 1 cup sliced peaches
- 1 tablespoon vanilla extract
- 1/4 cup honey

**Directions:**
1. NOTE: Freeze your ice cream bowl for at least 24hrs prior to starting!
2. Puree the peaches in a food processor or blender.
3. Place the milk and cream in a bowl, and mix them together until well combined. Use a whisk to mix in the sugar. Continue to whisk for about 4 minutes until the sugar dissolves. Then mix in the vanilla extract honey and peach puree.
4. Pour the ingredients into your ice cream maker, and let it churn for 25 minutes.
5. Put the gelato in an airtight container and place in the freezer for up to 2 hours, until desired consistency is reached.

### 463. Lemon Lime Soda Milkshake

Servings: 6
Cooking Time: 25 Minutes
**Ingredients:**
- 2 cups heavy cream
- 1 cup milk
- 3/4 cup sugar
- 1 teaspoon vanilla extract
- ¼ cup lime juice
- ¼ cup lemon juice
- ¼ cup 7up or Sprite
- Zest of one lemon
- Zest of one lime

**Directions:**
1. NOTE: Freeze your ice cream bowl for at least 24hrs prior to starting!
2. Place the milk and cream in a bowl, and mix them together until well combined. Use a whisk to mix in the sugar. Continue to whisk for about 4 minutes until the sugar dissolves. Then mix in the vanilla extract, juice, Sprite/7-Up and zest.
3. Pour the ingredients into your ice cream maker, and let it churn for 10-15 minutes, until desired consistency is reached.
4. Serve immediately.

### 464. Matcha Ice Cream

Servings: 6
Cooking Time: 2 Hours 50 Minutes
**Ingredients:**
- 2 cups heavy cream
- 1 cup milk
- 3/4 cup sugar
- 1 teaspoon vanilla extract
- 1 tablespoon matcha

**Directions:**
1. Refer to note at the beginning of the chapter about freezing bowl.
2. Place the milk and cream in a bowl, and mix them together until well combined. Use a whisk to mix in the sugar. Continue to whisk for about 4 minutes until the sugar dissolves. Then mix in the vanilla extract. Finally whisk in the matcha until well mixed.
3. Pour the ingredients into your ice cream maker, and let it churn for 25 minutes.
4. Put the ice cream in an airtight container and place in the freezer for around 2 hours. Allow the ice cream to thaw for 15 minutes before serving.

### 465. Strawberry, Nectarine, Orange, Banana Sorbet

Servings: 8
Cooking Time: 10 Minutes
**Ingredients:**
- ¾ cup sugar
- ¾ cup water
- 1 cup strawberries, hulled
- 1 cup orange wedges, peeled and seeds removed
- 1 cup nectarine, peeled and seeds removed
- 1 ripe banana, peeled

**Directions:**
1. Place the water and sugar in a saucepan. Bring to a boil until the sugar dissolves.
2. Remove from the heat and place in the fridge to chill for at least 3 hours.
3. Place the rest of the ingredients in a blender and add the chilled sugar mixture. Pulse until smooth. Allow to chill for another two hours.
4. Turn on the Cuisinart and pour in the mixture.
5. Churn for 10 minutes.
6. Transfer in an airtight container and freeze overnight.

**Nutrition Info:** Calories per serving: 78; Protein: 0.7g; Carbs: 20g; Fat: 0g Sugar: 14g

### 466. Black Raspberry Clementine Sorbet

Servings: Makes 1 Quart
Cooking Time: 4 Hours 35 Minutes
**Ingredients:**
- 20 chilled, peeled, and segmented clementine's
- ½ cup Black Raspberries
- 1 cup sugar
- ¼ teaspoon salt

**Directions:**
1. NOTE: Freeze your ice cream bowl for at least 24hrs prior to starting!
2. Use a food processor or blender to puree the Clementine's and black raspberries. Strain the puree until you have 4 ½ cups of juice. Place the juice and sugar back in the blender or food processor. Process until sugar dissolves. Then pulse in the salt until combined.
3. Pour the ingredients into your ice cream maker, and let it churn for 25-30 minutes.
4. Place in an airtight container for up to 2 hours, until desired consistency is reached.

### 467. Coconut Guava Raspberry Sorbet

Servings: 6
Cooking Time: 5 Hours 35 Minutes
**Ingredients:**
- 3 cups packed, cubed guava
- 1 cup fresh raspberries
- 1 cup full-fat coconut milk
- 1 cup sugar
- Pinch of salt
- 1 teaspoon lime juice

**Directions:**
1. NOTE: Freeze your ice cream bowl for at least 24hrs prior to starting!
2. Puree all the ingredients in a food processor or blender. Then transfer the mixture to a bowl, and refrigerate covered for 3-4 hours.
3. Pour the ingredients into your ice cream maker, and let it churn for 25-30 minutes.
4. Place in an airtight container for up to 2 hours, until desired consistency is reached.

### 468. Peanut Butter Plum Sorbet

Servings: Makes 1 Quart
Cooking Time: 4 Hours 35 Minutes
**Ingredients:**
- 2 pounds pitted, quartered plums
- 1 tablespoon light corn syrup
- 3 tablespoons peanut butter
- 1 cup sugar
- ¼ teaspoon salt

**Directions:**
1. NOTE: Freeze your ice cream bowl for at least 24hrs prior to starting!
2. Use a food processor or blender to puree the plums. Put in the sugar and corn syrup, and process for about another 30 seconds. Then blend in the salt and peanut butter. Strain the

mixture into a bowl, and refrigerate covered for 2-3 hours.
3. Pour the ingredients into your ice cream maker, and let it churn for 25-30 minutes.
4. Place in an airtight container for up to 2 hours, until desired consistency is reached.

### 469. Vegan Soy Vanilla And Carob Chip Ice Cream

Servings: Makes 1 Quart
Cooking Time: 35 Minutes
**Ingredients:**
- 1 pound silken tofu
- ½ cup plus 2 tablespoons organic or granulated sugar
- ½ teaspoon kosher salt
- 1 vanilla bean, split lengthwise
- ¾ cup refined coconut oil, melted, cooled slightly
- 1 cup vegan carob chips

**Directions:**
1. Refer to note at the beginning of the chapter about freezing bowl.
2. Put the first 3 ingredients in a blender. Then add in the vanilla bean seeds. Puree the mixture until its smooth, around 15 seconds. Turn the blender to medium speed, and slowly drizzle in the coconut oil. Blend the mixture until its thick, but don't over blend it.
3. Pour the ingredients into your ice cream maker, and let it churn for 25 minutes. About 5 minutes before the ice cream is done churning add the carob chips to your ice cream maker.
4. Put the ice cream in an airtight container and place in the freezer for around 2 hours. Allow the ice cream to thaw for 15 minutes before serving.

### 470. Honey Cinnamon Blackberry English Muffin Ice Cream Sandwich

Servings: 2
Cooking Time: 15 Min
**Ingredients:**
- 1 pack of English muffins
- organic honey to pour atop
- small pack of blackberries
- 1 tsp. cinnamon

**Directions:**
1. Toast your English muffins in a toaster just like you would for breakfast.
2. Spread about 4-5 blackberries on top of your warm muffin.
3. Squeeze out and drizzle honey over both inside pieces of the English muffin.
4. Sprinkle a little cinnamon on top
5. Add a scoop of Ice Cream (that you made from this book) between the two pieces of English muffins. Enjoy!

### 471. Peach Sorbet

Servings: 8
Cooking Time: 15 Minutes
**Ingredients:**
- 2/3 cup sugar
- 1 cup water
- 2 ½ pounds peaches, peeled and halved (seeds removed)
- 3 tablespoons fresh lemon juice
- ½ teaspoon lemon zest

**Directions:**
1. Place sugar and water in a saucepan. Bring to a boil until the sugar dissolves. Add the peaches and simmer for another 3 minutes.
2. Remove from the heat and place in the fridge to chill for at least 3 hours.
3. Place all ingredients in a blender and add the chilled sugar mixture. Pulse until smooth. Allow to chill for another two hours.
4. Turn on the Cuisinart and pour in the mixture.
5. Churn for 10 minutes.
6. Transfer in an airtight container and freeze overnight.

**Nutrition Info:** Calories per serving: 121; Protein: 1g; Carbs: 31g; Fat: 0g Sugar: 25g

### 472. Honey Mint Heaven Milkshake

Servings: 6
Cooking Time: 25 Minutes
**Ingredients:**
- 2 cups heavy cream
- 1 cup milk
- 3/4 cup sugar

- 1½ teaspoon mint extract
- 1/3 cup honey

**Directions:**
1. NOTE: Freeze your ice cream bowl for at least 24hrs prior to starting!
2. Place the milk and cream in a bowl, and mix them together until well combined. Use a whisk to mix in the sugar. Continue to whisk for about 4 minutes until the sugar dissolves. Then mix in the mint extract, and honey.
3. Pour the ingredients into your ice cream maker, and let it churn for 10-15 minutes, until desired consistency is reached.
4. Serve immediately.

### 473. Chili Lime Mango Sorbet

Servings: 6-8
Cooking Time: 2 Hours 40 Minutes
**Ingredients:**
- 3 peeled, pitted, and diced large mangos
- 2 cups simple syrup
- 1/4 cup fresh lime juice
- 1 tablespoon chili powder
- Pinch of salt

**Directions:**
1. NOTE: Freeze your ice cream bowl for at least 24hrs prior to starting!
2. Puree the mangos in a food processor or blender. Then add in the remaining ingredients and blend on low until combined.
3. Pour the ingredients into your ice cream maker, and let it churn for 25-30 minutes.
4. Place in an airtight container for up to 2 hours, until desired consistency is reached.

### 474. Sweet Pumpkin Gingerbread Frozen Yogurt

Servings: 1 Quart
Cooking Time: 2 Hours 35 Minutes
**Ingredients:**
- 1 quart container full-fat plain yogurt
- ¼ teaspoon salt
- 1 cup sugar
- 1 teaspoon vanilla extract
- 1/2 cup pumpkin
- 2 tablespoons molasses
- 1 teaspoon cinnamon
- ¼ teaspoon ginger

**Directions:**
1. Refer to note at the beginning of the chapter about freezing bowl.
2. Place all the ingredients in a blender and blend on high until pureed and sugar dissolves.
3. Pour the ingredients into your ice cream maker, and let it churn for 25 minutes. About 5 minutes before the ice cream is done churning add the chocolate to your ice cream maker.
4. Put the frozen yogurt in an airtight container and place in the freezer for at least 2 hours, until desired consistency is reached.

### 475. S'mores Ice Cream Dream Cookie Delight

Servings: 6
Cooking Time: 35 Minutes
**Ingredients:**
- 1 graham cracker
- 1 scoop ice cream (of your choice)
- 1/4 c. toasted mini marshmallows
- Chocolate sauce, for drizzling

**Directions:**
1. Get a box if Graham Crackers and break them into squares.
2. Then scoop ice cream onto one square and top with toasted marshmallows.
3. With the chocolate sauce just drizzle on top. (should be a little messy!)

### 476. Frozen Pistachio Ice Cream Dessert

Servings: 6
Cooking Time: 30 Minutes
**Ingredients:**
- 1 cup cold whole milk
- ¾ cup granulated sugar
- 2 cups cold heavy cream
- 1 teaspoon vanilla extract
- 45 pieces Ritz crackers, crushed
- ¾ cup melted butter
- 2 small pistachio pudding mix
- Chocolate chips

**Directions:**

1. Put ice water in a large mixing bowl. Place a small bowl on top of the large bowl with ice. Pour cold milk and sugar into the small bowl and whisk until the sugar is dissolved. Stir in the cream and vanilla. Stir to combine.
2. Place the cold freezer bowl in the Cuisinart Ice Cream Maker. Turn on the machine and pour in the mixture. Add one package of crushed Oreos five minutes before the time ends.
3. Stop in 25 minutes until the mixture becomes soft and creamy.
4. Transfer into an air-tight container and freeze overnight.
5. In a bowl, combine the crackers and butter. Mix until combined.
6. Press dough in individual bowls or ramekins. Set aside.
7. Place ice cream in another bowl and add the pudding mix.
8. Scoop into prepared bowls and top with chocolate chips.

**Nutrition Info:** Calories per serving: 563; Protein: 4.8g; Carbs: 41.9g; Fat: 42.5g Sugar: 24.6g

### 477. Peach Frozen Yogurt

Servings: 5
Cooking Time: 10 Minutes
**Ingredients:**
- 4 cups fresh peaches
- 3 tablespoons honey
- ½ cup plain Greek yogurt
- 1 teaspoon vanilla extract

**Directions:**
1. Place all ingredients in a food processor and pulse until smooth.
2. Turn on the Cuisinart and pour in the mixture.
3. Churn for 10 minutes.
4. Transfer in an airtight container and freeze overnight.

**Nutrition Info:** Calories per serving: 109; Protein: 3g; Carbs: 24g; Fat: 3g Sugar: 23g

### 478. Tart Frozen Yogurt

Servings: 4
Cooking Time: 10 Minutes
**Ingredients:**
- 2 cups plain yogurt
- 2 cups plain Greek yogurt
- ¾ cup sugar
- 2 tablespoons honey
- Fruits for topping

**Directions:**
1. Place the yogurt, sugar, and honey in a bowl. Whisk to combine everything. Place in the fridge to chill.
2. Turn on the Cuisinart and pour in the mixture.
3. Churn for 10 minutes.
4. Transfer in an airtight container and freeze overnight.
5. Top with your favorite fruit before serving.

**Nutrition Info:** Calories per serving: 362; Protein: 21g; Carbs: 61g; Fat: 3g Sugar: 60g

### 479. Chunky Cherry Apple Sorbet

Servings: 6
Cooking Time: 2 Hours 40 Minutes
**Ingredients:**
- 6 cups frozen pitted cherries
- 1 apple
- 1/4 cup sugar
- Juice of one lemon

**Directions:**
1. NOTE: Freeze your ice cream bowl for at least 24hrs prior to starting!
2. Puree the sugar, cherries and apple in a food processor or blender until smooth. Put in the lemon juice and pulse a few times to mix the ingredients.
3. Pour the ingredients into your ice cream maker, and let it churn for 25-30 minutes.
4. Place in an airtight container for up to 2 hours, until desired consistency is reached.

### 480. Kiwi Strawberry Gelato

Servings: 4-6
Cooking Time: 2 Hours 35 Minutes
**Ingredients:**
- 1/2 cup heavy cream
- 2 cups milk
- 3/4 cup sugar
- 1/2 cup sliced strawberries
- 1/2 cup finely chopped kiwi
- 1 tablespoon vanilla extract

**Directions:**
1. NOTE: Freeze your ice cream bowl for at least 24hrs prior to starting!
2. Puree the strawberries in a food processor or blender.
3. Place the milk and cream in a bowl, and mix them together until well combined. Use a whisk to mix in the sugar. Continue to whisk for about 4 minutes until the sugar dissolves. Then mix in the vanilla extract and strawberry puree along with the finely chopped kiwi.
4. Pour the ingredients into your ice cream maker, and let it churn for 25 minutes.
5. Put the gelato in an airtight container and place in the freezer for up to 2 hours, until desired consistency is reached.

## 481. Pineapple Sorbet

Servings: 5
Cooking Time: 10 Minutes
**Ingredients:**
- 1 small pineapple, peeled and cored
- 2 tablespoons fresh lemon juice
- 1 cup sugar

**Directions:**
1. Place all ingredients in a blender. Pulse until smooth.
2. Place in the fridge to chill for at least 2 hours.
3. Turn on the Cuisinart and pour in the mixture.
4. Churn for 10 minutes.
5. Transfer in an airtight container and freeze overnight.

**Nutrition Info:** Calories per serving: 170; Protein: 1g; Carbs: 44g; Fat: 0.2g Sugar: 25g

## 482. Cherry Chocolate Pretzel Gelato

Servings: 4-6
Cooking Time: 2 Hours 35 Minutes
**Ingredients:**
- 1/2 cup heavy cream
- 2 cups milk
- 3/4 cup sugar
- 1 teaspoon vanilla extract
- 2 ounces pitted cherries
- 3 ounces semi-sweet chocolate
- 4 ounce pretzels

**Directions:**
1. NOTE: Freeze your ice cream bowl for at least 24hrs prior to starting!
2. Melt the chocolate, and allow it to cool a little bit.
3. Place the milk and cream in a bowl, and mix them together until well combined. Use a whisk to mix in the sugar. Continue to whisk for about 4 minutes until the sugar dissolves. Then mix in the vanilla extract. Finally mix in the chocolate and cherries.
4. Place the pretzels in a food processor, and process until the cookies are no bigger than chocolate chips. If you don't have a food processor place the pretzels in a large resealable plastic bag, and seal it shut. Use your hands, a mallet, or a rolling pin to crush the pretzels.
5. Pour the ingredients into your ice cream maker, and let it churn for 25 minutes. About 5 minutes before the ice cream is done churning add the pretzels to your ice cream maker.
6. Put the gelato in an airtight container and place in the freezer for up to 2 hours, until desired consistency is reached.

## 483. Summer Sorbet

Servings: 6
Cooking Time: 15 Minutes
**Ingredients:**
- 2 pounds fresh fruit of your choice
- 8 ounces sugar
- ¼ cup lemon juice
- ¼ cup vodka

**Directions:**
1. Place all ingredients in a blender. Pulse until smooth.
2. Place in the fridge and allow to chill for at least 3 hours.
3. Turn on the Cuisinart and pour in the mixture.
4. Churn for 10 minutes.
5. Transfer in an airtight container and freeze overnight.

**Nutrition Info:** Calories per serving: 268; Protein: 0.8g; Carbs: 67.4g; Fat: 0.8g Sugar: 54.6g

### 484. Lime Sorbet

Servings: 7
Cooking Time: 15 Minutes
**Ingredients:**
- 2 cups water
- 1 cup sugar
- 4 limes, zest
- Juice from 8 limes

**Directions:**
1. Place the water and sugar in a saucepan. Bring to a boil until the sugar dissolves.
2. Remove from the heat and place in the fridge to chill for at least 3 hours.
3. Turn on the Cuisinart and pour in the water-sugar mixture, lime zest, and lime juice.
4. Churn for 10 minutes.
5. Transfer in an airtight container and freeze overnight.

**Nutrition Info:** Calories per serving: 74; Protein: 0.3g; Carbs: 20.6g; Fat: 0.1g Sugar: 13 g

### 485. Matcha Frozen Yogurt

Servings: 6
Cooking Time: 10 Minutes
**Ingredients:**
- 2 cups Greek yogurt
- ¾ cup sugar
- 2 tablespoons matcha powder
- A pinch of salt

**Directions:**
1. In a cold bowl, combine all ingredients.
2. Turn on the Cuisinart and pour in the mixture.
3. Churn for 10 minutes.
4. Transfer in an airtight container and freeze overnight.

**Nutrition Info:** Calories per serving: 106; Protein: 3.1g; Carbs: 18.1g; Fat: 2.7g Sugar: 16.2g

### 486. Berry Frozen Yogurt

Servings: 12
Cooking Time: 10 Minutes
**Ingredients:**
- ¾ cup whole milk
- ¼ cup sugar
- 4 cups Greek yogurt
- 2 cups frozen mixed berries, thawed and pureed

**Directions:**
1. Place all ingredients in a food processor. Pulse until smooth. Place in the fridge to chill.
2. Turn on the Cuisinart and pour in the mixture.
3. Churn for 10 minutes.
4. Transfer in an airtight container and freeze overnight.

**Nutrition Info:** Calories per serving: 109; Protein: 4.2g; Carbs: 14.2g; Fat: 4.2g Sugar: 13.6g

### 487. Mint Guava Milkshake

Servings: 6
Cooking Time: 25 Minutes
**Ingredients:**
- 2 cups heavy cream
- 1 cup milk
- 3/4 cup sugar
- 1 teaspoon vanilla extract
- ½ cup mint (pulverized)
- 1/2 cups guava juice

**Directions:**
1. NOTE: Freeze your ice cream bowl for at least 24hrs prior to starting!
2. Place the milk and cream in a bowl, and mix them together until well combined. Use a whisk to mix in the sugar. Continue to whisk for about 4 minutes until the sugar dissolves. Then mix in the vanilla extract, and juice.
3. Pour the ingredients into your ice cream maker, and let it churn for 10-15 minutes, until desired consistency is reached.
4. Serve immediately.

### 488. Feta Frozen Yogurt

Servings: 6
Cooking Time: 10 Minutes
**Ingredients:**
- 1 cup plain Greek yogurt
- ½ cup feta cheese
- 1 tablespoon honey

**Directions:**
1. Place all ingredients in a food processor. Pulse until smooth.
2. Turn on the Cuisinart and pour in the mixture.
3. Churn for 10 minutes.
4. Transfer in an airtight container and freeze overnight.

**Nutrition Info:** Calories per serving: 161; Protein: 7 g; Carbs: 12g; Fat: 10g Sugar: 11g

### 489. Chocolate Bacon Frozen Yogurt

Servings: 1 Quart
Cooking Time: 2 Hours 35 Minutes
**Ingredients:**
- 1 quart container full-fat plain yogurt
- ¼ teaspoon salt
- 1 cup sugar
- 1 teaspoon vanilla extract
- 4 ounces chopped dark chocolate
- ½ cup olive oil
- ½ cup crispy bacon

**Directions:**
1. NOTE: Freeze your ice cream bowl for at least 24hrs prior to starting!
2. Place the yogurt in a bowl. Use a whisk to mix in the sugar and salt. Continue to whisk for about 4 minutes until the sugar dissolves. Then mix in the vanilla extract, olive oil and bacon.
3. Pour the ingredients into your ice cream maker, and let it churn for 25 minutes. About 5 minutes before the ice cream is done churning add the chocolate to your ice cream maker.
4. Put the frozen yogurt in an airtight container and place in the freezer for at least 2 hours, until desired consistency is reached.

### 490. Applesauce Waffle Cookie Ice Cream Sandwich

Servings: 6
Cooking Time: 5 Minutes
**Ingredients:**
- Simple Applesauce
- 3 pounds apples combination of McIntosh, Golden Delicious, Granny Smith, Fuji, and Jonathan
- 1 cup water
- 2 tablespoons lemon juice
- 1 3-inch cinnamon stick
- Add-Ons (As an option)
- 1/2 cup brown sugar
- 2 tablespoons butter
- 1/2 teaspoon ground cinnamon
- 1/2 teaspoon vanilla extract

**Directions:**
1. Simple Applesauce Directions
2. Cut up apples into small pieces, but peel and core it first. Move the apples to a large pot.
3. Add in lemon juice, a stick of cinnamon and water, when it starts to boil over high heat reduce the heat to low and cover to let simmer. About 20-30 min. The apples should be soft.
4. Use a blender to puree the applesauce., You can also use a food processor, or immersion blender for a smoother applesauce.
5. Add-ons: (Optional
6. Stir in brown sugar. Cook uncovered till the applesauce thickens up a little bit. about 5-10 minutes. (Sweeter option)
7. Mix the butter, until butter is melted, with the ground cinnamon, and vanilla extract, Yummy!

### 491. Chocolate Olive Oil Frozen Yogurt

Servings: 1 Quart
Cooking Time: 2 Hours 35 Minutes
**Ingredients:**
- 1 quart container full-fat plain yogurt
- ¼ teaspoon salt
- 1 cup sugar
- 1 teaspoon vanilla extract
- 4 ounces chopped dark chocolate
- 1/4 cup olive oil

**Directions:**
1. Refer to note at the beginning of the chapter about freezing bowl.
2. Place the yogurt in a bowl. Use a whisk to mix in the sugar and salt. Continue to whisk for about 4 minutes until the sugar dissolves. Then mix in the vanilla extract, and olive oil.
3. Pour the ingredients into your ice cream maker, and let it churn for 25 minutes. About 5 minutes before the

ice cream is done churning add the chocolate to your ice cream maker.
4. Put the frozen yogurt in an airtight container and place in the freezer for at least 2 hours, until desired consistency is reached.

### 492. Apple Cinnamon Almond Butter Top Roman Ice Cream Sandwich

Servings: 2
Cooking Time: 10 Min
**Ingredients:**
- 1 pack top roman noodles (remove season)
- 1 tsp. cinnamon
- 1 tablespoon of almond butter
- ½ apple (peeled, cored, and finely diced)

**Directions:**
1. Open the pack of top roman. Break it in half so you have 2 slices.
2. Spread some of the almond butter on top of both slices of Top Roman.
3. Spread the finely diced apples on top of the almond butter (apples warmed is amazing!!!)
4. Sprinkle a little bit of cinnamon on the almond butter.
5. Add a scoop of Ice Cream (that you made from this book) between the two pieces of Top Roman, almond butter and apples... A real treat indeed! Enjoy!

### 493. Oreo Ice Cream Cake

Servings: 16
Cooking Time: 25 Minutes
**Ingredients:**
- 1 cup cold whole milk
- ¾ cup granulated sugar
- 2 cups cold heavy cream
- 1 teaspoon vanilla extract
- 2 small packages Oreos, crushed
- ¼ cup butter
- 8-ounce whipped cream
- 16-ounce hot fudge

**Directions:**
1. Put ice water in a large mixing bowl. Place a small bowl on top of the large bowl with ice. Pour cold milk and sugar into the small bowl and whisk until the sugar is dissolved. Stir in the cream and vanilla. Stir to combine.
2. Place the cold freezer bowl in the Cuisinart Ice Cream Maker. Turn on the machine and pour in the mixture. Add one package of crushed Oreos five minutes before the time ends.
3. Stop in 25 minutes until the mixture becomes soft and creamy.
4. In a bowl, mix the remaining crushed Oreos and butter to create a dough.
5. Press the Oreo dough in a spring form pan.
6. Spread the ice cream over the crust and freeze for 4 hours in the fridge.
7. Before serving, top with whipped cream and drizzle with hot fudge.

**Nutrition Info:** Calories per serving: 689; Protein: 10g; Carbs: 82g; Fat:35 g Sugar: 67g

### 494. Chocolate Almond Butter Top Roman Ice Cream Sandwich

Servings: 2
Cooking Time: 10 Min
**Ingredients:**
- 1 pack top roman noodles (remove season)
- 6oz. Hershey's milk chocolate
- 1 tablespoon of almond butter

**Directions:**
1. Open the pack of top roman. Break it in half so you have 2 slices.
2. Spread some of the almond butter on top of both slices of Top Roman.
3. Melt the chocolate in the microwave at ½ power for 1 min. (repeat if necessary).
4. Add a scoop of Ice Cream (that you made from this book) between the two pieces of Top Roman, drizzle on some of that melted chocolate... and Enjoy!

### 495. Frozen Banana Split

Servings: 15
Cooking Time: 25 Minutes
**Ingredients:**
- 1 cup cold whole milk
- ¾ cup granulated sugar
- 2 cups cold heavy cream
- 1 teaspoon vanilla extract
- 4 bananas, split lengthwise
- 16 ounces whipped cream
- 1 cup salted peanuts

- 1 cup chocolate syrup

**Directions:**
1. Put ice water in a large mixing bowl. Place a small bowl on top of the large bowl with ice. Pour cold milk and sugar into the small bowl and whisk until the sugar is dissolved. Stir in the cream and vanilla. Stir to combine.
2. Place the cold freezer bowl in the Cuisinart Ice Cream Maker. Turn on the machine and pour in the mixture. Stop in 25 minutes until the mixture becomes soft and creamy.
3. Transfer into an air-tight container and freeze overnight.
4. Once the ice cream is frozen, assemble the banana split.
5. Place two slices of the banana on each side of a serving dish and place three scoops of ice cream in between.
6. Top with whipped cream and garnish with peanuts.
7. Drizzle with chocolate syrup on top.

**Nutrition Info:** Calories per serving: 334 ; Protein: 6.5g; Carbs: 32.6g; Fat: 21.2g Sugar: 19.5g

### 496. Turtle Brownie Ice Cream

Servings: 8
Cooking Time: 25 Minutes
**Ingredients:**
- 1 cup cold whole milk
- ¾ cup granulated sugar
- 2 cups cold heavy cream
- 1 teaspoon vanilla extract
- 1 package commercial brownie

**Directions:**
1. Put ice water in a large mixing bowl. Place a small bowl on top of the large bowl with ice. Pour cold milk and sugar into the small bowl and whisk until the sugar is dissolved. Stir in the cream and vanilla. Stir to combine.
2. Place the cold freezer bowl in the Cuisinart Ice Cream Maker. Turn on the machine and pour in the mixture. Stop in 25 minutes until the mixture becomes soft and creamy.
3. Transfer into an air-tight container and freeze overnight.
4. Once the ice cream is frozen, assemble the frozen brownie.
5. Slice the brownies into 2x2 inch squares.
6. Spread the vanilla ice cream in between two brownie slices.
7. Serve immediately.

**Nutrition Info:** Calories per serving: 200; Protein: 1.9g; Carbs: 19.1g; Fat: 13.3g Sugar: 17g

Printed in Great Britain
by Amazon